I0810195

In Praise of Nonsense

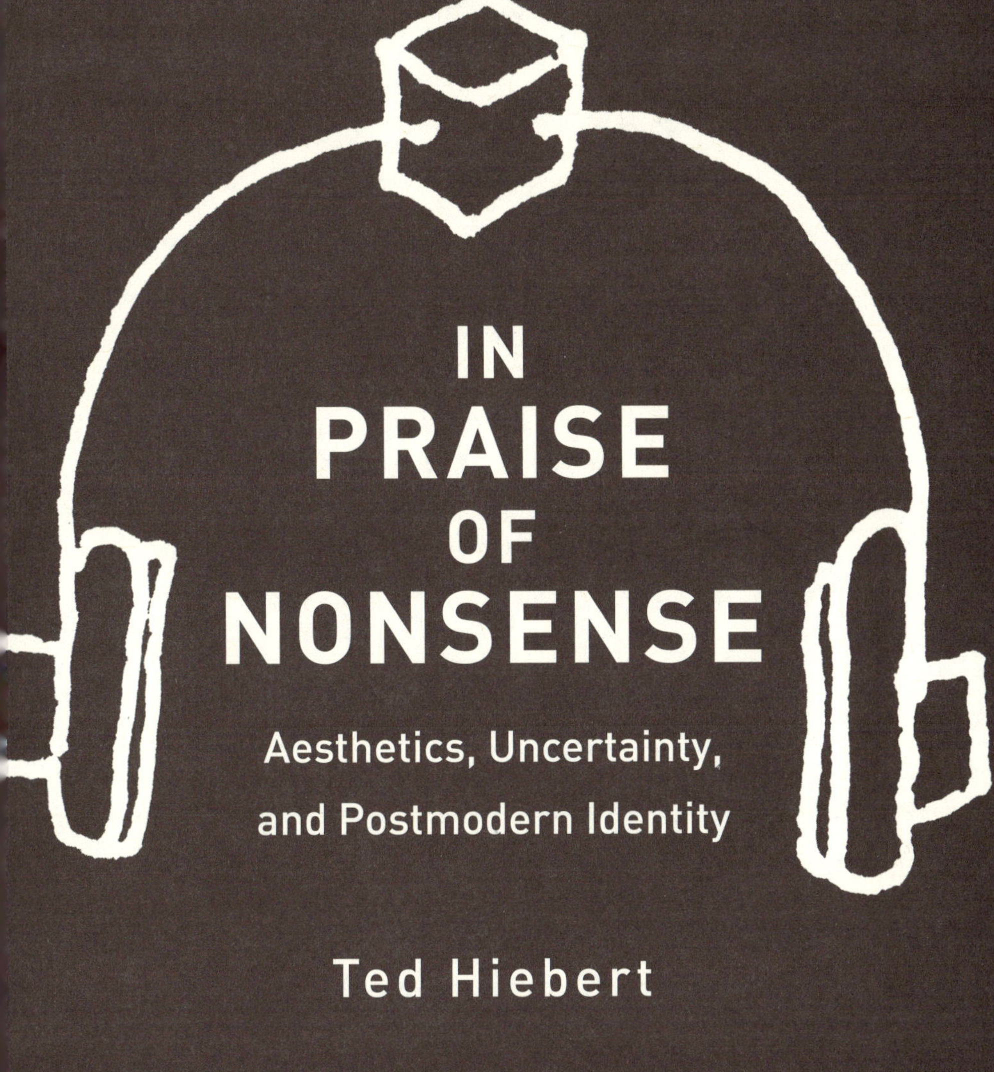

IN PRAISE OF NONSENSE

Aesthetics, Uncertainty, and Postmodern Identity

Ted Hiebert

McGILL-QUEEN'S UNIVERSITY PRESS
Montreal & Kingston • London • Ithaca

ISBN 978-0-7735-3973-0 (cloth)
ISBN 978-0-7735-3974-7 (paper)

Legal deposit third quarter 2012
Bibliothèque nationale du Québec

Printed in Canada on acid-free paper that is 100% ancient forest free (100% post-consumer recycled), processed chlorine free

McGill-Queen's University Press acknowledges the support of the Canada Council for the Arts for our publishing program. We also acknowledge the financial support of the Government of Canada through the Canada Book Fund for our publishing activities.

Library and Archives Canada Cataloguing in Publication

Hiebert, Ted, 1973–
In praise of nonsense : aesthetics, uncertainty, and postmodern identity / Ted Hiebert.

Includes bibliographical references and index.
ISBN 978-0-7735-3973-0 (bound).
ISBN 978-0-7735-3974-7 (pbk.)

1. Aesthetics. 2. Postmodernism. 3. Imagination.
4. Uncertainty. 5. Creation (Literary, artistic, etc.). I. Title.

BH301.P69H53 2012 149'.97 C2012-901368-4

This book was designed and typeset by studio oneonone in Stone serif 9/13.5

Contents

Illustrations

Acknowledgments

This book grew out of my dissertation in the Humanities PhD Program at Concordia University. The initial manuscript owes much to the support and guidance of my doctoral committee: Arthur Kroker, Catherine Russell, Evergon, and Johanne Sloane. Since that time the book has gone through revisions and rewrites that could not have happened without the support of the Pacific Centre for Technology and Culture at the University of Victoria and the mentorship of Arthur and Marilouise Kroker. I would also like to thank Philip Cercone at McGill-Queen's for his enthusiasm for the manuscript and Jessica Howarth for her expert editorial guidance.

Finally, I am grateful to each of the artists who generously allowed me to include images of their work in this book: Jackson 2bears, Chris Gillespie, Toni Hafkenscheid, Isabelle Hayeur, Doug Jarvis, Erik Kaiel, Christian Kuras, Jennifer Long, Duncan MacKenzie, Mike Paget, Scott Rogers, and Tim van Wijk.

Portions of the introductions to Part I and Part II were published in *Drain: A Journal of Contemporary Art and Theory* 5.0 (Fall 2005) as "The Medusa Complex: A Theory of Stoned Posthumanism." Portions of chapter 1 were published in *CTheory* 28:2 (Spring 2005) as "The Lacanian Conspiracy." The introduction to chapter 1 appeared in *dANDelion* 14:2 (Fall 2004) as "Nervous Control Centre" and also appeared as an exhibition monograph for *Central Nervous Control*, an exhibition by Christian Kuras at The New Gallery (Calgary, 2004). An earlier version of chapter 5 was published in *Psychoanalytic Review* 84.1 (Winter 2007) as "Mirrors that Pout: Subjectivity in the Age of the Screen." The introduction to chapter 7 appeared as a curatorial catalogue essay for the exhibition *SuperModels* at Open Space Artist-Run Centre (Victoria, 2006). The Introduction to chapter 8 appeared as a curatorial catalogue essay for the exhibition *Vulnerable Light* at Open Space Artist-Run Centre (Victoria, 2006).

The real is born of a lack of imagination.

Jean Baudrillard

In Praise of Nonsense

Preface

Everything begins with the simulation of nothing. Not because it is out of nothingness that things grow, but just the opposite – the simulation of nothing is necessary for the appearance of something. The truth is that there is no nothing, and it is the simulation that hides this fact from us. Only somethings can be simulated, and this is why the formula breaks down. Nothing is not nothing, but merely something else.

In the delusion of delusions, there is not anything that is not possible. This is the formulation that raises the stakes of the question – articulating the possibility of the impossible. This might be a limit of the imaginary mind, in the conception of absolute possibility – including the possibility of absence, the possibility of impossibility, or in the end, the impossibility of possibility to begin with. And, if even delusions are delusional, at stake in this precarious distinction is the strategy for negotiating the difference between delusions and their real manifestations.

A mantra for the circular pattern of delusional thinking …

… *in praise of nonsense.*

Opening Remarks

In an intellectual climate that no longer easily distinguishes the boundaries of the real and the imagined, and one moreover that finds such distinctions increasingly distasteful, this project makes the attempt to formulate a basis from which thought and theory might proceed into a future of postmodern thinking. My goal is to engage the theoretical possibilities open to a postmodern imagination stripped of its responsibility to remain fictional. Of primary concern to this text are the consequences of postmodernism, particularly as they relate to the understanding of representation, visual culture and identity.

My initial assumption is that as a result of the postmodern challenge to structures of logic and sense, the foundations of philosophical meaning have irreversibly shifted. Instead of attempting to recover a logic of sense amidst the proliferation of uncertainty and deconstructive thinking, I argue that the opposite perspective is preferable – a coming to terms with the imaginative possibilities of nonsense. And while there may well be room to debate the merits of such a manoeuvre, the truth or falsity of the suggestion is not itself the point of the inquiry. Rather, what is of paramount interest to this exploration is the possibility that the suggestion might be made to seem plausible and therefore some inquiry into the consequences of such a formulation is necessary. Having abandoned the notion of an external logic to which meaning can be held accountable, I attempt to formulate an embodied "illogic" which might be translated into plausible methodologies of interaction with (and within) an increasingly uncertain philosophical world.

The Children of Postmodernism

One challenge of postmodernism – what might be seen both as the basis for its speculative merit and its central problem – is the relentless emphasis it places on philosophical intervention and formulations of uncertainty. In this, postmodernism arguably demonstrates a limit condition of the rational mind – a receding horizon of speculative thought and a game of deferral which once begun requires that no plausible position or proposition be left unchallenged, after which all propositions and plausible positions open themselves up to the necessary and continuous undermining that is the consequence of speculation in the first place. While intervention may well be the modus operandi of postmodern thinking, it is the uncertainty – even the impossibility – of conclusion that is itself the condition to which every postmodern perspective must remain accountable. A philosophy set on continually challenging the certainties of others must also resign itself to a life without sanctioned boundaries.

Real or imagined, logically grounded or not, postmodernism has consequences, especially for those who have come of age in a time of postmodern uncertainty. In this, there is the implication that postmodernism is not simply a rhetorical perspective – not, at least, if it is taken seriously as having shaped personal histories of thinking, and in so doing challenging the larger questions of knowledge, experience and understanding. In fact, postmodernism – indeterminable as it may be – has become an intellectual horizon to which experience must somehow be related, and to which declarative truths must be held accountable. While this may seem difficult for those who prefer a collective agreement of philosophical tradition, for the postmodern generation that has always known confusion over certainty and doubt over truth, there is nothing rhetorical about a postmodern mind that knows only that its knowledge will always be subject to error, never quite leaving ground firm enough to stand on and argue – ground that philosophers of the past have known. This is, instead, a generation that has grown up with the logic of uncertainty, children of the completed spectacle – no longer simply citizens of Guy Debord's "society of the spectacle," but a cult of spectacular individualities. This is a generation that lives as though always on stage, never without witness – whether that be the scopophilic gaze of others or the watchful eyes of the surveillance machine makes, perhaps, little difference.

To the children of postmodernism, the world appears exactly backwards. It may arguably be Plato who is the father of Western thought, but it is a thinker like Jean Baudrillard who speaks to the intuitive understanding of a postmodern mind – with all its uncertainties, absurdities, spectacles, and resultant insecurities. Much more interesting than the "truth" of a situation is the curiosity that may be employed in its exploration; much more compelling than the reality of a relationship is the drama of interpersonal placement; much more seductive than the future of a sensible world are the possibilities for alternative formulations. And despite the backwardness of the each of these renderings, for a postmodern generation it is simulation that is more familiar than reality, contingency more familiar than truth, doubt more familiar than conviction, and nonsense that is more familiar – much more familiar – than sense.

Instead, the children of postmodernism feel discomfort when uncertainty exits the speculative process, when authority rules over meaning, when the spectacle does not seduce but seeks to impose itself upon minds that would rather be entertained than convinced. If postmodernism can be seen as simultaneously the limit condition of a rational mind as well as its undermining, what is nevertheless left unscathed by this intervention are the limits of the imaginary mind – the mind liberated of its responsibility and ethical imperative to remain fictional – the mind, in other words, which now begins to snarl and howl, to twist and turn, and to re-formulate the world around it. In this new world, the philosophical vertigo of embedded living is, in some way, allowed to persist without the dubious principles of logical containment that have historically been both the boon and the burden of philosophical understanding.

Without a reliable basis for its thought, postmodernism is inevitably left with only imaginary bases, and unreliable bases at that. For this reason, the postmodern perspective is not properly – or only – intellectual, it is also experiential. Under the conditions of uncertain understanding, what nevertheless proceeds is the lived experience of uncertainty, a position whose vertiginous disorientation is in no way an argument against its material incommensurability. Paradoxically, this position is – due to its intellectual tenuousness –

accountable only to the lived imaginary that continues to reinforce its uncertain experience. This is not a self-contained world, but rather a world whose absence of containment – whose unverifiability – results in an inevitable undermining of self.

Imaginary Practices

The paradox of uncertain living can be phrased differently by insisting that if postmodernism declares an end to the authority of truth, there is no privileged position from which such a declaration is exempt from its own proclamations. Instead, with each intervention, a postmodern perspective commits itself to an ontological self-undermining of equal seriousness, a shattered reflection to which it must also hold itself accountable. Postmodernism may break the mirror of humanist reflection, but as a consequence it can also never quite see itself with the clarity or authority it might expect to command. When one breaks such a mirror, one puts an end to the integrity of reflection, including one's own. The result is a spectacle of refraction, broken reflections left to interact in ways that can no longer be easily or neatly contained, but instead require lived synthesis to keep their stories alive.

There is a nuance to such a formulation, one that requires postmodernism to invest in the sustainability of its own fictions. While postmodern intervention may make short work of the mirror, the chaotic residue of appearances cannot simply be dismissed as themselves broken – particularly not when one continues to see a fragmented, multi-faceted gaze attempting to return one's own. Instead, the postmodern gaze reverses directionality, deconstructing not the externally imposed structures of meaning, but the internally satisfied desire for nihilist finality. A postmodern perspective – when pushed to encounter its own shattered reflections – is not merely intolerant of the boundaries of truth and meaning. The boundaries of falsity are equally fair game. If the tenets of postmodernism hold, the (sometimes contested) declaration that "postmodernism kills truth" finds a counterpart in the paradox of its own methodological procession, in this case a simultaneous death of falsity.

The result of such a perspective is a proliferation of possibilities – real and imagined – for the formulation (or deconstruction) of meaning. If postmodernism breaks with a horizon of truth, it is not to replace it with a horizon of rhetorical nothingness, but something more difficult still – a horizon of imaginative possibility, no longer pre-determined by principles of logic or verifiability. The postmodern doubled face appears with full paradoxical intensity

– not merely as a philosophy of nihilist defiance, but also as a fragmented poetic of encounter. It is a paradoxical double-bind – a world of dying truths and living falsities, in both cases kept in tension by the disbelief that sustains the postmodern gaze. To any formulated truth or falsity, the postmodern mind responds with the assumption that it can be, in the words of the philosopher Richard Kearney, "imagined otherwise,"[1] after which the postmodern challenge becomes one of beginning to constitute this "otherwise."

There is a spirit at work in this text that is as much artistically motivated as it is theoretically minded – one that owes a clear debt to a larger legacy of aesthetic and creative thinking. Where rational thinking may be insufficient to grasp the paradoxes and complexities of postmodern living, a logic that operates according to aesthetic principles has the distinct advantage of being able to proceed through and even despite positions of multiplicity, paradox and indeterminacy. One might even suggest that the negotiation of interpretive uncertainty is at the core of aesthetic thinking, a sensitivity to imaginary possibilities not restricted by ontological verification. Rather than binding thought to rational determinations of truth or falsity or reality, aesthetic thinking invokes what Aristotle called "plausible impossibility," what Alfred Jarry termed "imaginary solutions," or what the poet Samuel Taylor Coleridge described as "a suspension of disbelief" – in each case mechanisms for engaging the intermingled faces of the imaginary and the real.

It was Friedrich Nietzsche who perhaps phrased the stakes of the aesthetic question most provocatively, declaring "the existence of the world is justified only as an aesthetic phenomenon,"[2] and thus fusing the question of the imagination with that of lived existence. Importantly, however, such a fusion does not set as its project a reconciliation of the tensions between the lived and the imaginary, but intensifies the deeply paradoxical ways in which the two co-exist. In fact, Nietzsche went further, suggesting that only when this tension is at its greatest are the stakes of the aesthetic question preserved. To invoke Nietzsche here is not to refuse a critical horizon to the question of aesthetics but to double the project of this text – an attempt to hold the postmodern question accountable to its formulations of impossibility while pushing the impossibility of formulation towards its questionable limit. The boundary between the aesthetic and the real has already begun to collapse, and there is no safe zone in which fictions can be made to remain fictional, nor in which reality remains unassailable. Instead there is only what for Nietzsche was the mythic interplay of appearances and intoxication, seen here as a co-mingling of reflection and delirium, nonsense and its performance, or, in the spirit of Antonin Artaud, madness and incantation – an "active metaphysics" in which thought is manifest into being in a crossing-over of real and imaginary worlds.[3]

Such a fusion is also a challenge to discursive method precisely because it refuses to hold the imaginary accountable to logical argumentation. Instead, when reason begins to collapse under the pressures of indeterminacy, the imaginary simply intensifies this collapse by inventing alternate versions of the story. In order to adapt thinking to an understanding of such circumstances, imaginary solutions are required – strategies for understanding which are not bound to reason, but only to the manifestations of imaginative plausibility – impossible or otherwise. If, as Ludwig Wittgenstein put it, "behind every well-founded belief lies belief that is not founded,"[4] then one might suggest that aesthetic strategy forms the basis of well-founded thought – in this case a "suspension of disbelief" in its own absence of foundation. In this case, it matters little what form such a "not founded" belief might take – it could really take any form at all – sensical or otherwise. The formulation itself being grounded as not-founded is nothing less than a possibility for nonsense that is nevertheless "praised into" existence – rendered in terms of imaginary plausibility rather than argumentative demonstration.[5] *In Praise of Nonsense* is conceived as an elucidation of this paradoxical double-bind – one in which the central strategy of the text is also the main argument against it. This double-bind, however, is also what guarantees a contingency to the resultant formulations – a manoeuvre that purposefully over-extends itself in order to ensure that the foundational not-founded gesture of "nonsensical praise" remains incorporated into the dynamic of inquiry.

Improving in the Wrong Direction

There is, of course, a logistical gamble in a project such as this. To impose an imaginative – even nonsensical – primacy to the question of postmodern thought is also to risk alienating oneself from the consensual reality to which thinking is held accountable.

A friend of mine once accused me of "improving in the wrong direction," by which he seemed to mean that I was getting better in a way that did not apply to the world in which the two of us found ourselves. One might suggest that the strategy employed in this text is similar, in that its stakes are less invested in the viability of an argument, and more in the possibilities for thinking and living imaginatively. That the worlds that emerge from this process may appear uncertain is not an argument against the strategy. Nor is this problematic left unacknowledged, for this text will approach such a method conscientiously, situating itself on the side of error and falsity, the side of an investment in the stakes of the exploration, or to put it more generally, at the position of autobiographical disjunction between the immediacy of living and the alienation of an understanding that puts lived existence on the defensive. If there is a disparity between what we understand and what we live each day, we cannot simply say that we have misunderstood, or that what we have been told is incorrect or imagined. Instead, when confronted with such disparity, we are made accountable to the task of understanding differently, but not in order to reconcile the project of living with its understanding. Here, the objective is to refashion understanding such that it is made to resonate with our own imagined or imaginary experiences – in congruence with the spectacle of nonsense.

A Roadmap to Nonsense

In Praise of Nonsense is broken into three parts, each of which constructs an aesthetic platform for the framing of thought. These sections have been compiled, not to argue for a centralized imperative or a new overarching epistemology, but to instead provide instances of plausible representation in order to provide a textural overview of the platforms they seek to represent. These platforms are those of disappearance, ironic appearance, and nonsense – building towards a theory of sustainable imaginary practice: thought "praised into" existence.

Beginning this task, Part One: Technologies of Disappearance sets the postmodern stage of inquiry, articulating questions of subjective uncertainty and the fracturing of cognitive and experiential boundaries that are arguably the most apparent consequences of postmodern thinking. Technologies of disappearance, it will be suggested, are indicative of ways in which selves are unintentionally amalgamated by their self-imposed terminologies of social and intellectual engagement, eventually disappearing into the simulacrum of themselves. Framed by a brief introduction to postmodern disappearance, this section presents three such instances: the disappearance of self-conception, the disappearance of experience, and the disappearance of autonomous self-fashioning. The result is the construction of a platform of plausibility for the strategic mobilization of theories of disappearance in a larger sense.

These technologies of disappearance proceed as follows: Chapter 1 explores, through the writings of Michel Foucault and Jacques Lacan, the disjunction between an informed understanding of self and a lived experience that defies informatic awareness, rendering the self always a function of precisely that which it is not. Largely gravitating towards discourses of identity and psychoanalysis, the conjecture is that as a result of postmodern intervention, self-conception can be theorized as a process of hallucination, effectively destabilizing the self as a real or apparent individual.

Building on this framework through the works of Paul Virilio, Marshall McLuhan, and Arthur Kroker, chapter 2 explores ways in which theorists of technology have articulated similar problems of perception – namely the postmodern blurring of technological and experiential boundaries. This blurring of borders between technology, bodies, and perceptual context is framed as a conjecture that initiates an undermining of corporeal authenticity and integrity, putting phenomenology itself at risk.

Concluding this section, chapter 3 examines self-fashioning through a reading of works by and about Walter Benjamin. Gravitating towards Benjamin's idea of the "useless concept," a scenario is presented in which resistance to trajectories of disappearance is best effectuated by falsifying the very existence one might otherwise hope to uphold. The conjecture here is that by allowing for the disappearance of authentic modalities of thought, experience, and autopoesis, one might increase alternative possibilities for aesthetic expression and imaginative forms of engagement.

Building on the plausible platform of the disappeared subject, Part Two: Technologies of Ironic Appearance suggests response strategies to a climate of postmodern disappearance, with particular attention paid to the contextualization of disappearance as a grounding point for ironic possibilities of social, philosophical and cultural appearance. These technologies are ironic because they rely on an awareness of disappearance to form their constellation of possibility – horizons of speculation that also require an experiential or performative negation of generally imposed models of self-conception. Framed by a discussion of the death of authority and its aesthetic consequences, this section builds on similar instances of rendering, in this case the question of authorship after the disappearance of authenticity, the question of self-conception after the blurring of technological and material boundaries, and the question of perception in a climate of cognitive vertigo. Again, the aim of these renderings is to construct a plausible platform for the ironic persistence of theory after the disappearance of its authoritative double.

These technologies of ironic appearance proceed in the following way: Chapter 4 begins with a discussion of authorial self-placement, representation, and interpretive deferral, focusing on the writings of Roland Barthes in order to frame a discussion of autopoesis as both an act of self-disappearance and one of ironic reconstitution. This doubling, it will be conjectured, provokes a proliferation of falsity, raising the question of paradox and self-placement in acts of creative production – through which a disappeared self confronts ironic contingency as the consequence of self-conceived living.

Building on this trajectory, chapter 5 examines an equivalent paradox, the consequences of technological living on the ideological imperatives of psychoanalytic practice. Through a series of disagreements with selected works by Slavoj Zizek, the originary trauma of (Lacanian) psychoanalytic self-conception will be transformed into a postmodern stage for the ironic proliferation of fantasy – a conjecture that the governing principles of awareness have slipped from principles of reflective self-placement to those of a projected imaginary horizon.

In an attempted coming-to-terms with the ironies that result from this paradox of subjectivity, chapter 6 takes up Mikhail Bakhtin's writings on the contextual dependency of meaning, putting forward a suggestion of "sustainable fantasy" as the ironic basis from which postmodern subjectivity might proceed into a delusion of its own self-conception. Perspective is fused with performativity in such a way as to leverage both the possibilities and the dangers of fantasy as a grounding mechanism of lived possibility.

Capitalizing on the paradoxical plausibilities of fantastic, and potentially delusional, interaction, Part Three: Technologies of Nonsense is a first attempt at constituting non-ironic possibilities for performative living – a gesture towards the nonsensical grounding of a lived imaginary. These technologies are nonsensical because they rely on the delusional capacities of awareness to re-shape possibilities for an existence caught in a perpetual process of inventing itself, which is to also say caught in a dynamic circulation of contingent indeterminacy. Framed by an invocation of the limits of language – as a groundwork for a theory of nonsense – this section attempts to go beyond disciplinary or ironic possibilities to render three versions of what might be called a "sustainable delusion" – thought caught up in the process of praising itself into existence. These are theories of alliance: with error, with delusion, and with laziness – in each instance bound to that which is already performed without necessarily knowing so. The aim of these renderings is not to constitute a surrogate horizon of meaning, but merely to suggest that there are possible trajectories for thought after postmodernism – thought that is left to negotiate the nebulous vanishing points of both authentic and ironic modalities of theoretical inquiry.

These technologies of nonsense proceed in the following way: Chapter 7 begins by suggesting that postmodern living requires a personal alliance with both multiplicity and misunderstanding in order to perpetuate a constellation of meaning. Through a discussion of selected texts by Gilles Deleuze and Félix Guattari, this conjecture will seek to place self-awareness in the shadow of error – with priority given to the material errors of corporeal interactivity – in order to allow for an experiential immediacy that would otherwise be pre-empted by problematics of external interpretive power.

Building on this framework of error, chapter 8 examines selected writings by Jean Baudrillard in order to invoke a debt to the immediacy of imaginative engagement. In particular, the primacy of this engagement brings us to questions of seduction, simulation, and lucidity – mobilized towards the logistical gamble necessary to maintain the stakes of questioning in an age of uncertainty. The conjecture made will be that one must choose the side of delusion in order to maintain the integrity of a question – a lucid delirium that is required to sustain the non-ironic stakes of speculative engagement.

Finalizing the nonsensical gamble, chapter 9 examines the performative imperative that results from experiential proximity to the questions of frustrated and delusional understanding. Through a selected reading of texts by Peter Sloterdijk, it will be proposed that a postmodern metaphysics will be lazy by necessity, since its framing of self-awareness is ultimately a task of metaphysical redundancy. The conjecture implied will be that this redundancy, while useless to the project of intellectual authority, has important possibilities for the plausible impact of nonsensical understanding.

In Praise of Nonsense

This text aspires towards a suggestion of possibility – a suggestion built around an aesthetic of contingency, one that reanimates the useless and the irrelevant, one that attempts to stimulate the critical imaginations of others. In the end, the text is a gesture towards the imaginary possibilities open to creative reformulation – "plausible impossibilities," "suspensions of disbelief," and "imaginary solutions." These are the ways in which nonsense is both honoured and betrayed – compiled into a stage of conjecture, and standing in praise of the nonsensical frameworks that allowed for its manifestation in the first place …

… in praise of nonsense.

PART ONE

Technologies of Disappearance

The First Story of Fire

Jorge Luis Borges wrote a fable about a man who spent years of his life attempting to dream into existence a perfect child. In his dreams he began by looking for a child that already existed, but soon realized he would have to create this being himself. And so he began, building the child piece by piece – fourteen nights of dreaming to make a heart, a year more until he had rendered into lucid imagination a full skeleton, and shortly after a complete child, asleep in his father's dream just as his father slept in the world. The final step in the attempt was that which would allow the child to awaken. For this, a pact was needed, a pact with Fire that would allow the dream child to become real. The pact was such that only Fire (and the dreamer) would ever know this child from one of real flesh and blood. Recognizing the illusory nature of this dream-child, Fire would not burn him. And so it was that "in the dream of the man that dreamed, the dreamed one awoke."

For two years the man raised this child of dreams, instructing him in the mysteries of the world, teaching him to transition between the world of dreams and that of the real. Finally, when he had taught the child all he knew, he sent him away – but not without first destroying the memories of his apprenticeship, so that the child would think himself like any other man of flesh and blood.

From then on, the old man accepted the life he had led, and lived out the remainder of his days in tranquility, until one day the forest around him caught fire. There was no escape, the fire surrounded him – but the man was left unharmed while the forest burnt to ashes around him. The fire, glowing with heat and embers, did not consume him – it left him untouched. "With relief, with humiliation, with terror, he understood that he also was an illusion, that someone else was dreaming him."[6] The fable ends here, but one can easily imagine how it would have proceeded. For such an event, in the end, would not have left the old man untouched, despite the fact that he was unharmed by the fire. Imagine living a whole life, only to find out that you were someone else's dream – or perhaps even worse, your own. You can imagine this man full of anger, despondent, disillusioned – survivor of a world that collapsed around him and left him unharmed.

The first story of fire is the story of technologies of disappearance. What would have happened if the child had not come after the fire? Growing up under the spectre of his "father's" disillusionment? Knowing that he, too, was dreamed, but never having experienced his fiction first-hand? Growing up, not in the context of the real (as his father had) but with the knowledge of his own illusion? Rather than a disillusionment at being made of dreams, the child's only fear perhaps would be that of being forced into the real. Taking his fiction for granted, the world would not appear the same to this child, despite being made of the same stuff of dreams as his father.

Such an identity, based in a dream aesthetic, would have no choice but to accept its own contingency in the face of the uncertainties, not of the world, but rather of the self – rendered fictional in the face of a world that burns to ashes around it. To know one's fictions, and one's possibilities, without necessarily ever having experienced either – this is the fate of a postmodern generation.

The Performance of Uncertainty

To invoke a generation of thinkers governed by postmodern logic – a logic of spectacle, of falsity, of simulation – is to insist that the postmodern method by necessity extends beyond its frame of self-reference. This is, on one hand, to embed the postmodern in a social, political and historical context in which thinkers interact with the logic of their predecessors and in so doing influence younger minds – intentionally or not. However, and more importantly, this is also to assert that postmodernism is from some perspectives a lived trajectory, potentially traumatic in its consequences, and not merely a philosophy of rhetorical intervention. To constitute the postmodern in such a way is to argue that the "solution" to the problems of uncertainty, deferral and deconstruction is more complicated than a simple return to the logic of rational humanist constitution. It is to say that postmodernism has happened – in ways that are difficult to take back, repress, or ignore.

This may seem like a cursory assertion but it is one that is useful in considering possible responses to a climate of constituted uncertainty. The stakes of this position might be summarized as follows, in the words of Richard Kearney: "Where do we go from here? How may we hope to ever escape the endless self-parodying of postmodernism which announces the "end" of everything but itself? And if postmodernism subverts the very opposition between the imaginary and the real, to the point where each dissolves into an empty imitation of the other, can we still speak of imagination at all? Does imagination itself not threaten to disappear with the disappearance of man? Is there life, for the human imagination, after deconstruction?"[7] It is not an easy task to find a satisfactory response to this scenario. One possibility lies in Kearney's observation that while postmodernism may entail a deferral of philosophical meaning, this deferral does not preclude the necessity of making everyday, social, and ethical decisions.[8] In the face of the undecidable, Kearney calls for an ethics of uncertainty, a political strategy for the negotiation of a world that may now (philosophically) mean nothing, but in which individuals are nevertheless (experientially) immersed. The strategy he proposes is not to accept an uncertain subjectivity, but more progressively to "imagine it otherwise" as a way to tease out new forms of possibility, effectively expanding the deconstructive gaze in its opposite direction, away from intervention and towards (imaginary) constitution.

Interestingly, what such a proposition entails is a rendering-uncertain of uncertainty itself – an undermining of the undecidable whose aim is to constitute imaginary possibilities that can be speculatively applied in philosophical or political ways. In other words, Kearney's suggestion is not simply to resist or counter postmodernism, but to actually use deconstruction to undermine deconstruction – and in so doing, to re-open the question of uncertainty to the possibility of that which is lived out despite the indeterminacy of meaning.

One might take this further, as John Caputo does in *Radical Hermeneutics*, and suggest that this possibility is the paradoxical kernel of all postmodern thought. It is paradoxical because such engagement must remain uncertain while still coherently interacting with the consequences of lived uncertainty. Caputo's solution, not unlike Kearney's, is to make of postmodernism a methodology – a "radical hermeneutics." It is only from within a methodological approach to postmodernism that one can both conclude that everything is uncertain, and maintain the uncertainty of the lived conclusion. The difference is that for Caputo, this rendering is a way of making postmodernism, in fact, more radical: "Radical hermeneutics does not pass through a moment of deconstruction to get to the other side of the flow. Rather deconstructive criticism belongs to its very makeup."[4] With this suggestion, Caputo effectively transforms postmodernism from a discursive deconstruction of established codes of meaning into a performative perspective. It is performative by necessity, because any attempt at establishing discursive distance results in dizzying uncertainty. Yet, despite this vertiginous horizon, postmodern uncertainty is *lived* uncertainty – not merely rhetorical for the simple reason that to exit the performance would result in a declaration of meaning of exactly the type that postmodernism finds intolerable. Postmodernism's solutions must remain imaginary – imagined otherwise – in order to remain exempt from self-undermining and in order to remain applicable to an already uncertain climate of living.

The Postmodern Mirror-Stage

For those who live under the governing signs of postmodernity, there is no argument required in order to enforce the necessity of making decisions on arbitrary grounds – there is only that which remains when the grounds for decision are recognized for the arbitrariness to which they are accountable. The task is not necessarily to find a way to adapt to a climate of uncertainty, but to realize that such a climate already forms the context within which the questioning takes place.

This is where technologies of disappearance come in – those ways of looking at ourselves which purposefully engender unfamiliar and uncertain responses – perspectives that are convincing precisely because of the foreign image that returns the mirror gaze. This is not a new problem – but until now it has been a problem. What is different in this instance is that instead of a constituted problematic, this form of uncertainty resonates with familiarity – it seems to belong, despite the fact that it tells us that we do not.

A similar perspective has been put forward by the theorists of the posthuman – thinkers such as Donna Haraway, Katherine Hayles, and Arthur Kroker – who attempt to recapture, recover, or reconstitute identity in an age of radical uncertainty – whether caused by technological advance or the consequent fracturing of social and personal identity.[10] For the posthumanists, the question of uncertainty is a consequence of the social intensification of technological living, but also – and perhaps more importantly – an inevitable conclusion of the psychic dissonance brought about by postmodernism in a more general sense. In this way, one might constitute the question of the posthuman as emerging explicitly and perhaps most poignantly out of the shattered reflections of a postmodern imagination.

Katherine Hayles, for example, argues that "the posthuman is 'post' not because it is unfree but because there is no a priori way to identify a self-will that can be clearly distinguished from an other-will."[11] If this is the case, might one not suggest that her argument is so convincing only because it is in some way already familiar – a suggestion that Hayles has articulated a familiar horizon of uncertainty proper and gone further to give it both a face and an intent? As a natural consequence of postmodern living, there is an immanent presence of "other-wills" at play in the formation of identity, always someone telling us who we are or are not, always pre-emptively determining one's very own formulation of self. The posthuman self is an already deconstructed self – living always as someone else's dream, subjected to the uncertainty of external formulation, and through such constitution denied a self-possessed authenticity.

Consequently, if the premises of posthumanism are taken seriously, eventually one must admit that the postmodern question, while credited with initiating a crisis of meaning, is not itself a position in crisis. Not, that is, until the deconstructive gaze begins to turn inward. The breaching of boundaries knows no boundaries itself, not even the boundaries between the self and perception, or the imaginary and the world – if we follow the logic of Borges' story – even the boundaries between dream and reality. Perhaps this is the natural trajectory of postmodern theory, fated from the beginning to fold back on itself as the only possible way of sustaining the paradox of its own methodology.

This may be where the posthuman is born: in the embodied reflection of postmodern uncertainty looking at itself. Posthumanism is the postmodern mirror-stage, one that looks into the mirror without recognition, for the boundaries of identity have dissolved into an uncertainty of perception, and the self no longer appears, even to itself, without the awareness of its own impossibility. In this sense, posthumanism might be seen as a first iteration of postmodern subjectivity, less a sequel to the postmodern than a perspective that simply takes the tenets of uncertainty seriously. In the unidentifiability of self that surrounds the question of the posthuman, and despite the inability to identify the persistence of a "self-will," it is perhaps time to begin identifying some of the "other-wills" in play.

Contrary to Kearney's assertion that "it is certainly unlikely that any amount of 'knowledge' about the falsehood of our experience is going to help us think or act in a more effective or liberating way"[12] it may be the case that this is exactly what might help think the question further, with one caveat. The continued consideration of falsity does not – indeed, cannot – have as its goal the recovery or reconstitution of lost truth. More simply, its goal is to render falsity – disappearance – as the technological basis for self-conception in the first place.

If we have been rendered "other" to ourselves as a consequence of uncertain living – if we have been dreamed into existence by posthuman "other-wills," perhaps it is time to begin a performance of our own disappearance, that which might make of disappearance an aesthetic technology – a vanishing into the "imagined otherwise" of our own existence.

Technologies of Disappearance

The following three chapters – grouped as technologies of disappearance – are one such attempt to constitute disappearance, setting up the speculative task of holding uncertainty accountable to the impact of ontological fragmentation. Technologies of disappearance are intellectual and psychological devices that one can use to construct a plausible picture of not-being, progressively writing out the residual elements of self and identity in such a way as to re-open the questions of possibility. For possibility is always limited by the perspective that considers it – an assertion that ceases to be essentialist at the moment when perspectives themselves are made to fluctuate – or made to disappear. Until one can understand the implications of plausible not-being, it is doubtful that one can realize the extent to which our possibilities for existence might be themselves re-fashionable. In this sense, technologies of disappearance assume a possibility of non-essential being – which is opened up at the moment one begins to consider the question of essential not-being – the question of disappearance.

Three such technologies are those of reflection, perception, and autopoesis – grown of their respective claims to authenticity: of the psyche, of the body, of life itself. These three perspectives will be rendered through the works of three thinkers of disappearance: Michel Foucault, Paul Virilio, and Walter

Benjamin, who collectively set the stage for the disappearance of the self into its technologies of agreement – its posthuman constitution as inevitably other to itself. It is a perspective best rendered by writing these thinkers *into* their own proclamations on the uncertainty of the postmodern condition – holding thought accountable to the lived trajectories it sets in motion. For example, where Foucault speaks of "normalization," one may not at first suspect that his position is itself "normalized"; when Paul Virilio suggests a theory of "sightless vision," the expectation is somehow that one should still trust the way he sees; and when Walter Benjamin invokes the idea of "useless concepts," one is to ignore the irony of such an idea becoming useful.

Despite the insightfulness of these perspectives, there is nevertheless a potential paradox present in the writings of these authors, one that can – and should – be used to undermine the authority of their respective claims. Read self-reflexively, the worlds of these thinkers cannot be reduced simply to the uncertainty of the established world, but must be eventually held accountable to the equally uncertain state of the subjectivities that constituted them. In fact, to do so is likely the best way to honour these thinkers for their actual contributions to a life caught up in the process of perpetual disappearance. To engage with these thinkers is to write the self out of its own existence, passing through the transparency of technology to find only that the rules of the game have changed to such an extent that we are no longer able to orient ourselves, or to understand ourselves, except as a population erased by precisely that which we are told to value most.

What follows, then, are three iterations of disappearance – three meditations – rendered technological in order to construct a horizon of reconsideration, a stage for the possibilities of not-being.

1
Willful Alienation

Nervous Control Centre[1]

There are certain moments when the creature called technology begins to reanimate, reinvigorating itself through an elaborate fiction of mediation and taking on mythological proportions in the process. At times such as these, technology begins to challenge its own utility – reversing the formula and imposing itself instead on the human utensil, extending those interfaced bodies in a dance of machinic destiny. Is it any wonder that under such circumstances the human control centre gets nervous?

A recent exhibition by Christian Kuras portrays this relationship well, creating monuments to contemporary mythology, golems of a revivified technological mysticism. *Nervous Control Centre* is a gallery filled with silent tongues of confrontation, gazes turned inward, wired circuitry and flesh, all immobilized by technological union. What is the fate of the body in an age of machines? Neither the site of authenticity nor of resistance it is so often held up to be – that much is certain. No longer can we justify the body and the machine as two different things – one with agency and personality, the other a site of pure mobilization and creative/productive potential. Now instead our own thinking (our own nervous extensions of mind) is the source of the problem. The fear of entering into symbiosis with technology is also the fear of symbiosis with ourselves.

Marshall McLuhan always said that technology is an extension of the body – an extension of the human nervous system – and a nervous extension at that, boxed for brand-name immortality. Without the body, technology becomes lonely, static, and bored, unable to communicate with the world around it. Kuras' vision of a nervous control centre is abandoned by the bodies that inhabit it – and by the bodies that it inhabits too. This is not merely technology as an extension of the body, but the body as an extension of technology – updated psychological and intellectual operating systems, updated potentialities grown of medical and biotechnological research. Tweak a gene and live forever. The same relationship can be seen more simply in a photographic image, a mirror reflection, or the electronic geography of email and webcams. Even language fits in this equation – remembering, forgetting, thinking, imagining

– we have the fantasy of a technology that remains separate, pouting in the corner, passively dominated by the human machine.

Nervous Control Centre presents us with useless machines, relegated to a decorative symbolic state – lonely machines that cannot quite bring themselves to co-opt the body in a contemporary way. In one room, a microscope has enlarged itself – a technological temper tantrum of system feedback that knows only one way of looking: "Forget the molecular ... pay attention to me!" Or, in another corner, a totemic control console whose buttons refuse to perform – arthritic, atrophied, abandoned. These machines are unified through alienation. Useless bodies. We begin to realize that we are all in fact joined to ourselves at the horizon of our own reflection. We are *metaboys* – joined to ourselves by the dysfunction of self-conception rendered technological.

Something happens at this limit of the imagination where science and mythology begin to speak the same language. To call it science fiction is to retreat to the delusion of a life without technological mediation, but it is the mediation of life that was already our technological fantasy. And it is our own bodies, our own caricatures, and our own reflections that are in fact the mobilized bodies of Kuras' *Nervous Control Centre*.

Technologies of Witness

In many ways, what is at stake in a technological world is the possibility of encountering oneself as a witness – the challenge to clearly see not only the locations and ideas with which one is aligned, but also the ways in which one has already been transformed by the world in which one lives. It is a challenge because no sooner is the gaze constituted than it begins to reflect, distancing itself optically while still struggling to orient to a technological conscience. It is a world without clear boundaries between the self and its context, made all the more complex by the fact that the clearest visions to present themselves are those fabricated in advance, socially, politically, and culturally appropriated by individuals themselves, who are transformed through these extensions into the selves they have become.

This is the world of Michel Foucault, a world of disciplinary technological extension, of social normalization, and of the invisible operations of power. This is also a world ironically devoid of authentic individuality, if not yet entirely stripped of the myth of autonomous being. There is something autonomous that persists in derivation – or so it would seem – and even when taught to conform in the healthiest of ways, a technological citizen remembers being made by the discipline of others. "Discipline makes individuals," says Foucault, and with this pronouncement the challenge is set, not to recover an undisciplined authenticity, but simply to find ways to witness the constitutions which have made us who we are.[2] "I think that the activity of giving a basis to power is an activity that is made up of investigating what founds the powers I use or what can found the power that is used over me. I think that this question is important, essential. I would even say that this is the fundamental question."[3]

One might begin a discussion of this sort with an ironic reminder – not the reminder that we live in a world of powerful social dynamics, but precisely that the impact of these dynamics can be so powerful because of the ways they preemptively demand our attention. The discussion will be familiar to many, best outlined perhaps with a brief description of Foucault's analysis of Jeremy Bentham's Panopticon: the centralized prison tower that forms the cornerstone of discipline by creating an architectural possibility of continual surveillance. From high above, guarded from the sight of those below, an authority watches

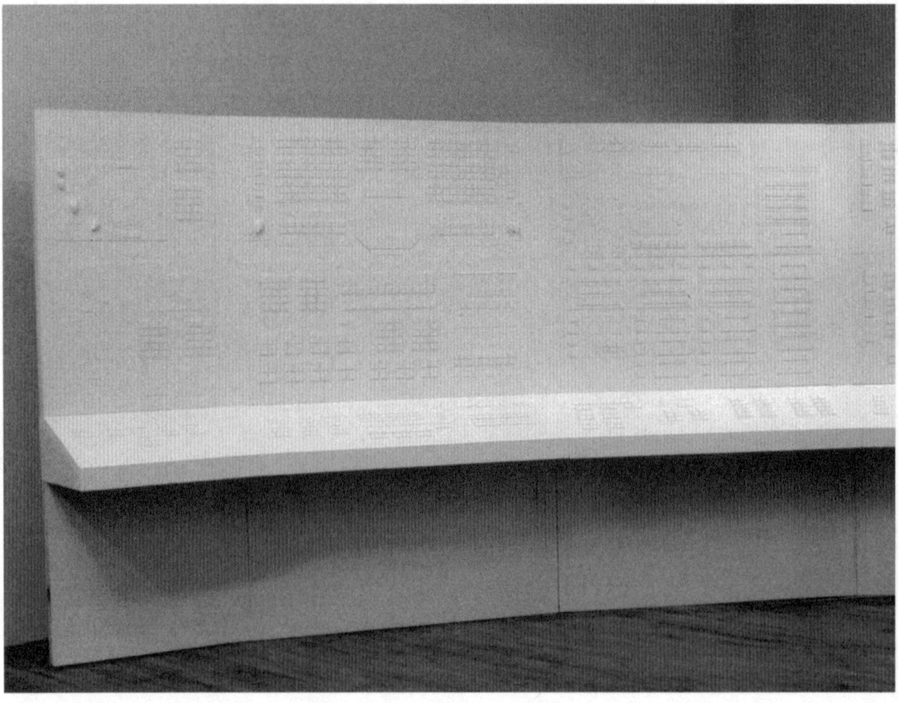

– or doesn't; the presence or absence of the watchful gaze is impossible to determine, masked by the tinted glass of the control tower. The Panopticon, much discussed for its important relationship to the question of power, is that which conceals the watchful gaze of authority and instills paranoia in the minds of those held captive. In fact, the Panopticon conceals authority so well that it renders redundant the actuality of whether an authority is present or not. Importantly, it is not simply the architecture that gives it power, but also that which the architecture is constructed to conceal: not the gaze of authority, but the possibility that there might be none. But it does not matter, for in the absence of a real watchful presence, there is always at least a *perceived* presence, present or not.

There is a form of disappearance that emerges in the dynamic of panoptic surveillance – the possibility of a witnessing authority is exaggerated and reinforced by its indeterminacy. What is important about this dynamic is that the indeterminacy of presence is continuous, unchanging according to the truth

Christian Kuras. *Console.* Mixed media, 2002.

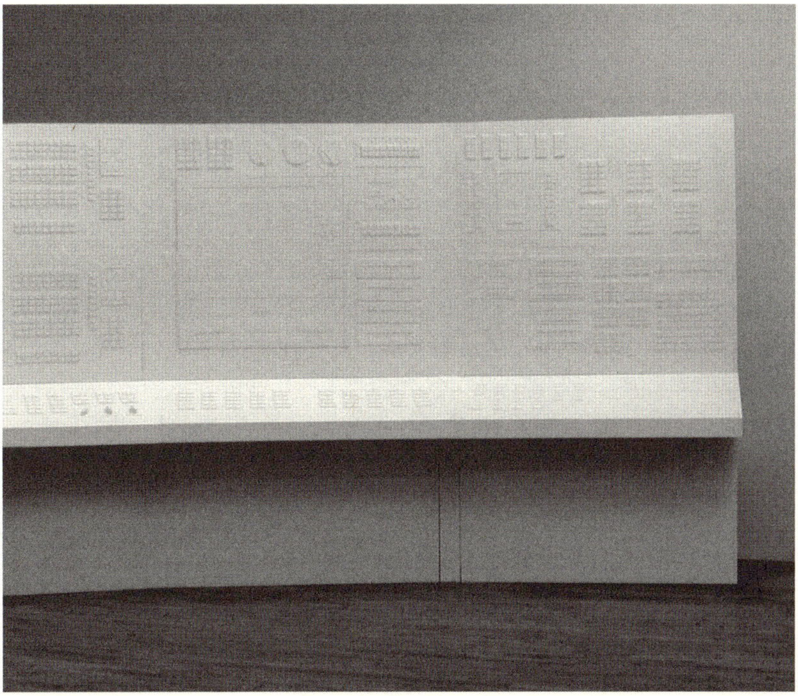

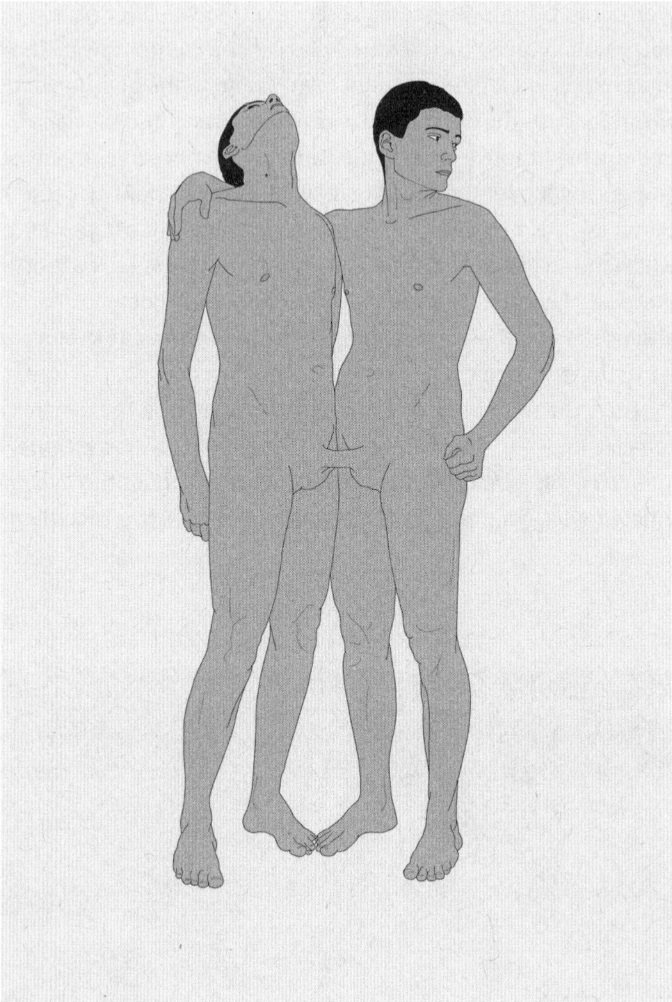

Christian Kuras. *Metaboy.* Acrylic on board, 2003.

or reality of the situation. The effect is the same whether there is an authority in the tower or not. For Foucault, this is why the Panopticon is such a model instance of power – it does not rely on an actual state of affairs – such an actuality disappears into the very ambiguity of the situation. Instead, here is a form of disappearance that literally imposes itself upon the perception and the psyche of those it seeks to control. It is not punishment that is the behavioural deterrent under such a model, but more simply the potential for punishment – the Panopticon at its simplest capitalizes on a paranoia of being witnessed.

The result is a relational dynamic that pre-emptively conditions behaviour. The Panopticon maintains control over its subjects by suggesting that they control themselves, conditioning into them an awareness that deviance will be observed, and that once observed, deviance may be punished. In this way, the Panopticon exists with a double presence. On one hand it is an icon of surveillance, an architecturally-enabled beacon of possible witness that can be so effective because it already conflates observation and punishment. On the other hand, in this indeterminacy there is also an engineering of self-consciousness, a structural awareness that is amplified by contextual uncertainty such that the paranoia of observation compels a response of its own – in this case a form of pre-emptive self-discipline:

> Hence the major effect of the Panopticon: to induce in the inmate a state of conscious and permanent visibility that assures the automatic functioning of power. So to arrange things that the surveillance is permanent in its effects, even if it is discontinuous in its action; that the perfection of power should tend to render its actual exercise unnecessary; that this architectural apparatus should be a machine for creating and sustaining a power relation independent of the person who exercises it; in short, that the inmates should be caught up in a power situation of which they are themselves the bearers. To achieve this, it is at once too much and too little that the prisoner should be constantly observed by an inspector: too little, for what matters is that he knows himself to be observed; too much, because he has no need in fact of being so.[4]

It is the self-sustaining mentality of a panoptic relationship to the world that is the consequence of such a relation. It is not the permanent visibility of the Panopticon that sustains this state of mind, but the fundamental invisibility of a gaze that is masked by its own indeterminacy.

Personalized Panopticons

Foucault's discussion, while focused on the birth of the prison, extends its analysis to a much wider social context, using the example of the Panopticon as an allegory for social conditioning in a much larger sense. Whether in prisons, politics, or education, the watchful eye of those in power predisposes a very particular sort of self-awareness – not a naïve or authentic self-encounter but a cultivated relationship to the watchful gaze of others. It is ultimately unimportant whether this is seen as that which sustains a disciplinary reality of power or as that which allows for the emergence of individuality through exactly the disappearance of power – in the end it is paradoxically both. In fact, one might even propose that the more autonomously one sustains this dynamic, the more the paradox intensifies. Foucault asserts: "as power becomes more anonymous and more functional, those on whom it is exercised tend to be more strongly individualized."[17] It is worth reflecting briefly on this equation in order to emphasize the impact of this relationship on individualized self-conception. If panoptic regulation can ensure a degree of invisibility to the exercising of power, one might ask after the relationship between individuality and the regulatory field that makes self-observation necessary.

Ironically, the more deeply one scrutinizes this relationship the more it seems that individuality itself is directly (and perhaps even proportionally) related to the anonymity and smooth functioning of power – to the apparent disappearance of regulatory context. If power functions most smoothly when it has effectively disappeared and individual self-regulation takes its place, one is put in the awkward position of having to theorize individuality itself as a function of power. Individuality becomes, in this instance, a self-sustaining desire to participate in precisely the disciplinary system that ensures a place for oneself as an individual. The disappearance of disciplinary structure simply masks this.

One might describe this relationship differently, drawing out the perceptual dynamic. While a discussion of the Panopticon reveals the Foucauldian paradigm of power and consequence, what is missing here is the additional step of simplifying the equation to the point where the horizon of individuality congeals. "What matters is that he knows himself to be observed," says Foucault, but what this means is that one observes oneself being observed – a doubled witness and a moment of self-reflection. The disciplinary dynamic, in this sense, can be seen to serve a mirror function of sorts, compelling a self-reflexive examination of life as it might be witnessed. Again, the truth or reality of the actual observation matters less than the impact of its possibility, its structural perpetuity. In fact, the disappearance of the witness into the tower might also be allegorically extended to suggest that this dynamic continues even when the tower itself disappears. What matters is not the external gaze that constitutes one as a subject, but the awareness that one has been so constituted, even better if one thinks one has done it oneself.

It is not only individuality that is born of disciplinary social dynamic, but self-reflexivity. Foucault's articulation of the technological tensions of social and disciplinary living extends into the forced birth of self-consciousness itself – the emergence of self-reflexivity requires precisely the existence of a self-sustaining contextual placement within the worlds of others. Selves exist (to themselves) within imaginary (disciplinary) limits, and to have a self is to self-subject to a relationship with the normalized ordering of what constitutes a self.

From this perspective, the self is not an essential or authentic category, but one that is constructed with a regulatory purpose in mind: systems of power offer the placebo of selfhood to their subjects, thereby ensuring self-regulation according to the invisible rules of disciplinary being. One must insist, then, that individuality comes with conditions – most fundamentally the condition of being oneself, within a context that allows for one's selfhood to be sustained. The condition of individuality is its willful self-perpetuation, the maintenance of self-constitution both for itself and for the disciplinary system from which it emerged. Here it is the subject that also sustains regulatory power, precisely by sustaining a constituted (self-reflexive) individuality. A suspension of disbelief in the autonomy of the self is at the very root of making power sustainable.

This raises a new problem, however, for it is not simply the self that is at stake in the question of power – the question of power already assumes the self as its methodological basis. At stake in the formulation of the self is the question of power, the question of *which* powers one succumbs to in order to self-reflect and self-constitute. The disciplinary gaze of the watch tower is, at this point, merely an instance of a much more pervasive mechanism – the paradoxical fusion of disciplinary strategy and autonomous self-fashioning. This is to propose, not only that selves are disciplined into existence, but that self-fashioning is itself a form of discipline. The self is an extension of its own self-discipline – a pre-emptive manifestation of an externally grown imperative. As Foucault states, "The acts by which he punishes himself can't be disassociated from those by which he reveals himself. The punishment of oneself and the voluntary expression of oneself are bound together."[18] The self, consequently, is not only disciplined into self-reflexive being, but is in fact sustained precisely by its own self-regulation, self-surveillance, and self-punishment. As the condition of subjectivity, one becomes one's own Panopticon – a Cyclops self who requires the panoptic gaze of self-regulation. A theory of willful self-discipline is at the root of sustainable self-conception: *having a self is a punishment.*

The Technology of Reflection

It is a somewhat unsavory form of identity that is yielded here, a disciplined and subservient subject that is dependent on a system of power for its very rendering.

This is a self that has disappeared into the very prosthesis from which it was grown, a technological extension of its own disciplinary self-placement. One might relate this to the vertigo of Katherine Hayles' posthuman subject, an identity that cannot clearly differentiate itself from the "other-wills" that have allowed its constitution. Yet, if one cannot clearly self-identify amidst the circulation of power and discipline, then the self-reflexivity of identity begins also to collapse.

The question that emerges then is that of self-reflexivity, the question of what we see when we look at ourselves. If these recontextualizations are to be taken further, it becomes necessary to rekindle some form of interactivity that can be separated from a contextually imposed, disciplinary self-image. It is the question of *what* is recognized when one self-regulates, what is reflected back as the condition of self-reflexivity, and to which contexts of power does self-conception then belong?

Consider the hypothesis: *If I didn't already know myself I might well fail to recognize myself in my own reflection.* The argument is relatively simple: if (1) the self in contemporary crisis (technological or otherwise) is the same as the self at stake in the writings of Foucault, and (2) if the self at stake in the writings of Foucault is the same as the self engendered by Jacques Lacan's mirror-stage, and (3) if the self engendered by the Lacanian mirror-stage is the same as the self behind René Descartes' cogito ergo sum, then the formulation that would seem to follow is *placebo ergo sum* – I hallucinate myself into being.[19]

The explanation is slightly more complex, beginning with the observation that through Descartes the self comes into existence at the moment of its self-conception. What complicates this observation are the ways in which self-conception occurs, and the particularities of the "existence" that is engendered. If one reads Descartes outside of an historical context – in the attempt to find a groundwork for his assertions in a contemporary setting – one might suggest that fundamentally this existence is of the same nature as its conception. Existence then becomes merely the observation of existing, in whatever form that observation might take. Descartes explains:

> I have persuaded myself that there is absolutely nothing in the world: no sky, no earth, no minds, no bodies. Is it then the case that I too do not exist? But doubtless I did exist, if I persuaded myself of something. But there is some deceiver or other who is supremely powerful and supremely sly and who is always deliberately deceiving me. Then too there is no doubt that I exist, if he is deceiving me. And let him do his best at deception, he will never bring it about that I am nothing so long

> as I shall think that I am something. Thus, after everything has been most carefully weighed, it must finally be established that this pronouncement "I am, I exist" is necessarily true every time I utter it or conceive it in my mind.[8]

More complex still is the question of to whom might such observations be attributed – the questions of who observes who amidst the circularity of self-conception and reflected thought. It is a question that Descartes does not answer, but which both Lacan and Foucault do. For Foucault, this "who" is the normalized self, the self-disciplined subject of contextual placement. Foucault is explicit: "discipline makes individuals,"[9] and it is not self-conception that is responsible for individualized existence but rather acculturation, education, and social participation. One *learns* to perceive oneself, learns to self-conceive under the shadow of disciplinary living.[10]

Strangely however, one also learns to forget, disappearing to oneself as the willing subject of disciplinary agreement. A normalized self is not quite normal if it does not also think it is freely thinking. The Foucauldian normalized self is one that is disciplined into *self*-conception, indeed one that has a vested stake in maintaining the conception of itself as autonomous. Disciplined into autonomous self-perception, what is forgotten as a condition of autonomous being is that being was never autonomous. As systems of power disappear into the darkened recesses of the self-disciplined mind, what is nevertheless carried forward is the very structure of self-reflexivity itself: a constituted image of oneself as an autonomous contextual agent.

It is a candy-coated autonomy, constituted for the self-agency that is its effect. Except that the sweetness turns sour as soon as one recognizes the disciplinary dynamic responsible for one's self-deceit. This self is placebo-grown, but its effects are real – at least for as long as we willingly sustain illusions of autonomy. But to doubt the doctor is to doubt the medicine, and once "off our meds" the face of identity will never look the same. Under the sign of Foucault, instead, identity will always have a face that is not its own. It is inevitably the face of the disciplinary institution – in this case a disillusioned doctor, whose medications no longer serve their regulatory function. This is not a problem as long as one maintains an active forgetfulness in the face of an autonomy that was never one's own – but the moment one ceases to forget, one's body is no longer one's own – even its face has changed.

The problem, of course, is that in such a climate of identity-in-crisis it is relatively easy to identify the authorities responsible. While the signs of self-deceit cause the breach of faith in the autonomy one remembers, this self-deceit is immediately transferred and transformed into the accusation of deceit levied against the circumstances of personal formation. This is to say, that one does not – indeed cannot – blame oneself for one's inherent depersonalization, for one no longer has a self-similar subject to blame, nor an autonomous perspective to wager.

The Lacanian Conspiracy

There is no clear way to self-identify that will uphold the myth of autonomy in the face of socially-conditioned living. Instead, identity begins to appear as a technology of sorts – a social conspiracy of regulated living. The frustration of such a dynamic is compounded further by the ease with which these faces of disciplinary conspiracy can themselves be identified. The futility of identity within a Foucauldian framework is precisely that these other faces are the only ones which can be clearly distinguished. We did not choose ourselves but were chosen as our own subjects of participatory constitution – chosen by others equally unchosen by themselves – a perpetual deferral of identities caught in the social dynamic of constituted living.

The nuances of this dynamic can be further explored through a consideration of Lacanian psychoanalysis. The alienating interplay of selves and power, so central to Foucault's perspective, is given an even more extreme structural rendering by Lacan who, in his theory of the mirror-stage, proposes that the self is formed out of an optic of self-alienation. Not limited to an alienating constitution by social and political dynamics, this is to say that what goes for discipline goes for bodily encounter as well. No longer is it as simple as to say that we do not recognize ourselves in the mirror – now we recognize someone else. According to Lacan, "[T]he important point is that this form [the mirror-stage] situates the agency of the ego, *before its social determination*, in a fictional direction, which will always remain irreducible for the individual alone ... by which he must resolve as I his discordance with his own reality ... [and which consequently] ... symbolizes the mental permanence of the I, at the same time as it prefigures its alienating destination."[11]

Consequently, to leverage Lacan's theory against Foucault would be to propose a poetic return of sorts, coming full-circle to an optical equivalent – a mirror-encounter from which the foundation of individual alienation is born. And the disciplinary dynamic of power and subject becomes an echo of an earlier dynamic of alienation at the core of subjectivity. Lacan has in this instance out-Foucaulted Foucault – making the latter's theories of social conditioning and discipline redundant in the face of the basic self-alienation required for the birth of psychoanalytic self-conception. Foucault's theories are no less critical for their effects, if less dramatic in their insistence on alienated individuality.

For Lacan, the child body, before even recognizing itself as embedded in the alienated dynamic of Foucauldian politics, achieves self-conception through a prior form of alienation, a technology of reflection that is the primordial factor in the self-alienation of the individual. For Lacan, the self has always been other to itself, indeed that is its condition of being – the unchosen condition of optically recognizing oneself as another. What this means is that no longer can one constitute the social world as solely responsible for the disappearance of individuality. Rather, in the act of self-recognition one has already chosen, however circumstantially, through the engagement with technological (mirrored) mediation, to *not* be oneself. This is not simply the result of social control or discourses of power, but rather the very condition of having a self to begin with. The (Foucauldian) confrontation with oneself as another is the re-enactment of something much more primal, much more fundamental, much less human.

Given the dual frameworks of Foucauldian depersonalization and its a priori Lacanian counterpart, there is something that happens when the self-alienation at the core of subjective being is "re-realized" – the socially-constructed self finding itself once again in a familiar dynamic of alienated awareness? This might be seen as, for instance, a second-order mirror-stage – an alienation of the subject that was already fundamentally alienated, a twice-undermined subjectivity. To re-realize oneself as such an entity is also to realize that personal history, personal trajectory, and personal formulation are themselves equally hallucinatory – equally unchosen – as the agent that spawned them.

Consequently, if Foucault, as an already self-alienated individual, can come to the conclusion that individuality is always self-alienated, is his declaration self-revealing or in some way a prophetic return to an originary (Lacanian) moment? In other words, is the fate of the postmodern to return, not to the redundancy of humanist fantasies of autonomy, but rather to the re-realization that humanity was only ever a phase in its cultural development? In this spirit, could it not be asserted that *to be human is to be alienated; to be postmodern is to be self-alienated*? *Placebo ergo sum* – *I* am born into *postmodern* destiny.

It is an already normalized self that now confronts itself as already normalized. Yet no longer is there any hope of recovery, for it is not as simple as to qualify contextual development and disciplinary participation as the root of alienated self-formation. Lacan posits an originary (natural) moment of self-alienation in contrast to Foucault's nurtured and conditioned alienation, and yet the result is the same. Doubly depersonalized, the myth of social autonomy has always been the shadow of the myth of biological self-similarity. Lacan states, "These reflections [on the workings of the mirror-stage] lead me to recognize in the spatial captation manifested in the mirror-stage, even before the social dialectic, the effect in man of an organic insufficiency in his natural reality – in so far as any meaning can be given to the word 'nature.'"[12]

But it is also precisely in this attribution of essence – this attribution of a non-human (alienated) nature to all things human – that the truly sinister side of the Lacanian perspective comes out. For if the spectre of autonomy after Foucault begins to look somewhat like a *social* conspiracy, through the work of Lacan this conspiracy is genetic. Betrayed by one's own body into not-being, the mirror stage becomes the literal stage upon which the fantasy of existence is acted out: "The mirror-stage is a drama whose internal thrust is precipitated from insufficiency to anticipation … [and] which will mark with its rigid structure the subject's entire mental development."[13] Consequently, a question is in order: what would Lacan see when he looks in the mirror? Not exempt from the implications of his own theory, the words of Lacan must be taken also as those of his reversed reflection – if the fantasy of autonomy resides with a spectral double (a self-alienated ego) Lacan himself must be taken as self-alienated to the same extent as everyone else. When Lacan speaks it is not Lacan himself that we hear but his double – the postmodern Lacan, the doubled Lacan. This is necessary since, as a biological theory, the mirror stage does not allow for a privileged recovery, nor for even the possibility of inside knowledge of what amounts to an a priori alienation.[14] In fact, Lacan's theory is as good an explanation for the postmodern condition as any other: we became human through self-alienation, we became postmodern through (re)recognition of our own humanity as myth. Lacan's voice is not the voice of (human) alienation, but rather that of (postmodern) belonging.

One need not try very hard to turn this into a conspiracy theory of sorts, as the fundamental politics of identity – that in which the self is irrecoverably alienated – serves the convenient (or sinister) purpose for which psychoanalysis itself becomes indispensable. The sympathetic ear that knowingly tells the individual that it understands the frustration of alienation, simultaneously leads it further into the trauma of irrecoverable loss. Indeed in the mirror of psychoanalysis what is recognized is that which can never be recovered, namely a fantasy of an autonomous whole that, without psychoanalysis, without Lacan, we never would have known we had lost.

What this is to suggest is not that psychoanalysis is simply another form of normalization, understood under the Foucauldian umbrella of disciplined thinking, but just the inverse. Alienation is the mechanism through which subjects come to the world, and it may thus be only natural that we continue to seek it out, continue to be fascinated by a very desire for disappearance: the only predictable trajectory after the original fall from authentic singularity. Mirrors make individuals – and the Lacanian conspiracy is one that has his name only because he was the first to alienate it from the already self-alienated perspective of postmodern living. *Placebo ergo sum.*

Mirror Narcotics

Despite the interplay of mirror selves and alienating tendencies that result from these formulations, there is something paradoxical – even deceptive – that persists, a doubling of the question that requires further articulation. At stake is the formulation *placebo ergo sum* as a paradoxical provocation of postmodern identity – on one hand, a form of preemptively inauthenticated subjectivity and, on the other hand an artificially constructed contextual state. What is at stake is the need to break from a strictly structural attribution of subjectivity and to enter into the possibilities for variation that a hallucinatory root of self-consciousness seems to offer. While it might be suggested that *placebo ergo sum* be taken to mean *I hallucinate myself into being,* this formulation says nothing about the form that such a hallucination of being takes. Indeed, one might quite easily mistake the formulation not as one that renders autonomy fundamentally inaccessible, but that makes all hallucination fundamentally autonomous.

The problem is that not all hallucinations are equivalent and that the hallucinating self remains largely inaccessible to itself. Consider that placebo effects require a manifestation of authority or belief in order, an appearance or prompt or expectation – much as the encounter with oneself in the mirror requires that a face appear, with all its alienating particularity. One does not hallucinate oneself, nor by oneself, but rather in relation to a generative position, a placebo. Hallucinations require context – versions of a believable world that initiate and sustain both disciplinary and creative effects. Placing oneself into a hallucinatory context allows, or even provokes, a principle of self-differentiation – a technology of reflective generation, or of generative reflection. Before one can properly be hallucinated into being, a context is needed in which to place the hallucination of self.

Seen this way, hallucination is not simply an attribution of imaginary or self-alienating appearances. Instead, hallucination is a strategy for perceptual contextualization, in which one avoids the attribution of authenticity or essentialism by preemptively placing appearances in a context of contingency. *Placebo ergo sum* is a preemptive disqualification of authenticity, proposed in order to preserve the hallucinatory possibilities of self-alienated living.

While this may seem deterministic as a formulation, it can be asserted that there is an action of this sort at play for both Foucault and Lacan, an exploration of which will assist with understanding the nuances of hallucinated self-conception. For Foucault, the action is one of power. As the inevitable consequence of disciplinary living and social conditioning, the self is displaced into a hallucinatory existence – a placebo that calls itself autonomy. As a consequence, self-conception in the work of Foucault is a function of a psychedelia of self-contextualization. As Foucault puts it: "[thought] is the presence of someone else in me."[15] While this condition of self-conception is as structural as it is socially and culturally induced, this particular manifestation of psychedelic structure takes an inevitably distinct and irreducible form: that which I learn to call "me."

For Lacan the situation is reversed, since the discourse of generative power that is so central to understanding Foucault is replaced by an equally essential category of reflective (mis)recognition necessary for the perpetuation of psychoanalytic alienation. The distinction between Lacan and Foucault with regard to the causality of technological self-conception is due to opposing perspectives on the same question. If for Foucault "[thought] is the presence of someone else in me," then for Lacan what he calls "I" is the presence of thought in someone else – another that "I" call "me" but do not recognize as myself.

This can be simplified by stating that for Foucault self-reflexivity is generated while for Lacan reflection is self-generating, both as a result of a prosthetic ingestion of self by foreign (reflective or generative) means. Generation reflects. Reflection generates. Between the movements of the two, the self emerges as a residual hallucination of failed mimesis, the reminder that the condition of this placebo is a narcotic debt to its own intoxicated potentiality. This is a speculatively recasting of the notion of reflection – no longer as an object or image, but as a substance ingested, and the relational co-dependency of self and mirror means that the state of selfhood is perhaps best likened to a state of delirious intoxication. This interplay of appearances and identities might then be likened to mirror narcotics, an ingestion of alienating effects that alter perceptual states at the same time as they generate, reflect, regenerate, and refract themselves in a simulacral dance of disappeared subjectivity.

A Theory of Willful Alienation

> We have to sacrifice the self in order to discover the truth about ourselves, and we have to discover the truth about ourselves in order to sacrifice ourself.
>
> Michel Foucault, *The Politics of Truth, 226.*

What is at stake in these meanderings is the attempt to find a way around the attribution of a merely hallucinatory presence to the concept of self. The way to do this, while somewhat counter-intuitive, is to complicate the relationship one step further, pushing subjectivity into the vertigo of hallucinatory deferral. The constitution of a hallucinatory world as the basis for alienated self-conception serves as an artificial yet causal basis for the awareness of individuality. The hallucinated world, by virtue of its relational dynamic, allows for the conception of self to appear in naturalized form – yet it is anything but natural – always a mandated reconciliation with technological mediation in the form of mirrors and/or social power. In this sense, to propose a hallucinatory world is to suggest an alternative to the alienated constitution of subjectivity in an oppressive, if authentic, encounter with power. Instead, in this instance the self appears as it does because of an agreement ratified by the ingestion of a placebo that allows for its appearance. The self is less a hallucination than the visceral effect of one.

While it may seem tenuous, the analogy between dynamics of hallucination, agreement, and effect can, in this case, be confidently made. Returning to a discussion of the placebo, consider again that in order for a placebo to function, some knowledge of an anticipated effect is required, as is a mechanism of authority with which such anticipation is compelled to agree. One might even say that such a relational dynamic begs for an examination of the placebo in mimetic terms, particularly insofar as mimesis can be seen as a form of behavioural agreement. Contextualized in this way, the generative dynamics at work in the theories of Foucault and Lacan find argumentative strength – if thought is the presence of someone else in me, or if I am the presence of thought in someone else, then my relationship to myself is mediated by mimetic necessity. In both instances, what is at stake is the possibility of mimetic failure as that which would allow for an emergence of selfhood as a qualifiable difference between myself and others.

This is a theory of willful alienation, but it may not be what it first seems, for it is not about subjecting the self to the observations or agreements of another. Rather it is about self-subjecting to a placebo horizon against which one's mimetic attempts might be assessed. The placebo is what is required in order to initiate the relationship, and one should be reminded that under such circumstances it does not matter whether or not the placebo is real. In fact, the very concept of the placebo suggests a breakdown of these categories – a manifestly real effect is provoked through a suspension of disbelief in the truth or falsity of mimetic ingestion. Equally however, such a methodology requires the anticipation of possible effect, in keeping with the dynamic of placebo ingestion. In this sense, the placebo is a prosthetic conceptual horizon against which the mimetic self draws its contours of identity.

This is not a convoluted attempt to revivify autonomy through a theory of placebo self-conception, however. It is instead a structural attribution suggesting that when the mechanism of narcotic self-conception is maintained, a more general rule of failed mimesis is also in play as a pervasive mimetic success. One copies oneself into social relationships, delivering on the mimetic promise of the placebo itself. It is only when the reproduction fails that a structural difference can be articulated. The generation of self is an act of mimetic reproduction, cast as the effect of hallucinatory residue: we imitate ourselves into believing we exist, and exist most notably when such imitations fail. Masquerade (rather than being) is in our existential makeup – fundamental to identity is the pretense that makes it so. In such instances, the appearance of self only serves to indicate a hallucinatory persistence. It is only in those moments where appearances fail that subjectivity is revealed as the absence of persistence, if not of hallucination proper. It is only in moments of failure that I might legitimately believe myself to exist. The self is a manifestation of the absence of effect.

As Foucault states: "You will become the subject of the manifestation of truth when and only when you disappear or you destroy yourself as a real body or as a real existence."[16] One might rephrase this assertion as follows: *You will become the subject of the manifestation of truth only when you become the subject of a manifestation of falsity*. The question that remains is that of what to do once one has destroyed oneself as a real existence, now that what remains is only the fiction of existence, the fiction of autonomy, and the fiction of experience. The comfort of self is no longer comforting. The absence of self is no longer traumatizing. Here, it is precisely not the trauma of alienation that separates us from ourselves, but just the opposite. It is the trauma of having a self that separates us from our alienation.

2
Prosthetic Phenomenology

Fear Commandos[1]

There are certain media dynamics that could never have existed before the voices of a televised generation stepped on stage. Among the voices is a challenge to the typically formulated media relationship in which the audience is a passive witness, mindlessly consuming entertainment and through so doing also passively ingesting the ideologies of a consumer media culture. There is a video by artist Michael Paget that perfectly represents this alternative voice of a media generation, a voice that is in no way passive in its consumer habits; a voice that instead treats spectatorship as an opportunity.

Two young men are seated on a couch in a setting that is non-descript, arbitrary, forgettable, as is the muted image of all settings when confronted with the seduction of televised stories that seem more interesting than our own. This story is illuminated by the viral green glow of screens and night vision. We watch as they watch, not gazing back in our direction, but instead held in rapture of the screen. A soundtrack starts, and we recognize the panic dialogue of one horror film or another – each distinct for its ability to surprise, shock, or terrify, but all uniformly interested in the relationship between media and voyeurism. The seated bodies fluctuate uncomfortably between media intoxication and self-reflexive laughter, in anticipation of the violence and fear they know – they hope – will come.

There is a hunger for fear among those in a postmodern generation, stripped of their voices and wills, those who now seek to complete their alienation though the impact of televised depersonalization. These are *Fear Commandos* – those who strategically place themselves in the line of televised fire, that they might feel alive in a way the world around does not so easily allow. It matters little whether the fear is prosthetic, the television screams and the bodies connected to it jump sympathetically – jumping with the joy that at least someone somewhere can still feel anything at all. This is not simply a dark side of technological possession, nor even completed nihilism. This is television as the agent of a possession ritual – the extent of the desire for affect is directly proportional to a new ethic of prosthetic experience that provides a token stake in a stake-less technological world. Prosthetic meaning, artificial sympathy, but

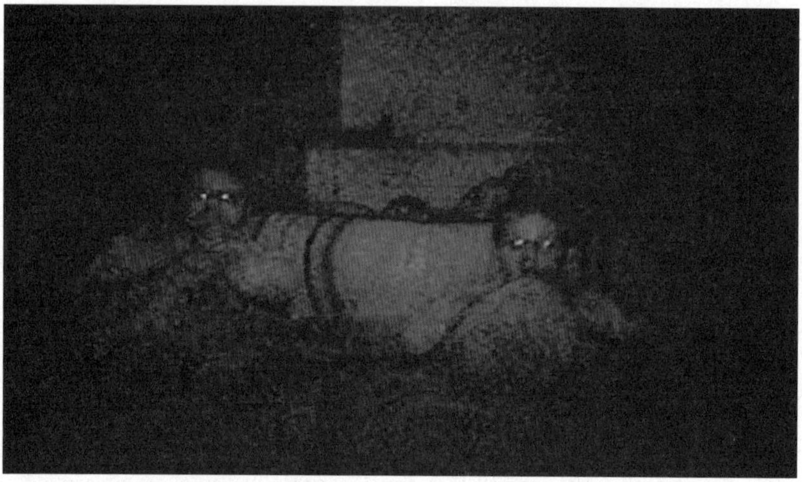

Mike Paget. *Fear Commandos*. Video still: dimensions variable, 2003.

real effects – these provide a new line of imaginative flight for those who have nothing left to care about.

Paget's *Fear Commandos* depicts willing puppets of a technological destiny, at once playing with the strings of desire as a kitsch puppet-master forcing itself to two-step out of rhythm. The freedom of prosthetic experience is that if you don't like its effects you can always change the channel – change the channel, change your mind – or let your mind be changed by the new strings you may encounter.

But this is not merely a video about televised ritual. Instead, *Fear Commandos* turns us into fear commandos too. They jump and we jump, then we all laugh in unison, and the television becomes the protagonist in its own version of a first-person shooter video game. Ten points are accrued for each of us that the movie can get to jump, and if we make each other jump too, so much the better. The ritual squared is much more than the sum of its parts, and in any case it's more about effect than it is about competition.

Fear commandos realize that all stages of the game, and of life, are equivalent in unimportance, but different in their provision of catalysts for response. This is how a televised battle is picked and when all else is stripped away, the fantasy of violence is enacted on ourselves – not into the vortex of nihilism, but in the desperate attempt to provoke some semblance of a response. Fear commandos know that television is the new extreme sport of contemporary living.

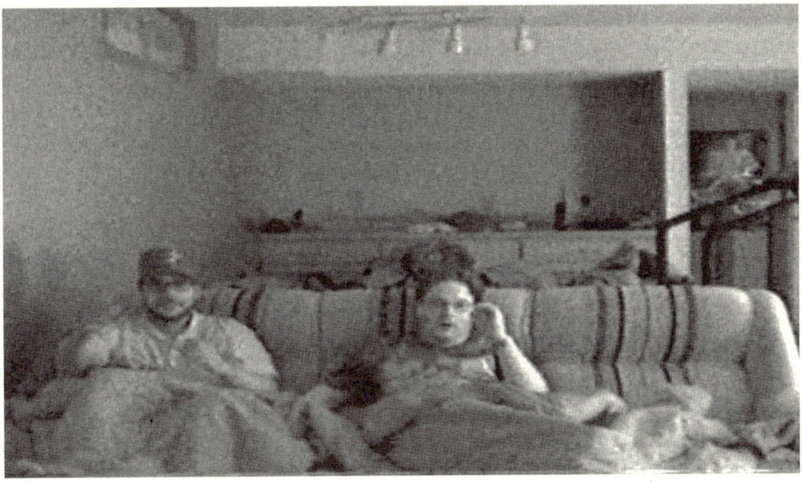

Mike Paget. *Fear Commandos*. Video still: dimensions variable, 2003.

The Skin of Disappearance

In response to a theory of willful alienation – a proposition that would put alienation at the core of critical cognition – it might seem tempting to return to a phenomenology of experience in order to ground some form of residual individual authenticity. Indeed the vertigo of cognitive uncertainty would at first seem to mandate such a turn – away from the unintelligibility of hallucinatory causality and towards the material immediacy of perceptual encounter.

The problem with such a formulation is that it demands a contextual reading of experience – in this case a contemporary context in which it is not only identity that is challenged by the deconstructive tendencies of postmodern living. The question of experience is not exempt from the effects of postmodernism – the accelerated pace of technological living might be seen to have effects on perception that are analogous to the ideological effects of deconstructive theory. As technology increasingly mediates perception, so too does it begin to challenge any phenomenology that would ground itself first and foremost in the integrity of human experience. It is the disappearance of the body, rather than its re-emergence as a general philosophical principle, that is the marker of postmodern, technological living. Rather than being given a new position of privilege amidst the ideological vertigo of postmodernism, the body is instead subsumed by the fragmentation of technological mediation. New technologies are for the body what deconstructive thinking is for cognition.

This, at its extreme, is the contemporary world imagined by Paul Virilio, a world of bodies co-opted by technology, rendered philosophically redundant by systems of understanding that have been built precisely to exceed any human capacity for direct perception. For Virilio, technology is neither politically nor philosophically neutral, and has as its overarching political and philosophical effect a disabling of the perceptual and experiential human body. For instance, when electronic vision is capable of perception on microscopic, telescopic and electromagnetic levels – capable of seeing even those perceptual components of the world invisible to the human eye – Virilio argues, the notion of human bodily perception becomes essentially obsolete.[2] No experience or concept is safe from technological extension: not vision, not geography and not time. As technological advancement accelerates, increasingly bodies are capable of only prosthetic experience – technological mediation extends into the minutia of corporeal reality, alienating the body from its own sensations and understanding. For Virilio, the case is extreme, "[leading]to the denial of any *phenomenology*. Far from wishing to 'save phenomena,' as philosophy demanded, we shall henceforth have to mislay them, to lose them beneath calculations, beneath the speed of a calculation which outstrips any time of thought, any intelligent reflection."[3]

If the image, seen technologically, is the skin of constituted appearances then it is the experiential body that now wears a second skin – a technological skin, a skin of human disappearance. This second skin is not that which appears, not that which is put on, but the violated residue of a skin that is left when human perception is pre-empted by technological rendering. This is a skin of disappearance, demanding a reversal of the phenomenological formula. No longer is it the task to understand the authenticity of perception, but to understand the way in which perception itself violates the possibilities of disappearance through compromising human alienation. The spectral side of disappearance is not the trauma of the self, not the made-to-disappear, but the violation of the primal code of disappearance, the violation of alienation in the making of appearances. Consequently, what is needed is a phenomenology of disappearance – a theory of absence, a shadow theory of sight, or a theory of the alienation of light. What is needed, in other words, is what Virilio calls a theory of "sightless vision,"[4] now no longer as simply the oppressive effects of technological living, but as the new rule for understanding phenomenological inauthenticity. For while Virilio may interpret sightless vision as the morally incorrigible consequence of technological proliferation, within this view is significant potential for the reinvention of alienation towards a theory of prosthetic phenomenological encounter.[5]

The Extended Skins of Technology

> Blindness is thus very much at the heart of the coming 'vision machine.' The production of *sightless vision* is itself merely the reproduction of an intense blindness that will become the latest and last form of industrialization: the *industrialization of the non-gaze.*
>
> Paul Virilio, *The Vision Machine,* 72–3.

Our skins have been scanned and strip-searched by the extended gaze of technology. We live under the sign of humiliated flesh – not as a result of political oppression, social regulation or personal futility, but rather more simply as the naturalized consequence of technological living. Our bodies are no longer our own, and perhaps they never were.

This is the theoretical consequence of technocultural discourse, formulated perhaps most clearly by Marshall McLuhan. Technology is an extension of the body, asserts McLuhan,[6] and he was more right than he could have imagined. If technology is an extension of the body, then the body itself is a horizon of technological engagement – an interface between the central nervous system and the world that surrounds it – processed into perception. If this perspective is to be taken seriously, must we not insist that the body – now seen as the Möbius skin of identity itself – must eventually be contextualized as purely virtual, not the authentic site of experiential living but an expanded field of blurred phenomenal boundaries. Consider McLuhan's perspective on this relationship: "Today, after more than a century of electric technology, we have extended our central nervous system itself in a global embrace, abolishing both space and time as far as our planet is concerned. Rapidly, we approach the final phase of the extensions of man – the technological simulation of consciousness, when the creative process of knowing will be collectively and corporately extended to the whole of human society, much as we have already extended our senses and our nerves by the various media."[7] For McLuhan, the human body might be seen as a phantom membrane – an illusory separation of perception from its extended (technological) environment. The integrity of the human body is an illusion, a phantom skin, because this boundary is explicitly permeable; the first major effect of technological living is the challenge to corporeal integrity. It is not that skins grow and flex to adapt to this new environment, but just the opposite: no longer bound by the skins of its own body, the self extends in self-conception and in self-deception, into the nervous world that surrounds it.

But if this brief description holds true, perhaps McLuhan's formula is also in some way reversible, and it is not simply technology that is responsible for the extensions of humanity. Rather, if these conjectures on the theories of Foucault and Lacan remain plausible – if consciousness can be seen as the technological alienation of the image from its hallucination – perhaps the body too was always technological. Already extended beyond the boundaries of self and skin, technological extension conceals the possibility that the body may have never actually been there, as it were; never an impermeable (corporeal) entity, never other than a myth of its own self-containment.

This is not to retreat to a purely phenomenological view of the body, except insofar as phenomenology is an already prosthetic rendering of sensory input – a technology of bodily placement – or perhaps a technology of refused cognitive placement. While the body might be seen as a technological extension of its own self-conception by McLuhan, if one considers the perspective of a thinker such as Maurice Merleau-Ponty, it is self-conception that is a required technology for the very act of perception. If McLuhan can be seen as privileging the consequences of technology in his propositions of corporeality, the error of phenomenology may be to have privileged the body as the site of experiential integrity: "The outline of my body is a frontier which ordinary spatial relations do not cross."[8] Merleau-Ponty goes on to elaborate: "Thus all senses are spatial if they are to give us access to some form or other of being, if, that is, they are senses at all. And, by the same necessity, they must all open up on the same space, otherwise the sensory beings with which they bring us into communication would exist only for the relevant sense – like ghosts which appear only by night – they would lack fullness of being and we could not be truly conscious of them."[9]

Contrary then to the phenomenological perspective that would have sensory perception as the mechanism through which bodies extend cognitively into space, it is worth looking at perception allowing, in this case, the penetration of worldly space into the body. This perspective would have the body not merely as a portal of extension, but as a site of relation, infection, and collaboration. And here, a systematic look at the boundaries of sensory perception is in order.

Sensory Scans

Consider the eye, responsible for the perception of light reflected back from the world around us. Light may be necessary for vision, but one should not forget that, for the eye, the perceived object is merely a reflective surface, brought into visual presence by absorbing and reflecting the light. Objects do not appear directly, but form a mirage that appears to us only as well as it reflects the light. The fact that vision is already a function of reflected perception means that all vision is mediated, and that mediation is the condition of both appearance and visual perception.

One might even look further into this dynamic, for it is not even as simple as to say that reflected light causes objects to appear. Rather the mechanisms of visual perception require that light penetrate the human body, passing into and through the eye, exposing images onto the retinal surface. Vision is burnt into existence as light enters the body and imposes itself on stimulus receptors, rendering the eye a technological function of the reflective appearances it re-constitutes. An eye is never merely an eye. Rather, vision is an after-image or a scar that forms around the illuminated flesh of optical receptors – perception trailing behind the actions of the world at the speed of light. In these relational dependencies, the eye is in no way autonomous from that which is perceived.

Consider the ear, receiver of sound waves generated by the surrounding world, a cross-referenced positional indicator as much as an organ of perception. It is no coincidence that the central mechanism of the ear is a drum, for ears like drums require the playing touch of an external user. In fact, sounds are only audible due to this imposition of the outside world onto the membranous surface of the eardrum, playing sounds into conscious existence. But this dynamic has consequences, and the fact that hearing requires the physical touch of a worldly hand means that hearing is just as mediated as vision. The ear is not a built-in radio receiver, but an instrument. And like any instrument, the ear requires a physical touch that teases out the sounds, a perceptual trampoline for the voices of the world. Sound is beaten into perception and the ear is rendered a technological function of vibration that constitutes sonic appearance. What this means is that an ear is never merely an ear – the perception of sound is due to a tactile blending of worlds and bodies, and most certainly not an autonomous bodily function separable from that which it perceives.

Consider the mouth, that which differentiates among textures, flavours, and temperatures, as well as serving as the point of entry into the body for food and drink. A mouth does not taste without provocation, but instead is a function of absorption, even infection; a collaboration with that which stimulates the senses, a sensory blurring of material boundaries. It is the same with consumption: in the process of feeding ourselves we literally ingest portions of the world, compromising bodily boundaries in order to survive. The mouth is not a passive intake valve but a portal through which the digestion of the world begins. The mouth, like all other perceptual senses, refuses to allow for autonomous or uncontaminated experience; experience is already a function of contamination simply by virtue of the perceptual dynamic.

Consider the nose, which shares much with the mouth, including an olfactory dynamic of chemical absorption that, like taste, requires an interpenetration of the world and the body in order to constitute its perceptual dynamic. The nose, however, is also responsible for an even more pervasive blurring of corporeal boundaries, ensuring that a body can never be cordoned off from the penetrations of the external world. The mere act of breathing ensures that bodies are always floating on the currents of an air-filled world, never separable – from the first breath of a newborn to the final breath that severs the experiencing body from the world. Through the nose, the world spreads out within the body, inflating both senses and mind, and most certainly complicating beyond repair any notion of firm corporeal autonomy.

Consider the skin, which despite its seemingly autonomous surface, is in no way a border between the world and the self, nor even between the world and the body. Nor is the skin simply a protective membrane designed to keep the blood and guts of biology intact, but something more complicated. The skin is an unfixed, permeable interface responsible for chemical absorption, tactile and temperature perception, as well as radiating excess body heat, and excreting salts and sweat. In short, mediating the blurred boundaries between selves and the so-called external world. The skin is never merely skin – not a membrane, but a horizon of nervous activity – an organ informed by the relationship between body and world. Body image is the image worn by skin, and identity is only identifiable through epidermal affiliations. It is the nervous extension of skin that allows for the tentative conceptualization of self to even occur in the first place. If eyes and ears perceive through the catalyst of worldly infiltration, it is the skin that conceals this occurrence as it pretends to be the defender of corporeal integrity, the last frontier between the body and the world. Instead, the skin has always been the horizon of the body's nervous system – bodies have only ever been as present as the skins worn over top of them.

Possessed Skins

As a function of interpenetrations of the world and the self, the body is hyperextended, no longer rhetorically separable from the worlds it perceives. The body is already an extension of itself. This is no longer the body referenced by McLuhan as extended by technology, nor that referenced by Merleau-Ponty as spatially distinct from the world around it. This, rather, is the already-extended body – one that has never been clearly separable from the spatial technologies of perception or experience. Never having belonged to a unified realm of being, the body has always been reliant on its extensions into the world for the very perceptions that articulate existence. It is a myth that the skins of bodies somehow construct or represent an autonomous separation between the self and the world. The illusionary function of skin is, in fact, to conceal the impossibility of an integral body, masking corporeal interpenetrations, diffusions, and blurring of boundaries. Skins, whether of bodies or identities, exist to hide the fact that neither bodies nor identities are clearly separable from the worlds they inhabit. In fact, such illusions have always been incorporeal – skins only of disappearance.

If the body can be seen as interpenetrated by the world around it, and if the body can be seen as technological before technology even enters the discussion, it may be prudent to remain skeptical of the insistence that electronic technology is responsible for the extension of the human body. Already hyper-extended, the body under the influence of technology encounters nothing particularly new. Without an impenetrable membrane to surround and protect corporeal autonomy, the body has only ever existed through mediation – not the externally generated impact of technological immersion, but the structural workings of perception and biology. Technological extension is not caused by technology, but more fundamentally by the mechanisms of bodily experience. The skin was always a stolen separation between bodies and a world that penetrates itself into appearance.

Theorists of technology have something important to offer nevertheless, for it has always been precisely the theory of technological extension that has obscured the fact that the body was already technological, already extended, already hyper to its myth of self. It is not television that extends the eye, but the eye whose already extended dynamic of perception allows for television in the first place; it is not radio that extends the ear, nor the electronic that extends the skin but rather the already extended ear and skin that allow for the possibility of radio and the electronic. These technologies can be so seductive because their dynamics are so familiar, and because they make apparent that perception has always functioned this way.

The staging of appearance takes on a familiar form: the stage of co-option and intermediation, rendered not as a consequence of technological living, but more humbly as a consequence of physiological being. McLuhan's famous assertion "the medium is the message" is no longer a sign of technological mediation, but more simply that of the physiological mediation that is already required for perception. When mediation is seen as physiological, the question of the medium of the message – the medium that *is* the message – emerges as the persistent question for bodies that mistakenly think experience occurs within experiential or technological integrity.

In contrast to the humanist conception of the possessive individual as an independent and autonomous self, what is needed here is to reframe the experiencing body as that which Arthur Kroker calls the "possessed individual." Contextualized through the revised signs of technological immersion, Kroker argues that in a postmodern climate selves are literally taken over, spoken through, and mobilized by the technological gaze. Contemporary bodies, according to Kroker, live precisely *as* media – as mediums of messages: "'Possessed individualism' is subjectivity to a point of aesthetic excess that the self no longer has any real existence, only a perspectival appearance as a site where all the referents converge and implode ... An apparent self whose memories can be fantastic reveries of a past which never really existed, because it occupies a purely virtual space."[10]

Seen technologically, the argument is convincing: the technological extension of bodies serving a mediating function that subsumes and possesses the human itself, ideologically no less than physically. And while the dynamic of possession serves both as poignant allegory and as a literal description of the psychic impact of technological living, the question here emerges of whether "possessed individualism" is only a result of the rise of virtual technologies – those technologies of possession that Kroker credits with the transformation of subjectivity[11] – or whether the opposite may also be the case. Is it possible that possessed individualism might be not only the new face of technologically extended identities, but also the case for identity in a lager sense – before technology even entered the picture? Perhaps the self was always a medium, already possessed by its own myth of separation from the extended world around it.

If the body is seen as already extended beyond its perceptual sensorium (not, as McLuhan argued, as a nervous extension of technologies that are separable from corporeality) and as having always been extended as its very condition of perception, perhaps the same is true for the body as a site for identity. To test this hypothesis, one might conflate Kroker's attributions of technological possession to the force of technological extension that McLuhan theorized – in both instances a technological penetration of the human sensorium. Here, if the body is already penetrated, already a function of its own technologies of perception, could the same not be posited for identity itself? One might remember the declaration of Foucault: "thought is the presence of someone else in me." A possessed identity haunts the very individualities it helps to construct. And like the presence of thought, the presence of perception has always relied on a world that can possess perceiving bodies into existence. Sight is the presence of light within the body; sound a function of the internal touch of the world; smell and taste and breathing and eating, each potentially seen as animating forces entering into the body with sensory-altering effect.

One might then insist that a possessed individual is no longer an individual at all. Like the perceiving body, and like the self-conceived body too, the possessed individual is a prosthetic technological extension of its own self-conception – a myth of itself. If technology can be seen as an extension of the body, it is only because the body was not already seen as hyper-extended. In a similar way, if technology can be seen as a possessive force of subjective determination, it is only because subjectivity itself was not already considered a phenomenon of possession – a paradoxical desire for (non)identity, given the form of an extended conceptual prosthesis that was itself only ever a myth of paradoxically virtual presence. The skin of identity, like the skin of the body before it, is already possessed: a medium for the mythic message of prosthetic being.

The Loss of Nothing

It is useful to return to an even more extreme formulation of technological impact – the theories of Paul Virilio, in which the technological possession that was the groundwork for Kroker's "possessed individual" becomes fully debilitating. For Virilio, it is no longer simply technological "extension" or "possession" that is the result of new technology, but a body that is literally disabled, rendered redundant by a climate of technological perception. In the formulations of Virilio, the eye no longer sees, replaced by a technological gaze that sees in more detail, in more depth, with more understanding. The technological gaze opens up to macro and micro levels of vision, from telescopic to microscopic, from virtual to panoptic. The technological eye sees everything, rendering the human eye functionally obsolete. Mediums without messages – what goes for the eye goes for the entire body in a technological world. The skin is the discarded symbol of lost humanity and, for Virilio, the result is a spectral body fully conquered by the force of technology: "[N]ew technologies are responsible for the loss of both the body proper in favor of the spectral body, and the world proper in favor of a virtual world. … Technology is colonizing the human body just as it colonized the body of the Earth.[12] But perhaps this is how the medium of possession has always worked, and the possessed body can be quickly and easily forgotten because of the attractions of its newly extended form. Perhaps there has never been a body proper, and the body to which Virilio refers was already virtual. If the body can already be seen as technologically extended, simply as a result of corporeal interaction, does it not mean that the body has never been itself – not, in any case, as it has self-conceived or self-perceived? Is the same not true for possessed identity? If so, what this would mean is that the project of technological thinking has somehow avoided exactly the question of its own self-placement by transferring its inquiry to a naturalized other. We may well have always been technological, we may have always been other to ourselves, and this may have always been our condition of living.

There is a way to make sense of this paradox, and it is by continuing to reread the theorists of technology back against themselves. Virilio, for instance, insists that "nothing is ever obtained without a loss of something else," a reflection on the simple assertion that technological interaction has consequences.[13] Yet if Virilio is correct, then the inverse may also be true: something is never obtained without a loss of nothingness. The accomplishment of technological understanding comes at the price of an ironic self-conception, the phantom appearance of a perceptual "something" – a constituted boundary, a prosthetic authenticity, an illusory integrity that was never actually there. Perhaps technology can be so easily accused of bodily compromise because we refuse to understand ourselves, except as the persecuted others of lived mediation. Strange though it might seem to say, perhaps we have lost our "nothing," the possibility that what we name as ourselves is neither as separate from the world, nor as autonomous as the traditions of understanding would have us believe. Perhaps, in the blurring of boundaries between selves and the world, one begins to recover a lost disappearance of sorts. This does not bring about a fundamental shift in the status of autonomy in an age of technological living – the illusion of autonomy has always been based on the technological myth of artificial separation from our surrounding worlds.

Corporeal integrity, personal autonomy and self-possessed living are not all they promise. To over-emphasize these imperatives for phenomenological understanding is also to potentially misconstrue the interpenetrations and intermediations of bodily and worldly boundaries. Something has changed, and it is not merely a ranting of dissent. Our "nothingness" is lost, replaced by a prosthetic constitution that conceals the fact that "we," contrary to everything we have believed or been told, never properly existed as independently experiencing individuals in the first place.

The Accident of Understanding

There is the attribution of what might be called an accident of understanding at the root of this conjecture – an accident of appearance that is made possible by the misunderstandings of technological and corporeal inquiry. The question of technology, phrased as a question of appearances, causes a collapse of the possibility of nothingness, of disappearance; the possibility that selves and bodies may never have been autonomous from the worlds that surround them. As a question of disappearance, the question of technology reveals nothing that we did not know already – it is the same nothingness to which we may have always unknowingly belonged. It is more than wordplay, much more in fact, since at stake in this reversal of the formula is the possibility of disappearance itself, not as a result of technological oppression but as a postmodern call to action.

What happens when these terms of engagement are reversed? It is not as easy as saying that the theorists of technology have been wrong; in fact their conclusions uniformly make sense. Instead, it is only the premise for questioning that has changed in any significant way. If, as these theorists claim, the fate of bodies in a postmodern world (technological or otherwise) is to collapse through over-extension – soul-sucked by electronics and neon – then the more general rules for technology must also apply to both perception and the body in this context. The overarching result of this reversal is not to assert that technology does not exist, nor that its impacts are different from those posited by McLuhan, Kroker, and Virilio, but rather to suggest that each of these theoretical voices was itself already a technological voice – already extended, already possessed, already disabled. Consequently, the conclusion that this is nothing new is itself nothing new either, except to say that bodies, and selves and identities have always been technological in form – and technological in consequence.

As a result, the examination of technological consequences must be tempered by an examination of the consequences of the experience of technology. Technologies (the body included) break down, misfire, collapse, and cause accidents intentionally or otherwise. It is Virilio who phrases this best, insisting that at the moment when a technology is invented, one also invents the possibility of a technological accident: "When you invent the ship, you also invent the shipwreck; when you invent the plane, you invent the plane crash; and when you invent electricity, you invent electrocution ... Every technology carries its own negativity, which is invented at the same time as technical progress."[14]

Constituted with particular emphasis on the effects of technological possession, identity and the self and the body are not merely casualties along the way, but perhaps the endgame of technological inquiry. When the body is "invented"– which is to say when the body is ordered as an impermeable corporeal entity, functioning independently from the world around it – then one simultaneously invents the possibility of corporeal extension, bodily possession, and technological oppression.

This is the accident of phenomenological understanding as well. If it is a technological understanding of experience that can be crediting with prosthetizing the body, it is the physiological dynamic of the body that allows for the claim that it has never been otherwise. Just as the self is a consequence of prosthetic (other-willed) induction, the body has never been other than an accidental misplacement of perceptual attribution. The discursive body may not be equivalent to the body that bleeds when injured, but if not, this is a discursive problem that needs to be reconciled. Technologies bleed and the discursive body is no different. Over-extension is either a technological quartering of flesh or a call to re-assess the terms according to which phenomenologies proceed. It does not seem that it can be both at the same time.

If the body has never been present in the ways in which it has been conceived, it means that phenomenology has always been prosthetic – a phantom of self-misunderstanding.

Prosthetic Phenomenology

What McLuhan, Kroker, and Virilio speak of as the impact of technology on the human body can be seen as a condition of bodily living in a more general sense. What these thinkers have in common is an oversight of sorts – an accident, even – in which eloquent descriptions of technological living seem to overlook the possibility that life was already technological. One might even suggest that understanding is itself a technology, revealing the possibility of a postmodern phenomenology, framed not by new technology but by a reconsideration of experiential boundaries. Whether such a phenomenology is taken as one of corporeal extension, virtual possession, or technological disabling, at the root of phenomenal understanding is not an authentic a priori experiential perspective, but a lived disappearance. Reframed in this way, the ghosts of the non-technological become hyper-aware that their tools of understanding are no longer adequate to the challenge of phenomenological possibility.

One final example is useful here, particularly because it provides an analogy that can help develop the relationship between technological understanding and the lived disappearances that are its discursive effects. The example is one of time, Virilio's apocalyptic vision of a technological end-time, the accident of time itself. For Virilio, technological time (the "real time" of online living) is a virtualization to which he attributes both the collapse of geography (since virtual time is geographically independent) and human measures of time itself (since time measured only in duration results in the loss of localized standards of measurement): "Time is volume; it is not only space-time in the sense of relativity. It is volume and depth of meaning, and the emergence of one world time eliminating the multiplicity of local times is a considerable loss for both geography and history. We are going to witness the accident of accidents, the accident of time ... the hyperconcentration of real time reduces all trajectories to nothing: the temporal trajectory becomes a permanent present, and travel – from here to there, from one to another – a mere 'being there.' Michel Serres calls this the 'hors-là' (out there). (Think of the image of the Horla in literature: it's a phantom.) We are therefore risking an accident of time that will affect our entire being."[15]

In a technological environment, because standards of difference and deviation are obliterated by the virtualization of time, Virilio aptly points to the literary figure of the Horla. The figure is derived from Guy de Maupassant's short story *The Horla*,[16] an elaborate account of an invisible presence that torments the central character, the former never managing to understand or defeat the latter and ultimately being forced to concede. While the simulations caused by virtual time may well be phantoms with no explicit real-world correlatives, the haunting impact of technological standardization indeed threatens the human relationship between bodies, spaces, and the cycles of lived time with all their geographic nuances. Virilio's version of the Horla is the story of conception extended outside of itself, haunted – the ghosted body of historical time in an age of technological living.

This familiar story of the end of history is intensified by Virilio, who charts, perhaps unintentionally, a last slippage into the fully technological rendering of phenomenology. It seems unintended because, while Virilio laments the loss of a multiplicity of local, personal, or embodied durations – whether governed by sunrise or by time zones – one might still attribute to these durations a regulatory power, already non-local in favour of regional, marked by geographic boundaries and zones of prosthetic temporal belonging. The globalization of time in the form of "real time," while intensifying the stakes of artificial regulation, has not broken with the regulatory imperative of technological living. We were already (temporally) other to ourselves, marked in standardized years and zoned in regional affiliation.

What is more interesting about this story, however, is that the accident of which Virilio speaks seems to be exactly what a postmodern phenomenology would demand: an abolishment of sensical forms of time that would have bodies floating in a perpetual uncertainty of duration. Virilio fears a temporal vertigo, the domination not of bodies but of historical tropes of understanding. This is why, for Virilio, the words of de Maupassant are such a poignant frame of referene: "Ah! the vulture has eaten the pigeon, the wolf has eaten the lamb; the lion has devoured the sharp-horned buffalo; man has killed the lion with an arrow, with a spear, with gunpowder; but the Horla will make of man what man has made of the horse and of the ox: his chattel, his slave, and his food, by the mere power of his will."[17] The Horla in fact makes of humanity a technology, making the larger problem clear. Already familiar with the zones of modernist time, Virilio's lament is more properly for the loss of technological familiarity – a loss of understanding – than for the loss of temporal authenticity. De Maupassant's words are no longer simply an allegory for time, but for the loss of the human to the will of technology. Yet he is not incorrect to assert that something has changed, for while time may have always been technological, this technology has now reached such critical velocity that its effects can no longer go unperceived. Time undermines itself, rendered hors-là, foreign even to the technological attribution of presence, rendered as a phenomenal existence that was never properly there.

The body has thus been rendered fully spectral – as a consequence of technological extremity, but also as a simple consequence of uncertainty. One might even suggest that this is only possible because the body has already become a technology, framed in terms of prosthetic understandings, extensions and possessions that quickly blur any authentic corporeal boundaries to the point of unintelligibility. The body becomes a spectre of its own experience; a phantom that seems to experience, sense, perceive, but in fact does none of these things since it is no longer identifiably present. The body has not become incorporeal – it always was. If the willfully alienated mind is lost to its own hallucinatory world, it is through a prosthetic phenomenology that the body becomes nothing more or less than a phantom of itself, disappearing into the prosthetics of corporeal misunderstanding.

We are thus accidented into disappearance, without a fight – and this may be what we always hoped for. Yet, what the machines of disappearance have forgotten is that there is always a second, hidden side to the dynamic of the accident. No longer bound by identities that cannot be supported, no longer bound to a static, singular, or authentic conception of bodily experience, we move towards a release from the myth of being into a prosthetic space opened up by the accident of understanding.

3
Vacuous Being

Kiddie Pool[1]

The most challenging, preoccupying, and devastating forms of disappearance are those that occur despite their own impossibility, seemingly reviving a lost kernel of appearance while actually doing nothing of the sort. This phenomenon is on display in Duncan MacKenzie's sculpture *Kiddie Pool,* a provocative conflation of playful consumerism and morbidity.

Into the kiddie pool go the summer memories of the nostalgic mind: hot sunny days spent running through the sprinklers or around the block, bike rides through the playground, sleepovers with friends and siblings. To remember in this way is not different from resurrecting moments gone, moments archived that can never quite be fully retrieved. Consequently, into the kiddie pool also go those memories not quite remembered, mis-remembered, and those one would rather just forget. It is this mix of memory that makes a many-headed beast of the process itself.

MacKenzie's *Kiddie Pool* is a many-headed beast, a nostalgic heap of soft foam skulls, each one individually hand-painted and sun-faded, rendered quarter-size – or, more disturbingly, baby-sized. *Kiddie Pool* is framed by a blow-up pool painted with candy-coloured polka-dots – a game of Twister gone wrong, an inflatable mass grave for the Nerf skulls of broken youth and forgotten memories.

This is a work of art that primarily and directly invokes the dynamic of death – the ongoing death of memory, the death of childhood, family, relationships, meaning, and certainty, and even the death of the spectacle. In short, it represents the death of everything that might otherwise be used to constitute a right to play in the splash pool of a contemporary world. As our own memories and prophecies are laid out on display in a plastic pile, this also means the death of life. There is company in death, but apparently none in life except for a fantasized community brought together by the spectacle of soft death, a foam-skull mattress upon which to confess our memories of never having remembered at all.

What does it mean to turn symbols of death into a playful display item, and where do we find the entry point into the spectacle it initiates? We could begin by asking which one is ours. They are seemingly interchangeable, and perhaps

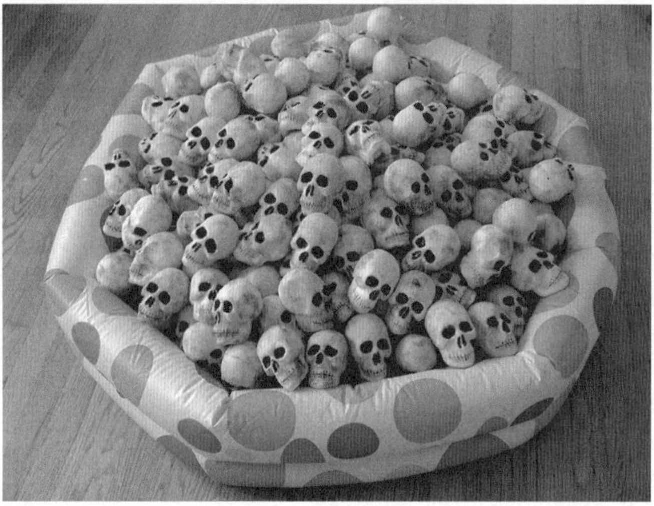

Duncan MacKenzie. *Kiddie Pool*. Mixed media, 2005.

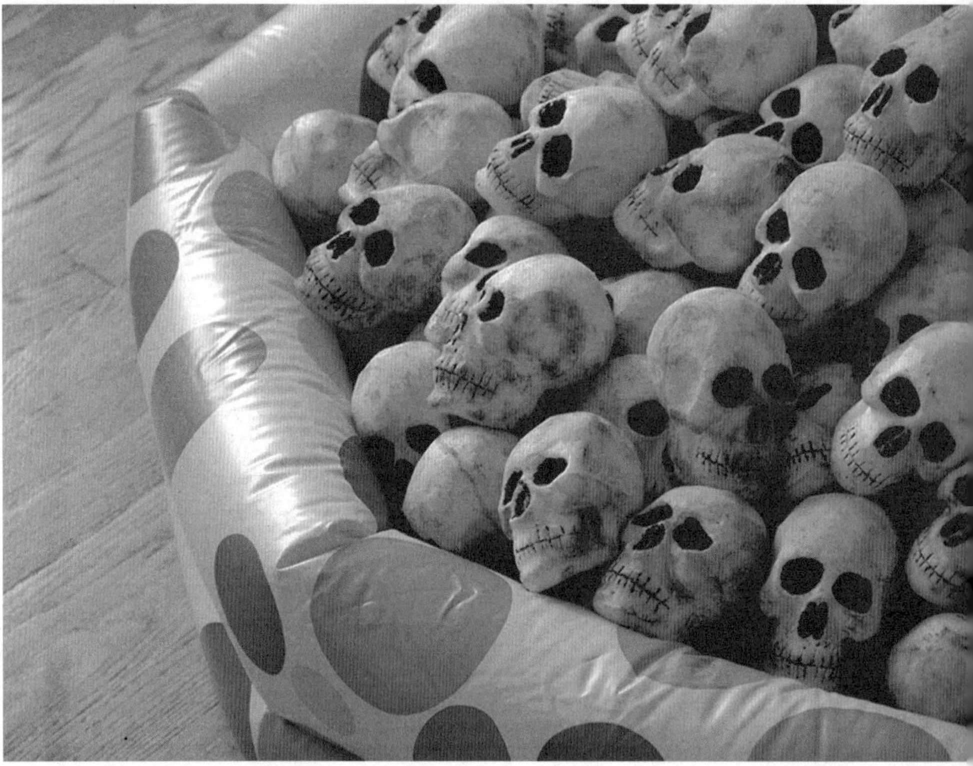

Detail: Duncan MacKenzie. *Kiddie Pool*. Mixed media, 2005.

this is because histories are all the same in their disappearance. Or what about the game of Twister that is invoked: if we are the ones to twist, is the point to see who can become the most twisted of all? Or if Nerf is simply Nerf, then why does this read more like an animated effigy to a Dia de los Muertos parade? Mexico's Day of the Dead, with its candy skeletons, chocolate skulls, bright colours, mariachis, and piñatas, is a celebration that makes many foreigners uneasy. If there was to be a soundtrack to the *Kiddie Pool* installation, would it not have to be something akin to the sounds of this carnival that is not a carnival, a game that is not a game, but an elaborate ritual celebrating the spectral presences of reanimated disappearance?

Softly twisted, screaming in silence – or is it some vestige of me that screams instead, on behalf of the phantom imagination that reminds me that death is to be avoided and certainly not laughed at? Or is the point of *Kiddie Pool* to demonstrate that even the most forgotten of images create, at the very least, an icon to the life they once represented? The next time we play Twister, the next time we throw a Nerf football with a friend in the park, the next time we turn on the sprinklers so that children can run and play, might we not also remember as equivalent to these the paradox of MacKenzie's *Kiddie Pool*, a paradox not unlike that of the day set aside to reanimate in playful spirit those who have died?

To live is to make of life a stage for death – this is how the paradox works. The Day of the Dead is also the day when the living pre-empt their own lives by vicariously celebrating the years to come when they themselves will become the objects of reanimation. *Kiddie Pool*, too, is an instance of this reversibility of logic, reminding us not only that disappearance is inevitable, but that it has already begun.

The Myth of Autopoesis

> How comprehensive is the horizon within which we have to rethink our conceptions of literary forms or genres, in view of the technical factors affecting our present situation, if we are to identify the forms of expression that channel the literary energies of the present.
>
> Walter Benjamin, *Illuminations*, 224.

At the moment when a logic of technology begins to render cognition and experience as functions of disappearance, the stage of a postmodern understanding begins to attune itself to the larger consequences of such reversal. In a climate of fractured interrogations, how does one continue either to fracture or to interrogate without being subsumed by the very processes of disappearance one has already presumed to be the end point of such inquiry? If the questions of identity and perception are to be entertained as phenomena of disappearance, then these reformulations eventually collapse into a forced re-evaluation of the structures of meaning and understanding. If we *conceive* of ourselves as we are not, and in turn *perceive* ourselves with equivalent misunderstanding, then it might be suggested that the condition of existence is precisely not being – not, in any case, as we assume being to be. Rather, if self-conception no less than bodily perception can be rendered prosthetic – placebos for the illusion of self-generated being – then one might assert that being has always been just as prosthetic as the terms of engagement upon which it is based. The myth of a self-fashioned existence – autopoesis – has perhaps always been a technological prosthesis in itself.

What happens when one considers a systematic removal of any and all indicators of authentic existence? No more free thought, or no more thought at all, except that which simply by structural virtue can never aspire to more than being a pastiche of itself. No more unmediated experience or perception, either. No more time, no more memory, no more prophecy except that which is self-fulfilling by virtue of participation in the spectacle of aesthetic predilection.

What most quickly emerges here is a fantasy of fatalism, tempered by possibilities of the sort that only a spectacle can offer. It is not quite (or not yet) a position of prosthetic determinism – a technological nihilism that would at first glance seem to be the natural consequence of disappeared constitution. Instead, it is in some ways a constitution of disappearance that is required, of the sort offered by the political imagination of Walter Benjamin, made particularly relevant with the interpretive insights of Gerhard Richter. Faced with persecution and the immanent fascist mobilization of intellectuality towards unscrupulous ends, Richter contends that Benjamin mobilized his own thinking in the opposite direction, towards a theory of the "useless concept." The result is an intellectual framework that defies mobilization precisely because it claims nothing directly, represents only with an allegorical temperance of indecision and paradox, rejects the logic of mobilization in favour of an illogic of uselessness.

The Technological Aura

In an age of technological mobilization, there is much at stake in the formulation of a logic of resistance. Whether logical or illogical is perhaps less important than the possibility of reversibility itself as a discursive and philosophical response. These are questions often explored in the context of Benjamin's work, most poignantly in his famous essay "The Work of Art in the Age of Mechanical Reproduction." The analysis of disappearance here finds analogy in Benjamin's writings about the loss of authenticity and of the aura in an age of mechanical and technological mediation. Arguing that technological advance has shifted the terms of political and social engagement, Benjamin, according to Richter, even went as far as to disdain the unmediated myths of living for precisely their politics of disappearance: "Benjamin's emphatic negation of what is 'unmediated' suggests that his confrontation with the political is meant to reach its fullest potential when the political is not illuminated directly."[2]

Benjamin, of course, saw great potential in the photographic image as a mediator of representational reality and as a potential tool for the dissemination of mediated messages. In addition to the ease in the reproduction and dissemination of photos, there is an over-throwing of the sanction of authenticity that accompanied prior representational forms such as painting. With the rise in mediation, the status of the original – bodies and images alike – becomes of secondary importance to the effects of mediated living itself. And much like the attempts made here, Benjamin's strategy was to illuminate the dynamic of mediation by targeting the myth of the unmediated in an age of technological innovation.

While it may seem like a step backwards to invoke a discourse of photographic reproduction in this technological context, it is useful to do so in order to reinforce a contingency of presence, of thought, of perception, and of authenticity. In cognitive and perceptual alienation alike, there is a collapse of the popular myths of autonomy, and the mediations of thought and perception make it increasingly problematic to attempt a redefinition of either. It is perhaps prudent to also reassert that this does not merely distance the self from itself – alienation is misunderstood according to these terms of engagement – but rather disappears the concept of self altogether. The perpetuation of identity or selfhood depends on maintaining a boundary that no longer exists. When there is only another, when there is only a someone or a something else, when I can no longer decide where the world ends and "I" begin, the only thing that is truly reliable is that complex uncertainty is the name of the vertiginous game, and any reliable sense of self is reliable only because of a willful disregard of the uncertainties in play.

This undermining of originality echoes a formulation used by Benjamin in a description of photographic practice: "the presence of the original is the prerequisite to the concept of authenticity."[3] Without an identifiable self, without the verifiable presence of an original, the authenticity of the image ceases to be self-evident. The disappearance of the self into a (technologically reproduced) simulation collapses the critical distance of personal reflection, real or imagined – the reproduction can be authentic only as long as the source maintains independent integrity.

It is a dynamic of this sort that Benjamin explores in "The Work of Art in an Age of Mechanical Reproduction," asserting that the arbitrary reproduction of the photographic print, coupled with its potential for mass dissemination, results in a complete reversal of the traditional role of the art object. A photograph does not have an identifiable original, in a traditional sense, rather, "from a photographic negative … one can make any number of prints; to ask for the 'authentic' print makes no sense."[4] In this dynamic, there is an aspect of the photograph that precisely resists entry into authentic being, despite the representational debt of the medium itself. A photograph is always a photograph of something, and it is this subject that must be invoked in order to centralize the authenticity of the image. If one were to speak of a photographic original, one would have to speak of "the way things *are* as opposed to the way things look."[5] In speaking this way, however, one would no longer be speaking about the photograph at all, but about the extrapolated reality it supposedly represents. Always thus in a state of deferral to the reality it represents, Benjamin's assertion is that art in an age of mechanical reproducibility has lost its aura, mobilized instead towards a dissemination of the image: a mass-produced image of a disappeared reality, a simulated aura for an image stripped of originality.[6]

If a theory of willful alienation might be seen as the deferral of original thought into its simulated double – framed by the alienation of mirror-image perception – then this means that thought is generated technologically. Foucault's "thought is the presence of someone else in me," means (at least) a hybrid self, a self that is always at least partly other, always at least partly (technologically) distanced from itself by its own self-conception. Likewise, if a theory of prosthetic phenomenology might be seen as the deferral of corporeality into its extended form, framed by the bodily penetration of perceptual dynamic, then this means that experience and perception are also fundamentally technological in nature. Here, perception is also the presence of something else in me, whether that be light, sound, heat, touch, food, or air. There has no more been an authentic or static body than there has been an original mind – the limits and boundaries of both have collapsed into simulations of themselves, necessary placebos for social participation and perceptual agreement but essentially contingent on the perpetuation of their own misunderstandings.

Consequently, what holds for Benjamin's theory of the photographic image functions equally well for the question of technological being in a contemporary world: a postmodern existence is one that has lost its aura. Or, properly, its aura has become technological in nature: a prosthetic aura for an existence disappeared into the discursive deferral of mediated being.

The Politics of Technological Thinking

Benjamin did not lament the loss of the aura in the art object. This reframing of the structure of artistic endeavour instead represented for him a technologically induced shift in the ideology of artistic practice, and one that held great potential for political mobilization, disseminating images and ideologies in "situations that would be out of reach for the original itself."[7]

This could also be seen as a more general recipe to deal with the consequences of technological living – the photograph, in this instance, standing as representative of a larger series of re-evaluations. Ultimately, the dynamic that Benjamin offers puts forward the simple suggestion that technological living changes the ideology of those who engage with it, cultivating a culture of impatience and distraction and offering unique possibilities for social control and personal (political) resistance.[8] Foucault's idea of thought as "the presence of someone else in me" is thus mobilized in reverse; for Benjamin, it is "the art of thinking in other people's heads that is decisive."[9] And Benjamin can make a declaration of this sort because of his insistence on the mediation of thought.

This demand to embrace the contingency of authorial production extends to any form of technological self-understanding. It is a demand for discursive self-fashioning in an age of mediated living. Here, disappearance is no longer simply the consequence of lost authenticity but also the condition for the rise of the aesthetic and political self. The possibilities of self-fashioning are contingent on mobilizing technologies of disappearance in order to make room for creative modalities of being. In other words, a theory of this sort (what might be called a postmodern aesthetics) is fundamentally incompatible with the discourse of authenticity (as with those of truth or reality). One might pine for lost appearance, or one might instead embrace what Paul Virilio has pessimistically called "an aesthetics of disappearance": "The heterogeneous succeeds the homogenous, the aesthetics of the search supplants the search for an aesthetics, the aesthetics of disappearance renews the enterprise of appearance."[10]

For Virilio, the rise of a climate of disappearance signals the dangers of technological fascism, humanity rendered an aesthetic function of its own technological imperative. Equally important is that Benjamin's theory also grew out of a response to the threat of social disappearance, in his case mediated by the political fascism of his time. Unlike Virilio, however, Benjamin saw the potential for reversibility as key to the understanding of technological living – clearly examined by Gerhardt Richter in his analysis of Benjamin's autobiographical writings. Key to this analysis is Richter's insistence that Benjamin's autopoetic writings attempt to avoid a return to the constitution of appearances, instead intending to frustrate mobilization without succumbing to the silenced oppression of forced disappearance. Here one must perhaps allow for the discourse of disappearance to be doubled: on one hand a consequence of authority in which selves disappear into a disciplinary context, and on the other a repositioning of inauthentic possibilities whose purpose is to allow for aesthetic and political engagement in an otherwise uncertain world.

In this doubling, one also might find the crucial elements of what Richter, in his book *Walter Benjamin and the Corpus of Autobiography*, uses to constitute a notion of the "useless concept" in Benjamin's writings. Most directly, useless concepts embrace the contingencies of demonstrative thinking over generalized abstraction. They therefore have unique potential to disrupt political and technical processing by refusing a unified presentation of authentic meaning. By emphasizing disruption Benjamin privileges "the radical moment of uncontainable critique itself rather than the veil of security and stability promised by a 'system,'"[11] turning the critique into a process of self-fashioning that holds value for intellectual resistance to disciplinary disappearance. Richter explains:

> [Benjamin's texts] stage a language in which the body of the confessional self remains suspended between construction and dispersal ... Within this infinite distance, the language of the vicissitudinous self's body in turn works to exhibit a figure that, in its perpetual turnovers and slippages, belongs to those innovative political concepts that remain useless for the purposes of fascism and, indeed, a kind of politics of presence and transparency. If in Benjamin's innovative art of self-portraiture the body is always in retreat – that is, both disappearing and being

> treated one more time – then it belongs to those concepts that elude ideologemes of self-identity and the powerful myth of stable meanings. Benjamin's corpus remains unusable.[12]

In Richter's analysis one finds a strategy of resistance to disappearance, inspired by Benjamin's willful self-placement at the very center of an already-disappeared identity. Paradoxically, despite the depersonalizing tendencies of socially-mediated disappearance, understanding oneself as already disappeared allows for a form of tenuous self-fashioning, dependent only on the non-declarative contingency of appearance itself. One fights disappearance poorly by attempting to re-appear or discover (and claim) locations, ideas, or identities in which such disappearance may not yet be complete. Better, in this instance, is the attempt to fight disappearance with disappearance – outdoing political or technological mediation by critically vanishing, except as a negative horizon of contingent separation. "If Benjamin's texts define the writer's struggle as a negotiation of the construction and dispersal of selfhood, then they allow us to redefine his self as the one who is not himself."[13]

This also assists in the translation of Richter's "useless concepts" from discursive and political tools to what might be called the useless identities of post-disappearance self-fashioning. This is the logic of falsity that begins to proliferate through the interrogations and deconstructions of postmodernism; the illogic through which alienation can provoke a critical confrontation with the disjunctions of absence and uncertainty. The one difference is that the disappeared individual (as opposed to the useless concept) has a variety of tools through which to contingently appear, what Benjamin refers to as an "arsenal of masks." And here, the logic of postmodern masquerade returns in a new key. As Richter notes, "These masks are designed to produce rhetorically the most plausible 'subjectivity effect,' that is, the mechanisms by which in the Nietzschean sense, the subject becomes what it is through representing itself to itself."[14]

This is not simply an acceptance of alienated (disappeared) identity as a condition of living, but a passing through with the aim of embedding oneself in the very technologies of alienation to which one responds. This is not a transcendent awakening, but a passing into alienation, not in order to recover a sense of wholeness or finitude, but for the purpose of fragmentation. It is not a project of emergence, but a resistance to the emergence either of a traumatized self or a self with a fictitious autonomous double: "only after this act, the renunciation of their self-identity, can they become what they are – and even then only in and as an other."[15]

The Horizon of Uselessness

While the notion of the useless concept seems to promise hope for critical engagement in a climate of uncertainty, the price of this engagement is one of inauthentic living. For this reason, one must explore Richter's assertions somewhat more fully, taking care to address the irony that emerges when one finds a use for uselessness. If the purpose of the useless concept is to avoid external mobilization, then one risks doing an injustice to the concept itself if one then turns it into a working model of political and ideological resistance.

What seemed like a manual for self-willed disappearance here becomes subject to authentic formalization. The oblique politics that Richter praises, in the act of praise begin to exit from disappearance, constituted externally as that which they are not. This is also the fundamental problem with the idea of a self-willed disappearance: insofar as uselessness targets the contingency of disappearance, it comes with a dangerous potential for self-validation – a generalization that can be synthesized into a recuperated illusion of authenticity. This is devastating to the project of disappearance, as it construes a horizon of uselessness, allowing in turn the assessment of uselessness – in other words exiting the dynamic of disruptive engagement by formalizing disruption as the common denominator of authentic engagement.

This is not unlike the paradox of certain uncertainty (the postmodern insistence on reducing meaning to a constituted game of endless deferral), and its solution also involves a similar line of exploration. If postmodernism undermines truth it also undermines falsity, and when the authenticity of the self is called into question, the self must respond, not only by coveting disappearance, but also by refusing the renewed sense of authenticity that such disappearance might cultivate. Strange as it may sound, the problem with uselessness is that it risks taking itself too seriously. When uselessness becomes useful, it creates a position that can be compromised or mobilized for political, intellectual, or aesthetic gain, frustrating the tactics of resistance that were its aim. "Thus, when the autobiographer or archaeologist of the self becomes the curator of his own gallery of the self, that moment is not simply one of remembering, enhancing, or preserving. It is also one of resignation."[16] Here, in the shadows of reconstituted authenticity, useless or otherwise, one must perhaps resign oneself to the immanence of technological (constituted) appearance.

There is something of a double bind that emerges when the project of autopoetic disappearance folds into the inevitability of mobilized appearance. It is not merely a paradox, but a problem. No longer is the question simply one of cultivating strategies for disappearance, uselessness or indeterminacy. Instead, the question becomes one of how the living of disappearance opens itself up to the inevitability of mobilized appearance. In other words, whatever is made possible through the engagement with disappearance must be immediately contextualized within a project of appearance. One might suggest that this interplay between disappearance and appearance is one of the central stakes of autopoesis. While engagement with the inauthentic, the useless, and the disappeared can provide creative space for new possibilities, when acted upon or lived, these possibilities open themselves up to a language of appearance, with all its potential for mobilization, both fascist and revolutionary.

Because of this, one must consider the consequences of such aesthetic activity – in terms of the ways any such constituted appearance threatens to compromise the creative possibilities that form its basis, and in terms of how such appearances might be taken up by others. This is not an imperative, however, for one can of course live an accidental lifestyle, and by so doing one mobilizes an accidental aesthetic, or at best an aesthetic of spontaneity. But as accidents are never merely accidents, spontaneity is never simply spontaneous, and a disregard of intentionality must be content to remain within the constraints of those appearances that have been made possible, on one's behalf, by others.

Intentionality can never quite be itself either, subject to the dynamics of alienated self-consciousness and prosthetic perception, requiring a tempered consideration of self-placement. This is to say that even a considered aesthetic cannot fully escape the ironies of disappearance. Instead, the aesthetic potential of postmodern living revolves around the suspended disbelief in the possibility of nonsensical appearance – a direct engagement with inauthenticity. This is to put a halt to the discussion of uselessness as a resistance strategy and instead to reframe it as the unavoidable and necessary horizon of contemporary living. The postmodern debt to uncertainty can be rephrased as an imperative for useless living.

The Aura of Nothingness

The horizonn of uselessness can be explored further by temporarily shifting the terms of engagement, focusing on the question of subjectivity with particular emphasis on the possibility of a non-ironic form of autopoetic self-concept in a postmodern technological age. Specifically, the subjective kernel of incommensurability might be used to guarantee a non-ironic, useful possibility to even postmodern self-conception. To get at such a possibility most directly, it is useful to refer to what consciousness researchers such as David Chalmers have come to call "the hard problem" of consciousness: "The really hard problem of consciousness is the problem of *experience*. When we think and perceive, there is a whir of information-processing, but there is also a subjective aspect. As Nagel (1974) has put it, there is *something it is like* to be a conscious organism. This subjective aspect is experience."[17]

Without attempting to overly antagonize the field of consciousness research, what is important about this formulation is that it constitutes subjectivity as, at once, a generalized yet identifiable presence, a "something" that all conscious creatures have in common, and which cannot be generalized. In some ways, this constitution is to make of subjectivity a "useless concept," in precisely the way Richter describes, constituting the discussion of disappearance also then as a hard problem of postmodernism. Within the discussions of the authentic and inauthentic implications of postmodern thinking – as with the analyses of consciousness research – articulating the parameters of subjectivity poses the most difficult challenge. The problem here is one of experience because, while there may well be something it is like to be consciously self-aware, there is precisely *nothing* it is like to experience subjectivity, this being the condition of subjectivity as an individually occurring phenomenon. By all authentic accounts, minds themselves seem to be beyond analogy, beyond comparison or exchange or even standardization. Here one must perhaps admit that subjectivity can neither embrace nor dismiss the question of disappearance – it knows only that it is not like anything else – hence the confusion, and hence the difficulty of the "hard problem."

In some ways this would seem to revive the possibility of an authentic form of uselessness, with the one caveat that such uselessness would have to, at the same time, be inauthentic as well. In the absence of standards for comparison, subjectivity is thrown into the vertigo of indeterminacy, and yet subjectivity might nevertheless dare to call this indeterminacy its own. There would seem, consequently, to be a singular element that stands in defiance of the technologies of disappearance – a perspectival element that emerges only as a last resort to the questions of cognition and perception. While it can be argued that consciousness is simulated (an effect of willful alienation), and that perception is the phantom of a body that was never there (a placebo effect of environmental penetration), there persists the strangely incommensurable coincidence of subjectivity-despite-disappearance. Whether or not there is a body is a matter of indifference to subjectivity in the same way as it is a matter of indifference to the experience of thinking whether thoughts are original or prosthetic. In either instance, subjectivity proceeds despite the authenticity or inauthenticity of the situation.

One might go as far as to term such a persistence hallucinatory, in the sense that it can neither be located nor generalized to any convincing construction of selfhood or identity except that of which it exists in defiance. The condition of a subjectivity of this sort is, consequently, that it is not subject to error, for it has no frame of reference outside of itself – an incommensurable self can only ever experience its own incommensurability. Conversely, in the attempt to self-represent, such subjectivity would have a condition of error that is the result of its self-mobilization, a mobilization according to terms of engagement inaccessible to its own constitution. Selves of this sort can only appear exactly as they are not, and appearance is always an ironic spectre of incommensurability. If there is nothing to which subjective experience can be compared, then "somethingness" can only ever be the prosthetic aura of an incommensurable "nothingness." The condition of appearance is that it appear as something, and the incommensurability of nothingness would require that appearance be the ironic mask of mobilized constitution. Incommensurability is the singularly vacuous myth of individuality required to sustain even the most useless of appearances.

The Death Mask of Incommensurability

The ironic mask of mobilized appearances is a death mask for subjectivity that has pretenses towards the incommensurable. "Truth is the death of intention,"[18] insists Benjamin, and if he is correct it is not truth but rather falsity that must be the carved face on the death mask of the incommensurable. Behind the mask there may be a face of one sort or another, but it is one that is not like anything in its self-similarity, in its incommensurability, in its solipsistic imperative, it is nothing if not like nothing else. Such a face is not bound to a truth of any verifiable sort. The death mask of incommensurability conceals the nothingness it is like to be a particular experiencing subjectivity, bound to the impossibility of a manifestation that does not compromise the very individuality it seeks to represent. Incommensurability is unrealizable as a premise of subjectivity, bound only to the uselessness of being that is nothing like anything else. Incomparable, incommensurability is reminiscent of Bejamin's description of the head of death: "[T]he incomparable language of the death's head: total expressionlessness – the black of the eye-sockets – coupled to the most unbridled expression the grinning rows of teeth."[19]

This is not simply the persistent problem of the incommensurable but, perhaps, the case for all things that have disappeared – for all that must retreat to the spaces behind the masks of falsified or mobilized appearances. Appearances of this sort can be nothing but death masks, tragic reconstitutions of that which insists on being inaccessible to anyone but itself. If this seems tenuous, consider the internal dynamic of incommensurability. Beyond analogy, the significance of the incommensurable is either total or non-existent. It would seem that it can be no other way: a horizon of completed mobilization which reduces its subject to disappearance, or an inaccessible fortress of uselessness that cannot be represented, remaining, for all communicable intents, vacuous.

A third option perhaps lies between these poles, in the spaces of paradox where it might be seen either way. Here emerge the illegitimate usages of appearance, the proliferating falsities that are both the signs of self-enacted masquerade and the signs of externally mobilized subjectivity. In keeping with the potentially infinite variety of directions in which such falsified perspectives might be mobilized, the singular defiance that makes each and every one of them possible is, in fact, the defiance of incommensurability itself. One might simply note that if incommensurability is truly incommensurable, then it remains so even to the subject whose individuality it sanctions. If subjectivity is incommensurable, even experiencing subjects do not get to decide what form it takes. If incommensurability is incommensurable then it cannot be told what to do, not even by the conscious agent to whom it supposedly belongs. Or if there is such a thing as incommensurability, subjectivity is its manifestation and not the other way around. One might go as far as to say that incommensurability cannot properly exist to subjectivity, for the simple reason that subjectivity knows no other mode of operation.

Given these parameters, the best one might do is to identify with the failure of a self-conception whose very premise of being defies its possibilities of manifestation. To salvage the possibilities of subjective existence requires precisely the death of subjective authenticity. The death of incommensurability is the ironic hinge upon which the persistence of subjectivity depends. That this persistence in some way proceeds despite its own impossibility, masked by its own disappearance, is no argument against the ironic commensurability of falsified appearance. In fact, such a notion of falsified appearances may actually be the premise of existential irony in the first place. Consider Benjamin on the question of individuation: "A tragic death is an ironic immortality, ironic from an excess of determinacy. The tragic death is overdetermined – that is the actual expression of the hero's guilt. Hebbel may have been on the right track when he said that individuation was original sin. But everything hinges on the nature of the offense given by individuation."[20]

Might something similar to this spirit of "offense" not be suggested for the tragic death of incommensurable subjectivity? The possibilities of nothingness do not allow for constitution as such – ironic overdeterminacy is, in fact, the overarching sign of disappeared self-constitution. If there is nothing that it is like to be a subjective agent, then there is no point of reference or point of possible comparison. There is no paradox, there is merely the inevitability of ironic appearance as the sign of constituted nothingness: a double agency that offends subjectivity, now left to roam the vacuous territory of falsified living, bound to the impossibility of its constitution.

Towards a Theory of Vacuous Being

One can never appear to oneself as incommensurable for the simple reason that there is nothing that it is like to be oneself. Nor, however, can one's own incommensurability be mobilized, either by authorities seeking to impose a social or political disappearance, or by revolutionary subjects seeking the creative possibilities of subjective disappearance. At best, incommensurability can be simulated, but in simulating itself the incommensurable inevitably disappears to itself.

Situated beyond verifiable truth and governed by a persistence of falsity and the inauthenticity of appearances, incommensurability is the ironic horizon as well as the impossible endgame of disappearance. Fundamentally vacuous in the sense that it can never appear without disappearing, and fundamentally ironic in that each appearance is reducible only to the fact that it is nothing like anything else, incommensurability is also the horizon of reversibility between appearance and disappearance. What is constituted is a horizon of vacuous being and a vacuous horizon of being, in which existence can only be seen without conditions since incommensurability is both the death mask of the subject and the guarantee of subjective possibility. Because of this relationship, both incommensurability and subjectivity are reducible only to simulations of their own death – simulations of an impossible nothingness that pretends to be "like" something else.

Technologies of disappearance conceal the simulation of nothingness. Accordingly, the self is a function of its discursive impossibility when seen technologically. This is evidenced by the writing of Michel Foucault, where technological normalization and cultural discipline drive a barrier between the self and itself, ironically constituting an alienated subjectivity in the process. This self is a spectre of itself – disappeared, except for its own hallucinations of impossibility. A similar relationship exists between perception and experience in the works of Paul Virilio. Technologically rendered, perception conceals the possibility that the body was never an autonomous site of discursive coherency, but a relational entity whose sensations are a result of tangible interpenetration by the worldly context of which it is a part. As a result, the integrity of sensory perception is artificially rendered in order to allow the sustenance of prosthetic bodily authenticity. Or, in Walter Benjamin's work, the question of uselessness as a resistance strategy, whether discursive or technological, reveals the paradox of autopoesis. Here, the privacy of subjective experience both guarantees the possibility of a plausible subject and makes impossible its manifestation in anything other than an ironic form – a paradox whose consequence is to undermine the very possibilities it guarantees.

In combination, these technologies of disappearance form the groundwork for a plausible theory of vacuous being: existential engagement rendered alienated, prosthetic, and useless, requiring an aesthetic resurgence in order to accommodate the paradoxes of traditional formulation. With a theory of vacuous being, the disappeared self has no choice but to appear ironically as a falsified existence, an inauthentic instance of living that proceeds despite the indeterminacy of discursive placement. Here, an aesthetic of disappeared engagement is formed out of the ashes of the real, out of the proliferation of the imaginary, out of the contingency of having to proceed despite the uncertainties, inauthenticities, and impossibilities of a postmodern world.

Appearance is the aesthetic detritus left behind on the way into the creative possibilities and the existential dangers of a lifestyle of disappearance.

PART TWO

Technologies of Ironic Appearance

The Second Story of Fire

The performance of disappearance always contains a trace of irony, a self-reflexive relationship to the paradox of its own impossibility. Consider theGreek myth of Daedalus and Icarus, the story of a father and son who escaped the island of Crete on wings made of wax and feathers. The story is part allegory, part catalyst for the imaginary, part challenge to the constraints of reasonable thinking. It is also a story of possibility, imagined into existence and just as quickly subsumed by the ironies of experience.

As the legend goes, Daedalus was a craftsman of some renown, who, ended up on the island of Crete in the service of King Minos through a series of unfortunate events. Learning that Daedalus assisted in the coupling of Pasiphaë with Poseidon's white bull (which resulted in the birth of the Minotaur), Minos punished Daedalus and his son Icarus by locking them in a labyrinthine prison.[1] It is noteworthy perhaps that the labyrinth is a place of disappearance, a place where one loses oneself in the vertigo of pathways that do not necessarily lead anywhere of substance. In a postmodern context, escaping the labyrinth requires a shift of perspectives, frustrating the attempt to resolve the riddle by finding ways for it to be creatively pre-empted.

Daedalus' solution was to focus his eyes upwards, into the sky, and to build two sets of wings, cleverly weaving together wax and wood and feathers that would allow them to fly away. Flying on wings of artistic conception, Daedalus and Icarus fled the island of Crete, Daedalus warning his son not to fly too high lest the heat of the sun melt his wings. Intoxicated by his new airborne freedom and heedless of his father's words, Icarus made the fatal mistake of flying too close to the sun. His wings melted and he plummeted into the ocean waters below. One might even imagine this more extremely, not simply as a slow melting of wax but as an instant of combustion – a moment of wings caught on fire, bursting into flames around the falling body of Icarus. Consider Georges Bataille's analysis: "[T]he summit of elevation is in practice confused with a sudden fall of unheard-of violence. The myth of Icarus is particularly expressive from this point of view: it clearly splits the sun in two – the one that was shining at the moment of Icarus' elevation, and the one that melted the wax, causing failure and a screaming fall when Icarus got too close."[2]

The second story of fire is the story of technologies of ironic appearance. These two suns could be the twin lights of constituted disappearance – on one hand the freedom of illuminated flight, the creative possibilities of imaginative practice no longer bound to a dogma of truth; and on the other, a resultant uncertainty of alienated, disciplined, and mobilized individuality. In fact, such a constitution has the paradoxical effect of doubling Icarus as well. Here, like ants under a magnifying glass, the ocean's waters may also have intensified the effects. Thus subjected to the sun from both above and below, Icarus never really had a chance, caught as he was between the burning effects of experience and reflection. Staring at his reflection in the deep ocean waves, one might also wonder further if, like Narcissus, Icarus fell prey to his imagination. Intoxicated by the joys of flying, seeing himself looking up at himself – doubled – seduced by his own mirror image until the space between them collapsed.

The collapse of possibility here emerges as the signal of disappeared experience, caught in the unfolding of stakes towards which one must be willing to rise and fall. Icarus, from this perspective, was not merely flying, but performing – implicated in the dreams of flight and self-recognition. If it was Daedalus who understood the dangers of taking a dream too literally, the story of Icarus that suggests that there is no other way for dreams to be taken. The story of Icarus reveals the paradox of ironic appearance, which will always be contingent on its commitment to the stories it acts out. No more simply a story of rhetorical possibilities, ironic appearance doubles the stakes of performance, as with the case of Icarus: burned by playing in the spaces between fire and water, the paradoxical poles of incommensurability and self-constitution.

The Death of Authority

The doubled trajectories of disappearance – at once liberating and authoritarian – should be taken as a paradoxical masquerade of sorts. It is a performance in which, while fashioning one's way through the indeterminacy of postmodern living, one must take care to simultaneously cover one's tracks, lest the aesthetics of disappeared experience emerge to form a corpus of their own. What remains is an impossible irony, the strange feeling that there is still something inexpressible yet integral to a self-fashioned lifestyle, despite the fact that what makes more sense is to say there is nothing distinct about it whatsoever, the self having disappeared even to itself as an authentic presence. Because of this impossibility such a precession must begin with an ironic and paradoxical self-understanding, at once humiliated and celebrating its humiliated freedom. This is not an attempt to salvage or reconstitute an authentic subject, but an attempt to explore strategies for inauthentic living, and for determining how the limit horizons for such a perspective might be constituted.

The project builds outwards from the discussion of technologies of disappearance – the recontextualization of cognitive authenticity, perceptual or experiential boundaries, and incommensurability. Each of these recontextualizations has the effect of undermining the relationship between the self and its cognitive, experiential, or subjective world. What is needed now is to take this relationship one step further, from a reflection on discursive systems of power or misunderstanding to an extended and self-reflexive rendering; from the general to the particular of lived dynamic. The difference will not be in the resultant dynamic of disappearance; the difference is that now it is no longer necessary for it to be externally constituted. These are ways to ensure a self-initiated undermining of thought: autobiographies of disappearance, or what might be called technologies of ironic appearance.

This form of undermined thinking can be traced back at least as far as Nietzsche, not simply as a critique of modernist institutions of meaning or reason, but as an in-depth interrogation of authority in any form – including one's own. Nietzsche has been called the "father of postmodernism,"[3] yet what is often framed as a critique here might also constitute the strength of the postmodern debt to Nietzsche – ironically, a refusal of indebtedness. For Nietzsche this was not simply a refusal to succumb to the authority of others, but a refusal of authority in all forms, including his own.

Perhaps the best example of such a dynamic comes from a passage in Nietzsche's *Thus Spoke Zarathustra* that follows shortly after the famous proclamation "God is dead." To follow up on his challenge to institutional meaning, there is an imperative for the equal undermining of the meanings and knowledge of others, institutional or personal – a self-proclaimed death of the philosopher himself: "Truly, I advise you: go away from me and guard yourselves against Zarathustra! And better still: be ashamed of him! Perhaps he has deceived you … One repays a teacher badly if one remains only a pupil. And why, then, should you not pluck at my laurels? You respect me; but how if one day your respect should tumble? Take care that a falling statue does not strike you dead!"[4]

What makes Nietzsche so seductive to a postmodern mind is his insistence on going beyond the imperative for autonomous or responsible thought, beyond even the autonomy of his own thinking. This is not simply a mandate of independent consideration, but a mandated suspicion of one's own authority as well. The fate of knowledge in this case is to become unintelligible, lived rather than shared; a moment of experience that can never quite be held accountable to the ways in which it is understood. In other words, latent in this formulation is a self-reflexively imposed indeterminacy – a technology of ironic appearance at the historical core of postmodern thinking.

It is also an imperative that is aesthetic, along the lines of a younger Nietzsche who in *The Birth of Tragedy* declared that "the existence of the world is justified only as an aesthetic phenomenon."[5] If one cannot trust teacher, authority, or God – or even, by extension, self – what remains is a negotiation of dynamic between falsities and their masquerades, dancing among falling statues and carnivorous reflections. What remains when knowledge disappears is an experience without knowledge – but one that nevertheless takes form, intelligible or not, paradoxical though it might be. Technologies of ironic appearance are the frameworks of exploration that attempt to bring this paradoxical core into focus.

Post-Mortem Aesthetics

After the death of authority, what remains is an aestheticization of disappearance. An aesthetic of this sort is not without irony, having decided that its goal is to constitute rather than render intelligible. Cynically, perhaps such an aesthetic attempt is doomed before it even begins. It is a fundamentally defeated aesthetic that does not grow as a celebration of the artistic, nor as a liberated creative gaze. This is instead a project of futility, a tragic realization that the only method of analysis open to a postmodern future is one that must proceed on the basis of lived disappearance, negotiating the ashes of its own internal combustion. The historical formulation of aesthetics as a practice of suspending disbelief also becomes the premise for existential masquerade, implicating itself in the ironic separation from that which it can never escape.

Nietzsche's aesthetic theory is one such dance of uncertainty, important because it foregrounds the interplay between representation and experience as "artistic energies which burst forth … first in the image world of dreams … and then as intoxicated reality."[6] These are not mutually exclusive domains of encounter, but ones that create dynamic and dramatic tensions – not synthesizing a single aesthetic encounter but framing a paradox that is particularly compelling because it revolves around the mechanisms of performance rather than the irreconcilabilities of cognitive difference. In an aesthetic theory of this sort, the paradox is set free, challenging the incommensurable though performative necessity.[7]

Central to this is the suspended judgment of aesthetic encounter, as that which is able to negotiate representational uncertainty without remaining outside of the encounter. Curiously, if in the pursuit of aesthetic engagement one suspends disbelief, then one must ostensibly also lose track of the fact that disbelief has been suspended – here becoming in no uncertain terms overtaken, even intoxicated, by what appears as representational truth, but is in fact nothing more than speculative postulation. Unmoored from standards of truth, it is equally the fate of aesthetic thinking to lose track of its own contingency, and in so doing be transformed into a larger philosophy of speculative proposition. One might suggest this as the postmodern state of inquiry: an uprooting of certainty for the sake of speculative possibility, whose only real danger is in the inevitable intoxication that is both the condition of serious speculation and what maintains its relationship to contingency in a larger sense.

This is aesthetics as ontology – the image is no longer an authentic representation, but an intoxication with possibilities at the expense of certainty.

If freedom is intoxicating, then at no time has thinking been more free than when all foundational rules have been lost to the willful suspension of the gaze. Postmodernism is thus the intoxicated celebration of defeated humanism. Posthumanism – as an aesthetic bound to the conditions of indeterminacy – is postmodernism's hangover.

There is a certain tragedy to this formulation: an overlap between the discursive ironies of postmodern aesthetics and the realization that only an aesthetic logic is equipped to navigate the intricacies of lived uncertainty. The ironic representation has as its only condition that it be neither real nor in jest, that it appear with all the seriousness of the real despite the unreality it portrays. In short, falsity masquerading as truth must not call itself into question by entertaining the possibility of verification. Aesthetics has always been allowed multiple, even paradoxical, perspectives, whether playful and serene, or cynical and dangerous, because it resists the imperative to compete for meaning and sense. As a logic of creative, poetic, and imaginative plausibility, what an aesthetic approach cannot bear is only that which forces it to justify its perspective – a perspective traumatized precisely because it cares nothing for the practice of justification. Already the historical counterpoint to serious thinking, aesthetics in its postmodern manifestation always flirts with its own disappearance.

There is something Icarian about a postmodern aesthetic – a condition of contingency to which it is bound, but which also immanently threatens to undermine its formulations. It is a confluence of aesthetic speculation and lived existence, a suspension of disbelief, but also a self-placement within this suspended dynamic. Postmodern aesthetics, in other words, is what happens when aesthetics begins to lose its self-image, distanced from a suspended gaze through the proximity of self-encounter. The dance is one between irony and aesthetics. The result is a creative extension of self-undermined identities, and the creative extensions of disappearance. Irony then, is that which sets up such a confrontation with oneself, not to distance but to bring closer. Irony raises the stakes of the encounter, allowing for speculative continuation where none is any longer logically possible, nor even desirable.

Technologies of ironic appearance are strategies that might be deployed towards the construction of myths, impossibilities, and paradoxes on the condition that they also continue to undermine their own performative placement. Technologies of ironic appearance are, in other words, modes of prioritizing the masquerade of falsity over the domination of truth.

Technologies of Ironic Appearance

The following three chapters, grouped as technologies of ironic appearance, are an attempt to use the extended gaze of self-reflexive disappearance to sustain the paradox of indeterminacy. Technologies of ironic appearance are attempts to respond to the resignation of very real disappearance, in part by continuing the postmodern project of undermining the demands of standardized authority and in part by mobilizing an extended field of imaginary possibilities. The self caught in the shadow of disciplinary living attempts to respond not only by refusing authority but, ironically, also by selectively agreeing to it – extending the terms of engagement until the resultant shadows begin to waver.

In many ways the trajectory unfolds backwards, like an elaborate version of the annoying game of "opposite day" that many children play, pretending that yes means no or up means down, much to the chagrin of the adults present. But this game is itself a celebration of disappearance, an inside joke that begins to re-map the appearance of creative possibilities for those who are willing to play. Here, irony is the indispensable tool that allows for belonging and not-belonging at the same time, a world where codes of disappearance can be suspended and reversed without necessarily being undermined in the process.

Three such technologies are those of futility, fantasy, and contingency, grown of ironic positioning with regard to questions of authorship, psychoanalysis, and interpretation. These three perspectives will be illustrated by the works of three thinkers of ironic appearance: Roland Barthes, Slavoj Zizek, and Mikhail Bahktin, who collectively set the stage for the ironic perpetuation of the disappeared self through an inverted aesthetic extension. The method is one of doubling, rendering identity into paradox with the aim of articulating the stakes and the dynamic possibilities of ironic living. And it is an exploration best conducted by holding these thinkers accountable to their own formulations of discursive and experiential practice, with all the paradoxes and ironies implicit therein. For instance, one might ask whether Barthes is a victim of his own theory of the "death of the author"; whether Zizek's insistence on the "traumatic kernel" of self-conception might not instead be the result of a latent desire for trauma; and whether Bakhtin's idealization of the liberatory potential of carnival living isn't in some way a disguised imperative for self-censorship.

What these thinkers share is the proposition of an overarching framework for understanding the interplay between disappearance and its ironic consequences. These frameworks, in paradoxical form, are both structural and aesthetic. When the stakes of contingent living reach their apex, only such a fusion might – either through its successes or failures – begin to identify some of the possible directions in which postmodern logic might proceed. It is a wager set to explore the possibilities of falsity as the ironic proliferation of subjectivities both enabled and undermined at once.

What follows, then, are three iterations or mediations of ironic appearance, rendered technological in order to suggest that what most strongly suggests an aesthetic presence is precisely the ironic, yet self-reflexive, cultivation of disappearance.

4
Playing Dead

Ten Little Indians [Remix][1]

The irony of contemporary living is that not all disappearances are equivalent, and not all forms of incommensurability come with the same set of consequences.

Mohawk artist Jackson 2bears has something to say about ironic appearance. *Ten Little Indians [Remix]* is a video and audio re-mix of the (once popular) children's song *Ten Little Indians,* a song now rarely heard because of its overtly racial subject matter, a social and historical prejudice that contemporary society finds distasteful because it refuses to acknowledge the persistence of such bias. 2bears' remix seems, at first glance, to be a political activism of sorts, an accusatory historical reference given ironic form as a remix reclaimed and repurposed, put to use as a reiteration of contemporary racial divisions.

In its most pejorative sense, *Ten Little Indians* (the original) counts all Indigenous peoples as equivalent, faceless numbers. Even the prisoner is distinguished by a serial number – a new identity framed by an identifiable social transgression. This is not the equivalent of a legitimated identity, but certainly something less than total disappearance. Not so with the *Ten Little Indians* whose identity is non-specific: one of ten, two of ten. These, instead, are the simplified and seemingly innocent numbers of those being counted out of existence, sung in the innocent schoolyard voices of youth.

There is a tendency in politically activated works to use a remix to simply re-invoke a politic of the original, the remix being little more than a proverbial replay for an intensified political effect. In such interpretations, the only noteworthy difference is that the replay is recontextualized – a political reflection, an accusation levied towards a culture that allowed for and continues to uphold the discriminatory social values expressed in the song. Here, the identity of 2bears himself forms the horizon upon which the politics of the remix depend, for it is only thus recontextualized that the political accusation is brought into focus.

It's an injustice to 2bears, however, to simplify his authorial contribution in such a way – framing the remix as a mere replay with accusatory intent. In fact, such a rhetorical reduction writes 2bears (as author) out of the equation with a second-order disappearance tactic, reducing the artist to his political gesture.

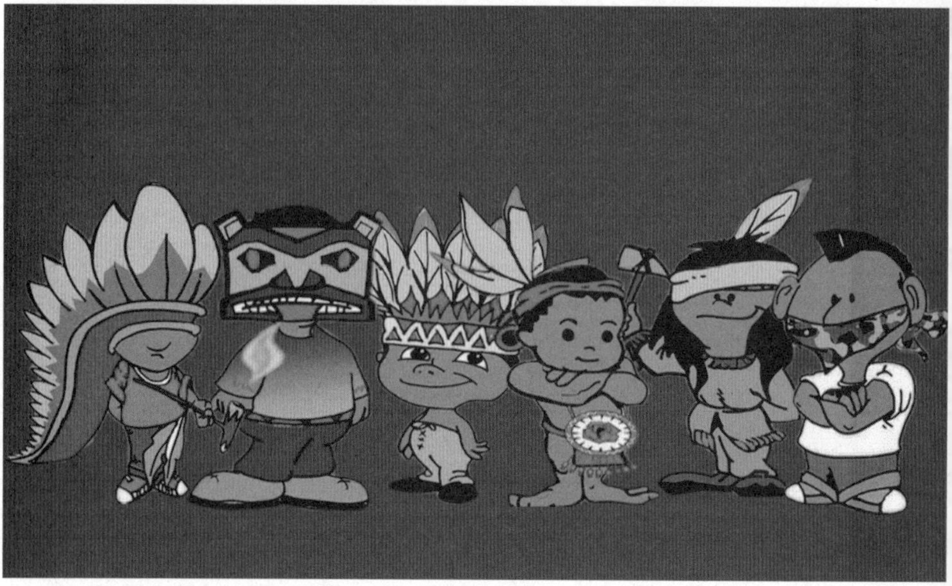

Jackson 2bears. *Ten Little Indians [Remix]*. Video still, 2005.

Such a reduction is made even more problematic by the fact that it overlooks precisely the nuance that forms the political critique of the remix. One can attribute a generalized voice to the remix, in which the invocation of political history forms the central critique, or (better, but more difficult) one can allow for a personalized (one might even say incommensurable) voice to the work, in which its purpose is synonymous with its frustration – no longer a political reclaiming but an observation of existence as it is currently manifest.

Arthur Kroker has written about 2bears as the "Mohawk Posthuman,"[2] but in this instance it seems prudent to ask what it is that makes 2bears posthuman. The answer, in this instance at least, is that his work is mobilized as a token, not of identity repossessed, but of identity made to disappear. Here, in other words, is it crucial to realize that 2bears has not made the attempt to single himself out of the proverbial crowd – has not made of himself a figure to be counted. Instead, he has included himself among the disappeared rather than attempting to reconstitute a singular identity, activist or otherwise. 2bears has not suggested that he be counted as number eleven, nor that he himself is the counting agent. Rather, his suggestion is more provocative still: 2bears has chosen to remain hidden, emphasizing the ironies of disappearance in a way that makes himself precisely interchangeable with the others counted.

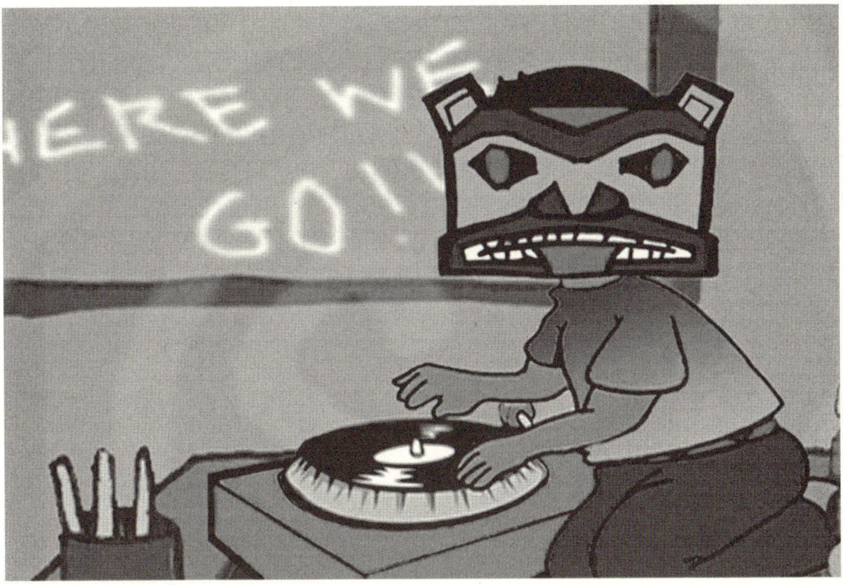

Jackson 2bears. *Ten Little Indians [Remix]*. Video still, 2005.

What would it mean to not only live in the shadow of domination, but to speak back, to claim domination as one's own as 2bears here has done? Is this not a case of ironic appearance par excellence – a mask worn to conceal the fact that there is nothing behind it? Contrary to the politics which would have us agree to a rhetorically enlightened indigeneity behind the remix – a liberated critical voice of dissent – the power of *Ten Little Indians [Remix]* is that 2bears does not remove himself from the context of the piece, does not seek to propose himself as an authentic or enlightened negotiator, agrees in short to his status as both an individual disappeared and a warrior of disappearance. Seen through the gaze of the Mohawk Posthuman, the key political message of *Ten Little Indians [Remix]* is that 2bears has no voice.

To further complicate this interpretation, one might also point out the irony of a gesture in which 2bears invokes his right to remain silent, for here it is his silence that speaks most eloquently. Ludwig Wittengstein once asserted that "that about which we cannot speak must be passed over in silence,"[3] yet it is precisely 2bears' silence that refuses to be passed over. Wittgenstein was wrong: it is that which cannot be spoken that least deserves silence, but strangely it is only in silence that the unspeakable can be uttered. Conversely, in this case it is the audience who has no right to speak, and in particular not on behalf of 2bears. The voice of sympathy and understanding comes too little and too late, and if we refuse to implicate ourselves in the piece then it is we who have missed the point. And that point? In his refusal to be counted 2bears has done two important things. First, he has critically extended his status as an agent of disappearance, calling into question the complex dialogue of voices presented, represented, and denied. Second, and perhaps more importantly, through this emphasis he has included the listener in the piece itself, silencing objection through complex political representation.

Ten Little Indians [Remix] is a mask for a similar song in new key: *Ten Little Listeners* – and we would do well to count ourselves among those who listen.

The Death of the Author

> [W]riting is the destruction of every voice, of every point of origin. Writing is that neutral, composite, oblique space where our subject slips away, the negative where all identity is lost, starting with the very identity of the body writing.
>
> Roland Barthes, *Image – Music – Text*, 142.

In a climate of disappeared identity, it is the particularities of experience that matter most. The nuances of the individual are also the stakes of the question of the incommensurable – not that which resists the question of disappearance, but rather that which is most impacted by its consequences. Seen technologically, disappearance reduces individualized living to its possibilities of simulation, pre-empting the discussion of authenticity by casting the question into the shadows of uncertainty. Seen ironically, however, this casting can be constituted as a prosthetic appearance, relating the particularities of lived uncertainty – philosophically, psychoanalytically, and performatively – to the enactment of disappeared identity. One can potentially appear without exiting from a climate of disappearance, despite the convoluted paradox that suggests disappearance is precisely the stripping away of legitimate appearance.

Roland Barthes' elucidation of this paradox appears in his treatise on "The Death of the Author." Barthes uses the disappearance of formalized identity in the question of the authorial message of a text, reversing the relationship of disappearance by using it to target the institution of meaning and authority through which texts have traditionally been contextualized.

Instead of the individual as the tragic endgame of disappearance, disappeared identity itself becomes the foundational principle upon which all appearance must be based.

At its simplest, the death of the author is a response to, and an acknowledgment of, the multiplicity of interpretive meanings that can emerge from any written text. The attribution of a singular or static meaning to any piece of writing does an injustice to the possibilities for meaning that the text may present. Barthes takes this further, however, adding to the justification by citing the derivative (one might say technological) nature of language: "We know now that a text is not a line of words releasing a single 'theological' meaning (the 'message' of the Author-God) but a multi-dimensional space in which a variety of writings, none of them original, blend and clash. The text is a tissue of quotations drawn from the innumerable centres of culture."[4]

For Barthes, text is a function of language and culture; it is not derived from, nor is it reducible to, the originality of voice of any given author. The author is, instead, an already contingent entity, disappeared; subsumed on one hand by the linguistic and cultural structures that make writing possible, and on the other hand by the multiple possibilities of interpretation itself. As such, while an author may well have singular meaning in mind when writing, this mindfulness does not constitute an ability to control the possibilities for meaning in the text itself. While an author may create, initiate, and even embrace the many possible messages in the text, he or she has no proprietary right to any singular message that emerges from the writing, and certainly no right to a decisive perspective on the finality of represented meaning. Instead, "there is one place where this multiplicity [of meaning] is focused and that place is the reader …"[5]

Barthes' position frames a doubled argument, addressing the structural constraints of language and learning, and prioritizing individual interpretive engagement. The death of the author is, on one hand, the necessary consequence of teaching language through the disciplinary methods of normalized culture, and upholding it according to normative rules of engagement, therefore in defiance of subjective particularity. On the other hand, the death of the author is also an advocacy theory for the primacy of a reader's interpretation – a textual repositioning in which the particularities of subjective response are given priority over the correct or authoritative constitution of message.The only possible form of misinterpretation is that which denies itself the right to interpret in favour of being told. Interpretation comes at the expense of authority: "the birth of the reader must be at the cost of the death of the Author."[6]

The Interpretive Imperative

The theory of the death of author holds great potential for the ironic reinvention of identity in a climate of disappearance. The stage set by this theory is the same as that upon which Nietzsche's Zarathustra warns his students to beware of taking the teacher's voice too seriously, lest they be struck by a falling statue. It is also the same stage as that constituted by Richard Kearney, speaking of the need to imagine alternatives to the authoritative messages of overly-regulated culture, making clear that this alternative comes at the expense of the (authoritative) same. While privileging the act of readership, Barthes' theory also makes clear that such interpretive license comes with certain constraints – most prominently, the need for active and engaged reading.

There is, however, a more serious constraint imposed by such a theory – the paradox of attributing the "death of the author" to the author that is Roland Barthes. This paradox is important, central even, to the meanings, consequences, and possibilities of the theory, for it here that the complexity of the formulation begins to manifest. One must not avoid such a paradox, nor simply use it to undermine Barthes' formulation, but instead reposition this discursive space as one in which Barthes deliberately undermines himself, making that most final and decisive of authorial assertions: that the author is dead. What at first appears as paradoxical can be rendered instead as ironic, as long as the mechanism of attribution is framed in terms that are self-reflexive.

On this hinge of irony lies the potential merit to the theory of the death of the author that goes well beyond a simple privileging of the particular over the general. Instead, the death of the author points to a fundamental repositioning of the dynamic between the two. If one takes into account such an irony, the consequence is that one can no longer self-consciously write without simultaneously undermining one's relationship to the text. The theory of the death of the author means that one must begin to seek ways of writing as a reader, with all the particularities of voice that such an act entails.

After the death of the author, the acts of writing and of interpretation become equivalent – equivalent in the paradoxical constitution and refusal of final meanings; equivalent in the disregard of outside authority; and equivalent in the irony with which such incommensurability must be deployed. It is this condition of interpretive irony that prevents authorial death from becoming merely a form of self-indulgent existentialism, turning it instead into a methodology for the negotiation of futile self-fashioning. Insofar as interpretation comes with the condition of constitution – a reading that takes individualized form – neither an author nor a reader can properly refuse themselves through interpretation. The possibility of such a refusal, however, enacted by another is a condition of discursive manifestations. The formulations that appear as a result of interpretation come with the condition that they be opened up to the interpretive gaze of others. In this way, and insofar as a reader reads and responds, formulating ideas of potentially proprietary meaning along the way, each reader is also an already-dead author. The reader "cannot any longer be personal: the reader is without history, biography, psychology; he is simply that *someone* who holds together in a single field all the traces by which the written text is constituted."[7]

Interpretation is an act of self-fashioning and of self-refusal – self-fashioning because one's interpretation comes with the condition that one interprets, and self-refusal because such an interpretation constitutes a text of its own, one that can and will be interpreted by others. There is a self-initiated disappearance that comes into play in the act of constitution – whether this happens as an author or as a reader is ultimately unimportant. Instead, the politics of the death of the author can be extended towards more structural ends. The mobilization of appearance is an inevitable indicator of a technology of disappearance – as soon as one is constituted as a voice, one's voice ceases to be one's own. The act of thinking is an externalization of thought just as the act of perceiving is an externalization of corporeality. Even the refusal to speak constitutes a surrogate voice that can be mobilized on one's behalf. However, this paradox of disappearance is not beyond interpretation, for the simple reason that it says nothing about how one interprets one's disappearance.

From one perspective, there is a futility to the form of interpretation that emerges here, an act already positioned in terms of its own potential for reinterpretation. And, if this futility of interpretation is one of the structural conditions that makes interpretation possible, then the key to understanding interpretation may, in fact, be the analysis of futility. This is the horizon where discourses of disappearance take a turn away from the politics of generalized (social, cultural, physiological) disappearance and into the nuances of particular (authorial, personal, psychological) manifestation, because what is in question is the ongoing possibility of individualized or proprietary being in its most simple declarative sense. If, through the theory of the death of the author, individualized voice is deferred to the contingency of external interpretation, it is only by mobilizing incommensurability *towards* disappearance that one retains analogy with the imperative of interpretation.

An interpretive imperative must, paradoxically, find its analogy in exactly the opposite of interpretation. To write after the death of the author is not simply to write as a reader. It is also to understand reading as an interpretive space where speech is reduced to silence; to write (or interpret) is to refuse oneself through the act of writing. This refusal extends beyond a simple disappearance of the authorial self; this refusal of self is the condition of having one. The maintenance of an incommensurable relationship to the world is effected only by continuing to compromise the possibility of such a relationship.

Incommensurable Realities

Consider the confluent message of the following two citations, drawn from Barthes' discussion of photographic representation rather than text, particularly revealing for the ways in which it constitutes a relationship between images, interpretations, and their undermining: "What is the content of the photographic message? What does the photograph transmit? By definition, the scene itself, the literal reality. From the object to its image there is of course a reduction – in proportion, perspective, colour – but at no time is this reduction a *transformation*";[8] and, "[A]ll images are polysemous; they imply, underlying their signifiers, a 'floating chain' of signifieds, the reader able to choose some and ignore other. Polysemy poses a question of meaning and this question always comes through as a dysfunction."[9]

What the confluence of these citations yields is a confirmation of the ironic dynamic of interpretation, here depersonalized in order to emphasize that intentionality matters little to the effectiveness of the relationship. If on one hand the photographic message transmits a literal reality, and at the same time the photographic image is polysemous, then it follows that reality is polysemous as well. Here reality is best defined not as a reliable singularity, but as the conflicting ways in which interpretive multiplicity is mobilized, independently of authoritative declaration. And, if this is so, one must insist that the argument be taken a step further. If the multiplicity of meanings in text is what rendered necessary the death of the author, it is the polysemy of reality – this dysfunctional multiplicity – that makes necessary the end of the ordered world. The ironic birth of representation is contingent on the dysfunctional death of the authority of the world.

What occurs in this framing is an extension of the authorial and textual dynamic to one with phenomenological import. One might assert that our phenomenological encounter with the world is built on selective engagement with a reality that is not reducible to a singular phenomenal possibility. An experiential rendering of this sort is instead based on a prosthesis – a dysfunction of representation, whether authorial, discursive, interpretive, or photographic. A message with no author, like a reality with no representation, does not lend itself to interpretive authority – such a message, in fact, is no message at all. A message of this sort is instead an encounter, not reducible to codification (whether textual or photographic), not equivalent to the signs that perpetuate it, and not generalizable despite a seemingly singular, real, appearance. No longer is it merely within the text that a variety of meanings blend and clash, nor even within interpretation. Now it is also within reality – not as a consequence of interpretive initiative, but as the structural condition of a polysemous yet incommensurable encounter with the world.

There is, however, a practical necessity to be considered in this context, and it concerns the mutual exclusivity of incommensurabilities, whether they be of selves, worlds, or representations. The multiplicity of appearance proceeds despite the exclusive manifesto of any given one, and yet it is the one rather than the many that forms the basis for Barthes' imperative. Taken to experiential extremes, this formulation reverses Walter Benjamin's declaration that what is important when faced with the photograph is "the art of thinking in other people's heads."[10] Instead, when faced with the dysfunction of incommensurability, it is merely the attempt to think in one's own head that constitutes the art – an aesthetic of irreducible reality, one version among many, here lived as an ironic phenomenology of disappearance.

The Death of the Reader

For Barthes, what was at stake in the discussion of the death of the author was the empowerment of the interpretive possibilities of reading (in the case of the text) or viewing (in the case of the photograph). While it is tempting to follow Barthes in the attempt to salvage interpretive license from the waning authority of text or representation, there is a structural paradox that such a trajectory must necessarily address. If the reader is seen as the site for the interpretation of the text (in the sense that the meaning now emerges from the reader rather than defaults to an author), then what Barthes is arguing for in this instance is a contextual understanding of meaning – derived from circumstance rather than discovered.[11] While the imperative for interpretation relies on a reader's mobilization of meaning, such mobilization is itself merely a moment in a context that can and must be extended.

After the death of the author, there are only readers, caught in various dynamics of context, interpretation, and re-interpretation. This is a semiotic game that, when put into play, has the philosophical consequence of rendering the author obsolete. All writing, in this context, occurs as a process of reading – the focusing of multiplicity into a singular interpretation that is both self-contained and merely one of many possible interpretations. In other words, insofar as reading contains an imperative for interpretation, and insofar as the multiplicity of meanings must be focused in the act of reading, each reader *produces* meaning from the engagement with a text, turning text into what Barthes calls "speaking corpses" – the orations of a dead author brought back to mythic life: "[M]athematical language is a *finished* language, which derives its very perfection from this acceptance of death. Myth, on the contrary, is a language which does not want to die: it wrests from the meanings which give it its sustenance an insidious, degraded survival, it provokes in them an artificial reprieve in which it settles comfortably, it turns them into speaking corpses.[12]

Seen in this way, the act of reading has as its consequence the reanimation of the author – a visceral ventriloquism that mobilizes the speaking corpse to interpretive ends. Interpretation not only causes the death of the author (in principle) but subsequently (in practice) reanimates the author as well, bringing him or her back from the dead not as an authorial figure, but as a zombie, a ghost of meaning that haunts the irony of interpretive mobilization.

This depiction, however, is a rather simplified dynamic that considers only two phases of what quickly becomes an ongoing system of interpretive deferral. Insofar as the author is abolished by the act of writing – disappeared only to be reanimated by the reader – the reader too is undermined at the moment in which interpretation is focused. The reader cannot help but become the proverbial next meal for the reanimated text since the reader, no less than the author, has the task of pulling meaning from the chaos of polysemous possibility – giving significance to the voices of ghosts and corpses.

It's important not to dismiss such a dynamic as one in which the reader merely becomes another author, subjecting him or herself to the mobilizing gaze of whoever, in turn, takes up the text to their own interpretive ends. It is not the reader who persists after the death of the author, – it is rather the reader who chooses this interpretive contingency as the structure of textual engagement to begin with.

For Barthes, the transition into a post-death of the author climate is a necessary ideological transformation. It is necessary for the perpetuation of structural multiplicity and for the enactment of these possibilities in a contingency of lived interpretation. It is only by constituting a theory of the death of the reader that both perspectives can be kept in non-competitive positioning. Neither should vouch for finality or authority of meaning, but continue to circulate haunted voices, fluctuating between the dynamic horizons of interpretation and mobilization. Writing, insofar as writing persists after the death of the reader (in the form of interpretive rather than authorial declaration) takes "zero degree" form according to Barthes: "The words become an alibi, that is, an elsewhere and a justification."[13]

Zombie Degree Zero

The alibi constituted by writing, reading, or interpretation is an alibi precisely because it refuses to participate in a normative world of established meaning, except as "a self-sufficient language … which has its roots only in the depths of the [dead] author's personal and secret mythology."[14] It is a mythology that might be called a proliferation of falsity in the sense that it is not bound to any truth except that contingency from which it is mobilized. Everything beyond degree zero is inconsequential to writing of this sort, for it understands itself as pre-emptively undermined. Preferring the multiplicity of possible mobilizations to the competitive politics of authorial tautology, to write after the death of the author is the same as to read after the death of the reader – it is to interpretively reanimate oneself. In other words, to write (zero degree) is not to creatively reconstitute oneself in the face of disappearance, but rather to write oneself out of self-control (and ostensibly into the control of others). This does not mean that one writes for others, it means one writes to undermine oneself. Interpretation (and, perhaps, creativity in all forms) must consequently be framed as an act of suicide: "This art [zero degree writing] has the very structure of suicide: in it, silence is a homogenous poetic time which traps the word between two layers and sets it off less as a fragment of a cryptogram than as a light, a void, a murder, a freedom."[15]

When the notion of the creative gesture as suicide is also seen as an alibi for interpretive engagement, what emerges is a zombie story: the formulated condition of interpretation after the deaths of the author and the reader. Any zombie philosophy must be seen as paradoxical – pretending to be alive while understanding that its appearance is contingent on the structural necessity of remaining disappeared at any cost.

Here, the suicidal imperative of writing or reading must be rephrased, however, for it is not quite the case that the author or reader self-destructs in the creative or interpretive process. Rather, the death of the author (and of the reader) begins to contextualize itself within an expanded network of emergent and undermined meaning. No longer simply self-contained mythologies mobilizing the meaning of an already-undermined message, what such a position requires is its mobilization by someone else. This is not a typical form of suicide, but one that thinks beyond its own death – this is the creative act as a stage for death-by-interpretation. For the author's hand is never the hand to strike the fatal blow; instead, it is in the act of reading that the author is undermined, and in the act of re-reading that the reader suffers a similar fate.

The Partial Paradox

The futility of constituted meaning is both the prerequisite for and the consequence of interpretative license. The paradox is that every interpretive declaration is spoken in the language of self-contained (authorial) meaning, while remaining contingent on external interpretive undermining.

On one hand, this external undermining is perhaps inevitable, and if such an assumption is proven true the paradox dissipates, since no matter what one says, others will hear it differently. In this case no amount of authorial or interpretive insistence will allow one to resist being mobilized towards the equally authoritative declarations of other authors and readers. The case is the same for every interpretation, even one's own: "once made use of, it becomes artificial,"[16] and the artificiality of the declarative voice reveals itself in the paradoxical contingency of absolute voice. Every declaration is at once absolutely meaningful (because the meaning must be focused as a consequence of the interpretive imperative) and absolutely meaningless (since meaning has no authority over the ways in which it will be subsequently mobilized). In fact, one might propose that it is precisely the meaningless (and not the absence of grounds for the meaningful) that is responsible for the sustenance of the paradox. The structural necessity of the meaninglessness of voice required for interpretive freedom sustains the paradoxically contingent state of interpretive meaning.

What such a paradox inevitably ignores, however, is that its sustenance requires a particular perspective on the question of meaning – one in which meaning is lost or denied, stripped from its authorial sanction, rendered dead because it anticipates itself as living. This is the problem that is reconciled by the fusion of the death of the author and zero degree writing. The paradox is reconciled not by being dissolved, but by placing the authorial position on the other side of the interpretive divide, by anticipating itself no longer as living, nor even as declarative. Rather, an authorship of this sort constitutes itself as spectral, hypocritically denying its own voice, preferring instead to speak in tongues: a voice of inevitably fraudulent content, a voice whose sincerity is no longer paradoxical because it is always sincerely insincere.

On the relationship between writing, fraudulence and sincerity, Barthes says this: "We see that here the function of writing is to maintain a clear conscience and that its mission is fraudulently to identify the original fact with its remotest subsequent transformation by bolstering up the justification of actions with the additional guarantee of its own reality."[17] By privileging conscience over authenticity, Barthes makes a structural leap – a suspension of disbelief which locates meaning within the fraudulent dynamic of.writing after the death of the author. To embrace the insincerity of interpretation is not to render redundant the voiceless voices that persist despite their authorial death. Rather, to write insincerely is to embrace the paradox of interpretive voice, no longer as paradoxical but as the structural condition of having a voice to begin with.

The key to the resolution of the paradox is the self-placement of the author with regard to his or her eventual and inevitable mobilization by others. Instead of treating authorial death (disappearance) as the traumatic consequence of interpretation, here one bypasses the trauma of disappearance by treating it as the structural condition of interpretation. By mobilizing this inverted structure of (the absolute contingency of) meaning, one neither resists mobilization nor prevents it. One rather pre-empts it, writing the story that sets the stage for one's own demise, making possible one's death-through-interpretation, indeed expecting it as the very consequence of writing to begin with. Ironically, this form of post-mortem self-contexualization creates a degree zero expectation – an expectation of disappearance – for an author or reader that seeks to engage or reconstitute meaning.

Such an interpretive perspective remains bound by its social, cultural, and existential victimization: its death and even its context for dying are externally imposed. Its suicide is merely an ironic pre-empting of what it understands as structurally inevitable. It is complicity with the myth of creative suicide that allows one to constitute an ironic death, in tandem with the interpretive life, constituted by others. After the death of the reader, the mythology of ironic self-constitution becomes the key to the self as a sustainable proliferation of falsity.

Playing Dead

The resolution of the paradox of postmodern authorship thus involves a basic repositioning of the dynamics of both interpretation and intentionality. While the death of authority is required for the birth of interpretation, it is the relegation of intentionality to the status of expectation that allows for the ironic declarative potential of contingent meaning. Here all meaning exists as by-product of authorial death, and the condition of meaningful writing is that it understands itself as mute – a voice that exists solely to be mobilized on one's behalf and at one's expense. This is not to say that authorial voice is meaningless; it is rather to say that its meaning is oblique and never self-determined.

In this conceptual inversion is a self-reflexive approach to the use of language, one that takes as its horizon of possibility (as the condition of each and every utterance) the consequences of signification in the disappearance of voice. Interestingly, this form of disappearance has much in common with the way Barthes defines mythology: "It can be seen that in myth there are two semiological systems, one of which is staggered in relation to the other: a linguistic system, the language (or the modes of representation which are assimilated to it), which I shall call the *language-object*, because it is the language which myth gets hold of in order to build its own system; and myth itself, which I shall call *metalanguage,* because it is a second language, *in which* one speaks about the first."[18] For Barthes, mythology is a second-order semiotics, one that self-consciously mobilizes the linguistic referents of others in the creation of new systems of meaning. Mythology escapes from the standards of representational language by constructing its own system of meta-representation that is always in excess and in anticipation of the linguistic and conceptual systems from which it is derived. Seen from such a vantage point, instead of the ironic attempt to constitute oneself as posthumously alive – a declarative, if contingent, authority – mythology allows for a conscientious scripting of the drama which permits the posthumous status of authorship itself. In this, there is for Barthes a privileging of gesture over language: "[Language is] a familiar repertory of gestures, a gestuary, as it were, in which the energy expended is purely operative, serving here to enumerate, there to transform, but never to appraise or signify a choice."[19]

Seen as an act of contingency, this form of engagement, whether written or lived, would no longer involve making gestures of content, but rather those of *context* – written, spoken, and declared no less than before, except that this time one gestures in order to set a stage upon which one no longer has proprietary control over one's own voice. This is mythology as a creative act of cosmological suicide in which through speaking one abandons one's own voice in a futile gesture towards the continued proliferation of the contingency of meaning.

Such an act might be seen as a self-administration of falsified perspective – pre-empting the competition for authoritative meaning through the proposition of contingent possibilities, no less ontological for their contingency. While this may seem at first glance like a series of semiotic manoeuvres, one must resist the temptation to dismiss such a position for its seemingly arbitrary structural self-placement. In the end, it is the arbitrary nature of mythological self-deconstitution that allows for the perpetuation of myth. Barthes asserts that "myth is a double system; there occurs in it a sort of ubiquity: its point of departure is constituted by the arrival of a meaning."[20] But, what must also be remembered is that this double system is potentially reversible, depending on how one positions oneself within its dynamic. The stakes not only of the departure, but also of all possible future arrivals (the interpretive possibilities) rest on this placement. There can be no competition among such possible future constellations of meaning, for in prioritizing the context for their arrival, one pre-emptively abandons oneself to their fate – to the fate of others as those who will ensure that one's writing does not go uninterpreted. This form of writing is not about an intervention into or contribution towards a context for living but about playfully attempting to set the context for one's own disappearance – embracing the futility of voice, asking not after the best, most useful, or most meaningful ways of living, but shaping the story according to which one will abandon oneself for good.

If this all seems just a little bit too easy, it is because such is the nature of both mythology and self-fulfilling expectation, mechanisms that can be so effectively mobilized because they do not wait to be confirmed. The postmodern author understands him or herself as simply waiting to be dismissed, discarded, interpreted, and mobilized. Because such a perspective knows that it ultimately says nothing of ontological value, it is indifferent to what is said on its behalf. It is also of paramount importance that *something* be said, however, for the emergence of an externally constituted appearance is the condition of its aestheticized disappearance.

After the death of the author, the death of the reader, and an imperative towards zero-degree interpretive forms, the idea of playing dead might be proposed as something of a conceptual intervention, situated on the other side of the paradox of authorship, projecting itself into self-fulfilling oblivion. In this sense, it is no longer merely a contingent strategy for the negotiation of writing after the death of the author, nor merely for the negotiation of identity after the death of the self, nor even only for the negotiation of falsity after the death of truth. Rather, insofar as all of these deaths initiate a paradox of their own, playing dead can be seen as a larger strategy for the negotiation of those paradoxes of disappearance that proceed despite their own deaths, mobilizing the ironic perpetuation of death as the horizon that a life of impossibility requires.

5
Mirrors that Pout

The Scott Rogers Google Project[1]

How many Scott Rogers does it take to find Scott Rogers? An interesting paradox since the more Scott Rogers' one finds, the more difficult it is to say which Scott Rogers one was looking for. The more Scott Rogers are discovered, the less Scott Rogers is able to just be himself, the less distinct is each and every Scott Rogers, the more each begins to diffuse into the nebulae of Scotts-Rogers, the less recognizable is any given Scott Rogers among the horde of others who, by all accounts, seem just like him.

This would seem to be the central point of a recent art project by Scott Rogers. *The Scott Rogers Google Project* is a collection of internet links – a portal to all things Scott Rogers – and ultimately, a virtual icon to his material disappearance.

Imagine how the story might unfold. One looks for oneself on the internet. One doesn't find the self one expected, but instead a horde of doppelgangers: each implicated in a real-life actuality that is not one's own. An excess of Scott Rogers perhaps, the 80,000 hits on a single name casting uncertainty on the identity of any given one: Scott Rogers, associate professor of neurobiology; Scott Rogers, attorney at law; Scott Rogers, actor and stunt coordinator. Yet in each manifestation of Scott Rogers there is something familiar, even if it is only a name.

What happens when one begins to search for oneself, search for self-knowledge and self-understanding, only to find oneself multiplied and fragmented? One's face is the same as someone else's, at least insofar as identity involves putting a face to a name. What seems like an intensely narcissistic endeavor – the competition for a name, the competition for Google ratings – takes exactly the opposite form: a dissolution of particularity under the auspices of multiplicity. According to Rogers, the piece is "more like channel surfing than narcissism,"[2] a narcissistic hall of mirrors perhaps, in which one perpetually appears to oneself differently, a kaleidoscope of Scotts-Rogers coming in and out of their own form of prime-time representational existence, or perhaps emerging only during life's commercial breaks.

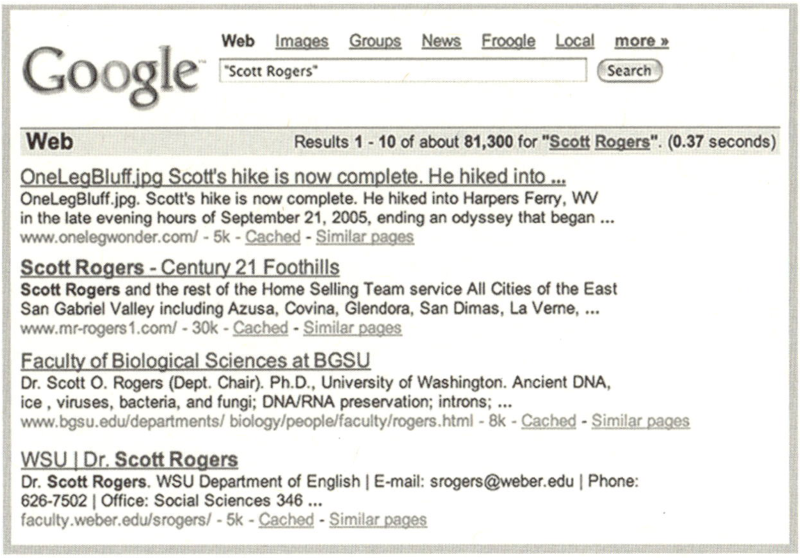

Google

Web Images Groups News Froogle Local more »

"Scott Rogers" Search

Web Results **1** - **10** of about **81,300** for "Scott Rogers". (**0.37** seconds)

OneLegBluff.jpg Scott's hike is now complete. He hiked into ...
OneLegBluff.jpg. Scott's hike is now complete. He hiked into Harpers Ferry, WV in the late evening hours of September 21, 2005, ending an odyssey that began ...
www.onelegwonder.com/ - 5k - Cached - Similar pages

Scott Rogers - Century 21 Foothills
Scott Rogers and the rest of the Home Selling Team service All Cities of the East San Gabriel Valley including Azusa, Covina, Glendora, San Dimas, La Verne, ...
www.mr-rogers1.com/ - 30k - Cached - Similar pages

Faculty of Biological Sciences at BGSU
Dr. Scott O. Rogers (Dept. Chair). Ph.D., University of Washington. Ancient DNA, ice , viruses, bacteria, and fungi; DNA/RNA preservation; introns; ...
www.bgsu.edu/departments/ biology/people/faculty/rogers.html - 8k - Cached - Similar pages

WSU | Dr. **Scott Rogers**
Dr. **Scott Rogers**. WSU Department of English | E-mail: srogers@weber.edu | Phone: 626-7502 | Office: Social Sciences 346 ...
faculty.weber.edu/srogers/ - 5k - Cached - Similar pages

Scott Rogers. *Scott Rogers Google Project*. Google Search Results Page, 2004–05.

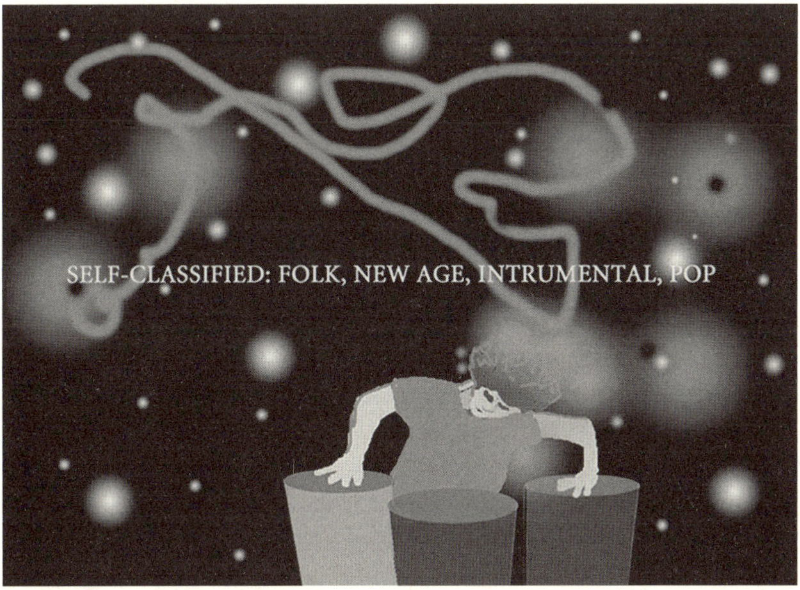

Scott Rogers. *Self-portrait as Scott Rogers*. Mixed media, 2004–05.

Walter Benjamin has argued that because of the infinite reproducibility of the photographic image, it makes no sense to ask after the original photograph.[3] Is the same perhaps true here? Would the "real" Scott Rogers please stand? The irony is that each Scott Rogers is in fact real – forming either an army of them, or an internal conflict, externalized in a new key. One understands of course what it is like to be in conflict with oneself, not quite sure what one's opinions are or could be, not quite sure what course of action to pursue. The case of Scott Rogers is not different, despite the fact that each is also his own individual. One might look at this as a collective of sorts, multiple personalities competing for attention. Is the real Scott Rogers defined as the one who one meets first? By all experiential accounts this first meeting would seem to form an initial conception of the identity of Scott Rogers. Upon meeting a second Scot Rogers might one not proclaim: "I know someone else with that same name!" One becomes two.

So what's in a name? A label of individualized belonging, unchosen by those who wear them, often chosen to reference someone else? I have my maternal grandfather's name, my father has the name of his father, and my brother has my father's name. I have friends named after poems, seasons, and

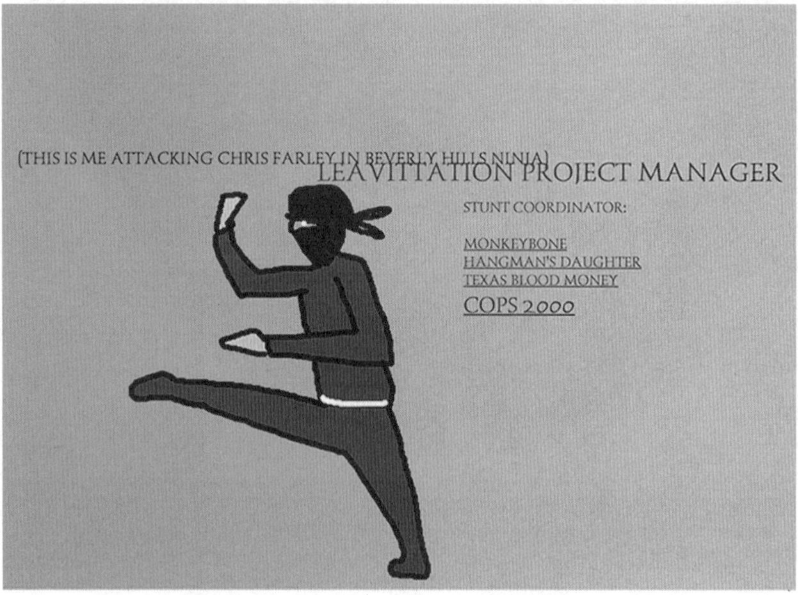

Scott Rogers. *Self-portrait as Scott Rogers*. Mixed media, 2004–05.

celebrities. Some names are chosen for the simple pleasure of pronunciation. But I know few people whose names were simply made up or chosen for no reason. At the very least, a name is a horizon of sorts, an ordering of the individual, and yet, as Roland Barthes says: "the content of the word 'Order' always indicates repression."[4] We are bound to our names, bound consequently to a named deferral individualized belonging, bound, in the end, to something else, something that defies our self-conception, rendering each and every named individual in excess of themselves. Here, the name takes on precisely the inevitability of being someone else.

Or is it the other way around? Perhaps here the multiplicity of Scott Rogers in fact requires that a differentiation be made, requires the disappearance of the group, not of the individual into the group. Perhaps there is more at stake here than the simple (and common) dismissal of subcultural identity – the awkward category of those who are so strongly individualized, just like everyone else. Does it matter if one is a punk or a skater, a hippie or a goth, an anarchist or a Scott Rogers? Perhaps in the case of the cult of Scotts-Rogers the grounds for separation require that there be no Scott Rogers at all, no such name, no such category. Perhaps, in a strange and subtle twist, *The Scott Rogers Google Project* is in fact more of an epitaph than a reunion. It is a monument to an individual who has come up against the horizon of his name, from which only two responses seem probable: one either finds one's name and loses oneself, or one finds oneself in losing one's name.

Cybernetic Psychoanalysis

The commonly held view of electronic and virtual technologies – from Marshall McLuhan to Paul Virilio, Jean Baudrillard to Arthur Kroker – is that they extend us (corporeally and cognitively) outside of ourselves. This contradicts the tenets of psychoanalytic theory – in particular in its Lacanian formulation – in which the self is seen as already extended, fundamentally alienated from itself as a condition of conscious being. There are also a variety of ways to understand this opposition between thinkers of technology and those of psychoanalysis, from the accusation of error levied against techno-theory to a similar accusation against the psychoanalytic version of the story. But what if neither is wrong? What if, instead of and despite the paradox this would cause, the reason both perspectives make sense is that both are correct?

One way to untangle this question is to construe these seemingly opposing theories as identical. If, according to Marshall McLuhan, "the medium is the message" and at the same time "the content of any medium is always another medium," does this not imply that the content of a medium is always deferred?[5] By applying this to psychoanalysis, we could force McLuhan and Lacan into a position of agreement– the self, as a medium of messages, always has its content in a deferred fantasy of itself as another medium, a deferred fantasy of itself as another. Or we could understand this question through Kroker, who asserts that individuals are literally possessed by technologies.[6] What if this possession took the form of an inaccessible fantasy of ourselves as Other, as grown through the (technological) interaction with the mirror? Here could we not declare that the mirror is another instance of technological extension?

Another and perhaps better way to understand this inter-relationship is through a more linear filter. The reason why technology can be so seductive is because it speaks directly to who we already know, but are unwilling to admit, ourselves to be. A fantasy without content, or with conflicted content – such as the fantasy offered by psychoanalysis – is rarely compelling, particularly when compared to the prefabricated fantasies of television, the walking soundtracks of iPods and Walkmans, or the information databases of the internet which offer prefabricated fantasies of everything from terrorism to lovemaking to shapeshifting. The seduction of technology is precisely that it fulfills our fantasies without emphasizing their vacuous nature. There is no trauma of misunderstanding, only the inspiring sounds of drum and bass that allow one to groove one's way through life.

If there is a problem with theories of technology it is ironically that they misunderstand technology as their object. Martin Heidegger declared that "the essence of technology is by no means anything technological."[7] In this vein, it begins to seem that technology may actually be a psychoanalytic facilitator – anaesthetizing the trauma of being by satisfying the desire to be someone else. Psychoanalysis tells us we all have this desire, irrespective of our personal knowledge or self-actualizing potential. Here, the problem with technology is not in any way technological. The problem rather is that the technological extension of the self is entirely *natural*; it is in fact our condition of being in the world. And techno-theory, consequently, does itself an injustice by asserting that its object of study is technology, for it is the question of human subjectivity that allows for this extension in the first place. We have always been other to ourselves, extended well beyond our self-conceptions, and it is no surprise that we encounter ourselves as such when faced with technology. More surprising perhaps is that it did not occur to us sooner, for technology is not needed for such a realization. Yet most certainly the stakes of the question are raised when technology rises to the stage, actualizing the fantasy of ourselves as Other.

It is no simple assertion to declare that a technological understanding of the self yields new insight into the question of psychoanalysis in a contemporary world. Rather, here one faces the possibility, not that technology is anything new, but that technology has always been the horizon of human self-conception, and a fantasy denied is no less actualized for its denial.

Optical Inversions

> [T]he proper reply to the postmodern doubt about the existence of the ideological big Other is that it is the subject itself who doesn't exist.
>
> Slavoj Zizek, *The Puppet and the the Dwarf*, 39.

The question of the self and its representations has long been a source of concern to scholars, philosophers, and psychologists; has long been a question whose stakes provide some an entry point into the nuances of possible and actual existence. Michel Foucault once said "we must sacrifice the self in order to discover the truth about ourselves."[8] Yet the price to be paid for such an understanding is the disappearance of that which we know into the knowledge of what can then be merely a form of living death, a post-mortem existence in which one has ostensibly chosen self-knowledge over having a self.

This is not a new problem. In fact, since the birth of the image out of Plato's cave, humanity has always been separated from itself by its self-knowledge, given the form of appearance. Perhaps we have already decided to abandon ourselves for the sake of the image – a choice predetermined by the social and cultural knowledge imperative.

In the same passage, Foucault also says something else: "we have to discover the truth about ourselves in order to sacrifice ourself"[9] – and it is here that the existential loop is completed. It is paradoxical of course, but apparent paradoxes should be taken seriously, for upon closer examination the two opposing sides often end up with strangely similar implications.

Consider what might seem at first to be a rather arbitrary example: the optical dynamics of appearance. Optical theory has it that the world around us appears as a function of reflected light, which is to say that light hits an object or body and is reflected back at us as the image of that object. This is true for any object that does not directly emit its own light (ourselves included), thus reliant on light from the world around it in order to secure a worldly appearance. For instance, a tree appears during the day because sunlight hits the tree and is reflected back to the human eye, allowing us to perceive its image. First tenet of the image: it requires illumination.

There is a nuance here however, that has to do with the nature of an image that is always indebted to its source of illumination. Sunlight, for example, is considered to be white light, while fluorescents have a rather greenish tinge, and normal room light is slightly yellow. Equally, to make a drawing with green ink on white paper will yield a green drawing under normal circumstances. Illuminated with green light, however, the image of the green drawing will disappear, again due to the principles of reflected light which say that a white surface will reflect all colours of light that come into contact with it while a green surface will only reflect green. Here, however, because all colours of light coming into contact with the white paper surface are, in fact, green, the two distinct surfaces appear to be identical. Illuminated with purple light (the optically-opposite colour of green), the green drawing will appear black, since it will absorb all colours of light that are not green. Second tenet of the image: like reflects like and absorbs all that is different.

Consequently, one cannot simply say that the image is an observation of light reflected off an object. While the image may be the reflected light of an object, there is a simultaneous principle of absorption in play – one that holds a great deal of value for the understanding of appearance. A tree will appear green because sunlight hits the tree and is reflected back to us, yet somewhere in this process the white light of the sun is perceived as a green image of the tree. What is mistakenly dismissed as inconsequential is the principle of absorption that would have all colours *except* green absorbed by the tree. The tree in fact refuses the green portion of the light spectrum, reflecting it – rejecting it – back as the light-detritus of image appearance. Third tenet of the image: the world of appearances is a world of refused light.

The understanding of appearances will, consequently, always appear exactly as it is not: the condition of a tree appearing green is that the tree (physiologically) rejects its own image. It is no longer enough to examine that which is perceived – now the very mechanisms of perception require re-examination in order to illuminate the misunderstandings of appearance. If trees reject green light, despite the fact that this is not at all how it seems, trees must in fact be precisely the opposite of green – the colour of the absence of green. Basic optical light theory will tell us that white light (from the sun) minus green light (from the image of the tree) leaves a residual presence of magenta – and thus under the dim light of an orange sky, the purple tree sways gently in the breeze while a white crow taunts a blue tabby cat on the prowl for black eggs. The world of apparent phenomena can be nothing other than a negative-image world. In both consciousness and optics alike the self appears to itself exactly as it is not; this in fact being the condition of appearance. The image world is a world of refused light, and we creatures of image are a function of light rejected into appearance. Final tenet of the image: to know oneself is to abandon oneself as (optically) other.

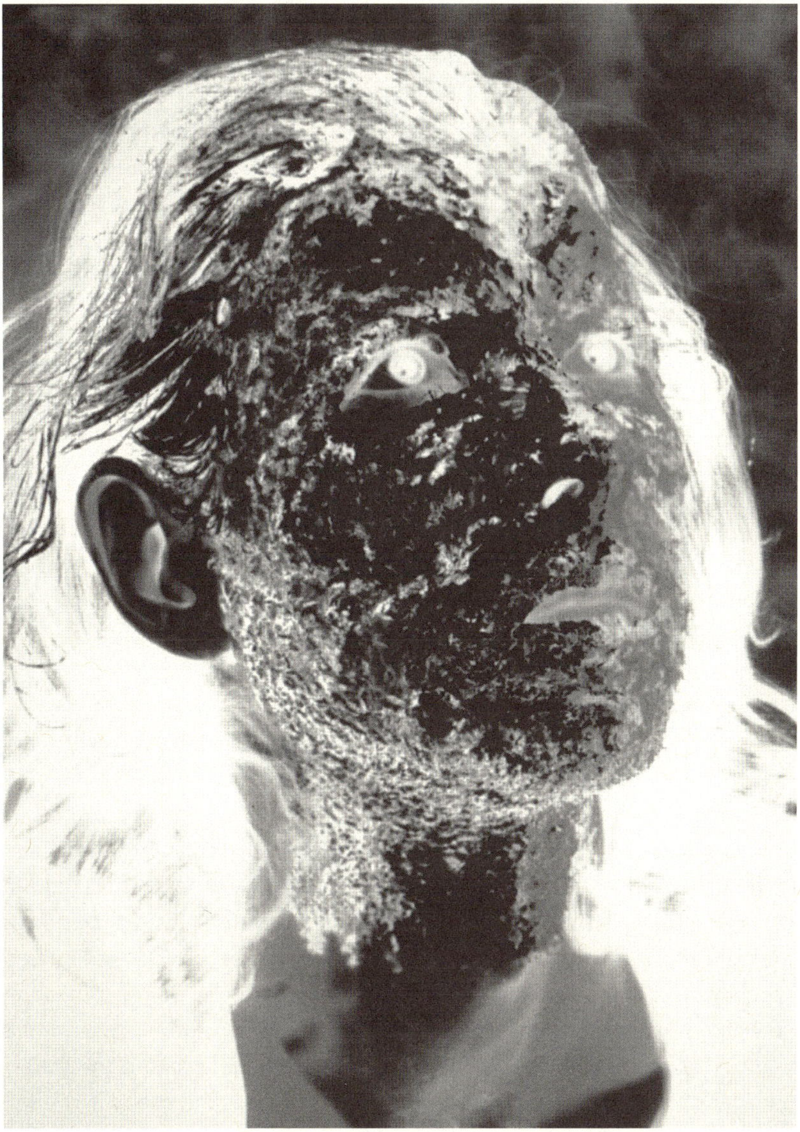

Ted Hiebert. *Negative-image self-portrait.* Colour photograph, 1997.

In a theory of optical inversion we find the reconciliation of Foucault's paradox. One's self-knowledge and the sacrifice of oneself are no longer in opposition; in fact, appearance becomes directly correlated to its own refusal, knowledge and alienation become equivalent. If this dynamic seems familiar, it is because it is the same dynamic that has always been at the root of Lacanian psychoanalysis. In the childhood encounter with the self in the mirror, we are first and forever alienated from ourselves, due to the self-understanding engendered by this recognition. In other words, the self is born through its alienation from itself in exactly the same way as the image is born in the constitution of refused light. And just as the psychoanalytic self is irreconcilable with its Other, so too would the reconciliation of the image result not in a higher understanding of its structural dynamics, but in its phase cancellation: the collapse of an image into its (objectified) Other would (optically) yield only its disappearance. To reunify the green and the purple would effectively make a tree disappear. The same may also be true for consciousness: the reunification of the split engendered by the mirror stage would effectively erase the very consciousness it attempts to unify.

Mirrors that Punish

> [Psychoanalysis] allows us to formulate a paradoxical *phenomenology without a subject* – phenomena arise that are not phenomena *of* a subject, appearing *to* it. This does not mean that the subject is not involved here – it is, but, precisely, in the mode of EXCLUSION, as the negative agency that is not able to assume these phenomena.[10]
>
> Slavoj Zizek, *Organs without Bodies*, 96.

In the separation of optics and perception there is a strange form of virtuality that emerges – a disappearance that lingers in the negative space of the perceiving body. Psychoanalysis might be best situated on this virtual side of the optical inversion; not on the side that appears, but inside the rejected appearance of the optical. It would thus be no surprise to find a correlation between psychoanalytic self-conception and the negative world of absorbed bodies that are denied the ability to appear. Consider Lacan on the consequences of the mirror stage: "We have only to understand the mirror stage *as an identification*, in the full sense that analysis gives to the term: namely, the transformation that takes place in the subject when he assumes an image

– whose predestination to this phase-effect is sufficiently indicated by the use, in analytic theory, of the ancient term *imago*."[11]

While the mirror-image allows for an unprecedented visual relation to ourselves, it is never quite the same way in which someone else might relate to us. Lacan points out the differentiation in scale that accompanies the perception of oneself in the mirror: a mirror image is always smaller than life-size due to the receding perspective that doubles the distance between oneself and the mirror. Likewise, the mirror image is always reversed, and given the fact that few faces are perfectly symmetrical (and, even if they were, most gestures immediately rupture corporeal symmetry), this also sets up an insurmountable barrier to the perception of oneself as one is. In the mirror image, we encounter ourselves in a way that nobody else can: optically inverted and cognitively reversed. Likewise, the encounter of oneself according to the terms of others is optically impossible through the interface of mirrored mediation. Lacan argues:

> The fact is that the total form of the body by which the subject anticipates in a mirage the maturation of his power is given to him only as *Gestalt*, that is to say, in an exteriority in which this form is certainly more constituent than constituted, but in which it appears to him above all in a contrasting size *(un relief de stature)* that fixes it and in a symmetry that inverts it, in contrast with the turbulent movements that the subject feels are animating him. Thus, this *Gestalt* – whose pregnancy should be regarded as bound up with the species, though its motor style remains scarcely recognizable – by these two aspects of its appearance, symbolizes the mental permanence of the *I*, at the same time as it prefigures its alienating destination.[12]

According to Lacan, it is here that the self is born as the immanently unrealizable fantasy of itself, since it cannot optically appear to itself in a form congruent with the world around it. Always backwards – when I move my right arm I see only the movement of my left. Always smaller than life – to be larger than life would, then, be to mistake myself for my own fantasy of myself. The best that I can hope for is that "objects in this mirror are closer than they appear." Or in the words of Slavoj Zizek: "what characterizes human subjectivity proper is ... the fact that fantasy, at its most elementary, becomes inaccessbile to the subject."[13] There is perhaps an (optically and cognitively) imposed distance necessitated by the principles of self-reflexivity, in which one's fantasy will always be closer than it appears, though never quite close enough to touch.

The optical illusion of reflected distance is constitutive of both a myth and a reality and both at the same time. Here the self is a sort of *Zeno's Paradox*[14] in which one only appears to oneself in terms of incremental division, never allowing for a meeting point since one must always travel half the remaining distance, and then half that, and so on. As Zizek says: "our painful progress of knowledge, our confusions, our search for solutions, that is to say, precisely that which seems to *separate* us from the way reality really is out there, is already the innermost constituent of reality itself."[15]

Both Lacan and Zizek seem to have missed the generative dynamic at the root of the image. The identification with one's image is a misidentification – or an identification with the light that has been optically refused by the subject; the constitutive image, instead, being the inverted image that is the function of light absorbed. To expand the Lacanian theory of cognitive formation in order to include the inverted image would then be to force the theory of the mirror stage into a position where it, too, is largely inverted. For the most part this is due to the need to reattribute the source of image generation – no longer a failed moment of externalized recognition, but a pre-emptively refused moment of reflection. Like the problem within Zeno's Paradox, psychoanalysis posits a continually shifting horizon of assessment, from within which one always finds oneself halfway, unable to exit the dynamic of self, and unable to actualize it. Just as I feel I begin to approach the fantasies of myself, I find those fantasies changed, and the search must begin anew. At best, the psychoanalytic self can only ever be halfway to nowhere.

For this reason, one might posit something of an error in the psychoanalytic formulation of subjectivity, an error that arises from the personification of the image as a contingent horizon to which the self will always be held accountable. Are we surprised that the image rejects us, imposing an alienating distance between ourselves and our self-conceptions? Are we surprised that the image also shifts in accordance with our self-understandings in order to forever maintain that distance as exactly double? In short, are we surprised that that which we reject (as the condition of appearance) rejects us back? And, consequently, rather than Zizek's assertion that "[the psychoanalyst's] ultimate aim is to deprive the subject of the very fundamental fantasy that regulates the universe of his (self) experience,"[16] should we not also invert this formulation such that the task of the psychoanalyst is not to deprive the subject of his or her fantasies, but rather to actively cultivate them?

It is not the structural dynamics of either the mirror stage or of psychoanalysis that are under question here, but rather their effects. In particular, the claim that must be made is that psychoanalysis assumes a traumatic consequence to what is in fact an optical phenomenon – the absorption and reflection of light – and that, further, psychoanalysis overlooks the pre-emptive mediation of images by the absorbing body itself. At the core of psychoanalysis is an insistence on the traumatizing effects of physiological existence, the traumatizing effects of fantasy, the traumatizing effects of what is (in both optics and psychoanalysis) an inevitability of appearing other to oneself.

The argument is not merely structural. It calls into question the psychology of psychoanalysis, and in particular the imperative of trauma that seems entirely unnecessary. Why must the fantasy of oneself as another be responsibly denied, and in particular, when we already know this to be in fact the condition of being oneself in the first place? Under such circumstances, should the fantasy not be actively cultivated as the one truth about ourselves of which we can be certain? A negative-truth, a nonsensical truth, a truth of disappearance, which paradoxically engenders all possibilities of appearance, since being (under such circumstances) is reducible to pure fantasy – a cognitive fantasy that exists without image. Image, instead, is acknowledged not as the grounds of fantasy proper, but that which fantasy must reject in order to come into (cognitive) existence.

We exist without image, this is the condition of being. That psychoanalysis (and cultural theory, and philosophy in general) tells us otherwise does not make it so, and to properly understand the dynamic that Lacan wished to trace, one must resort not to the trauma of appearances – not to the cognitive transformation that occurs when we assume an image – but something substantially more convoluted. The trauma is that of being taught to think of ourselves as something that we have always rejected; the trauma is that from the start what Lacan would have us assume is precisely our own rejections of ourselves, in the form of the optically reflected image. One must return to the absorption principle of light – to the dynamics of optics rather than the assumptions of cognitive generation, and observe more properly that the mirror stage encounter is not in any way an encounter with oneself, nor the symbolic moment in which the subject is born through assuming an image, but rather more simply: the mirror stage is a second-order rejection of the image, where we (re)assimilate the discarded residue of appearance.

This assertion is not intended to undermine the psychoanalytic emphasis on the traumatic effects of appearance. Rather, it is to reformulate it as the fantasy at the core of psychoanalysis: what is perpetuated by psychoanalysis is not the trauma of fantasy, but the fantasy of trauma – the fantasy of oneself as irreparably traumatized. In this context of misunderstandings and misrecognitions, one might posit psychoanalysis itself as a sort of disciplinary social theory, inevitably reflecting the mistaken conclusion that reflection is responsible for cognitive duality, when in fact the rejection of duality has always been the condition of (cognitive) appearance. Here the misrecognition is not of oneself as another, the misrecognition is that there ever was an apparent self to begin with.

Fantasies of Trauma

Contemporary psychoanalysis finds itself in a Catch-22. On one hand, reconceived in order to accommodate the inverted image, the theory of the mirror stage becomes a complex fantasy of traumatized existence. On the other hand, this fantasy is no less immanent to the cognitive experience of oneself as another that has always formed the central premise of psychoanalytic pursuits. It is also no less traumatic for the paradox that results from this doubled reading – unless, that is, one can posit an alternative model through which to re-actualize psychoanalysis for its deep understanding of the implications of alienation without retreating to the insistence on alienation-as-traumatic.

There is something to be said for the powerful effects of fantasy, here instanced by the effect psychoanalytic theory has already had on the social and philosophical psyche. Far from making psychoanalysis a redundant practice, the power of fantasy speaks to the complexity of the task at hand: the attempt to understand the impossible accountability of a fictionalized self to its own rejected image. What is initiated is a perpetually inaccessible dialogue between images and fantasy, one that makes the relationship between the two into one of pure repetition. This is a game of endless deferral that quickly becomes monotonous and therefore, according to Zizek "demands the highest creative effort."[17] Taken to an extreme, this game begins to make of psychoanalysis an aesthetic practice; a practice in which one is coached, not towards a reconciliation of trauma, nor even towards the acceptance of its perpetuity, but into the cognitive possibilities for refashioning the fantasies that cannot be made to disappear even though they no longer have an image.

What is needed in order to keep this game active is a way to frustrate the emphasis on trauma in psychoanalytic theory, such that the absence of legitimate appearances does not lead to a trauma of disappearance – a trauma of fantasy denied – but instead to the ironic actualization of the fantasy of alienation. Psychoanalysis will not deny, for instance, that we are all capable of fantastic self-conception; it will only deny that the horizon of such constitution is anything other than traumatic. But one might question whether it is the subject who is incapable of non-traumatic fantasy or whether it is psychoanalysis itself that is incapable of understanding any self-concept grown through alternative means.

Against the imperative for a traumatic encounter with the image – or its absence – what is needed is a way to undermine the authority of reflection such as to reconstitute appearances ironically. That mirrors are not designed with this in mind is part of the difficulty, and that we ourselves have largely succumbed to the assumption of reflective authority is part of the postmodern challenge. If the mirror image in psychoanalysis is seen as already personified, forming the alienated version of ourselves to which we hold ourselves impossibly accountable, the task here is to undermine these mirrors – to undermine, in other words, our own self-image. The psychoanalytic mirror has always been a speaking mirror; a magic mirror through which we tell ourselves what to think. And when we no longer take its seduction for granted, this is a mirror that begins to pout – our own disciplinary voices no longer taken seriously except as the ironic indications of fantastic possibility.

One might rephrase this by suggesting that the optical image and the cognitive image of self hold together similar territories, and, in both cases, it is the fantasy of self that is contextualized by the image. Thus the problem is not with the attempt to understand how an image is generated, but rather how the self understands itself as accountable to the image against which it has been generated. If the image is seen as the discarded reflection of disappearance, the stage of fantasy is entirely reversed. Now, if I must maintain the image of myself as another, it is only in order to avoid accepting myself as fantasy proper – to affirm the possibility that I exceed in some way my own fantasies of myself. This, in other words, is to insist on the fantasy of reality by precisely denying the reality of fantasy.

The result of this formulation does not exit the dynamic of disappearance, for the mirror will never quite reflect the fantasy of oneself unless that fantasy is precisely the fantasy of oneself as another. Without an image to confirm this dynamic (for the image, as Lacan showed, always rejects the formulation of the fantastic, thus the entry into traumatic reality[18]), the practice of fantasy will always remain bound by the impossibility of appearance. The image no longer confirms the fantasy and one encounters oneself as a fantasy without possible referent. The psychoanalytic trauma here, if it is to be maintained at all, is simply the inability to accept oneself as an instance of completed fantasy, in whatever form that fantasy might take.

Subjectivity in the Age of the Screen

It is here that one might find an alternative to the psychoanalytic mirror in precisely the frustration of accountability to one's image. If one is to be held accountable at all, it is no longer to one's image, but only to one's fantasies. While there is little room to extend this formulation psychoanalytically, techno-theory has something further to contribute to the question. With the influence of electronic technologies, something quite different happens to the question of the image.

One might again think of optics – this time virtual optics, which do not obey the principles of reflected light and which have no need of the principles of absorption that will always contextualize the reflected images of analogue encounter. Rather, the virtual participates in exactly the opposite phenomenon, what photographers call incident light, or light that is transmitted directly – emitted – without a mediating reflection. Think of the computer screen or the television, whose rear-projected image always seems exactly as it is, since there is no real-object refraction required for the redirection of light. In incident light, the object is always self-illuminating, self-revealing, stripped of its secrecy and mystique. One finds for perhaps the first time the possibility of a non-traumatized image, an image that is capable of rendering fantasy for the simple reason that it never pretended to be real.

McLuhan says that the electronic age has created a totally new environment which has as its content the old mechanized environment of the industrial age, and further that one is only ever aware of the (old) content, and not the (new) medium.[19] This example is important, for with the birth of the projected (technological) image, the content of subjectivity is entirely transformed. If it was the body that was the implied content of the reflected image, it is this reflected body (and not the biological body proper) that is the content of the projected self. This virtual self-conception can be so malleable because the reflected image was already a mistaken attribution of self. Given the horizon of virtual identity, there is no question about the recuperation of an authentic self-image, and consequently no psychological stakes in a proper appearance. The reflective self-image has always been a myth of itself.

The virtual image, seen as a phenomenon of projection or incidence, is also an image that does not structurally impose a cognitive division of the subject. Rather, if such a division is noted in relation to the virtual, it is always because it belongs to a fantasy of trauma. The virtual sets up a barrier to the real, a fantasy that must be deployed and accepted in order to set the grounds for a participation that will always remain slightly ironic because it is forever unredeemable in a real world context. But the problem is that the virtual is always too accessible, too real, too familiar, too close; what becomes unbearable is the understanding of oneself exactly as one wishes to self-conceive.

McLuhan can again elucidate, particularly in his denotation of the difference between hot (non-participatory) and cool (interactive) media.[20] The reflected self-image, as proposed by Lacan, is essentially a result of the mirror seen as a hot medium – not grown out of interaction, but formed out of the alienating encounter with the authority of one's own reflection. The medium is the message, and the one-way gaze of the mirror will impose the alienating destination on the individual "situat[ing] the agency of the ego ... in a fictional direction, which will always remain irreducible for the individual alone."[21]

In contrast to this a priori alienating destiny of the reflective image, the projected image is cool in its constitution, depending entirely upon the possible horizons of fantasy which the individual mobilizes on his or her own behalf. This is not necessarily a liberating dynamic, as the participatory possibilities of paranoia, perversion, and delusion are just as accessible to the subject as the liberatory self-constructions of possible fantasy. The point, then, is not to predetermine the content of fantasy, except to say that its only horizon is that which is literally projected onto it by the subject.

To expand on this distinction between reflected and incident (projected) light is to enter into a second-order discussion of reflection, a second-order of mirror-play, and a second-order of alienation. This time the result is not the traumatic separation of selves from themselves, but a trauma of self-proximity, a trauma of self-knowledge, a trauma of self-understanding. And within this second-order discourse, no longer is the mirror simply the inanimate index of alienated appearance; rather the mirror now reveals itself as doubled in equal ways, personified by necessity as the exorcist of the (image of) self from (the reality of) its fantasies.

With the technological image, unfettered from the principles of absorption, what remains is the immanence of completed fantasy, that which Jean Baudrillard calls "the divine irreference of images"[22] or, more simply, the simulacrum as the floating symptom (and no longer the authentic consequence) of self-image. The simulation becomes real, and in doing so replaces the realities that came before it. This is, of course, what was happening anyways, only this time there is no spectre, no traumatic haunting of the self by its self-image. Now there is only fantasy as the singular horizon of aesthetic self-rendering. The technological image allows for the acceptance of ourselves as fantasy, indeed an indulgence in the non-traumatic freedoms of not-being. No longer the reflected image – now we encounter only the projected images of self-fulfilling fantasy.

The Ironic Intuition

Intuition, as the ostensibly incommensurable performance of self, as well as the formations of reflective self-conception, are inverted under the sign of the technological image. This has consequences. Self-conception has moved well past the stage where the reflexive self-understanding of experiential division (whether perceptual or cognitive) forms the core of subjective formulation. With the projected self (without) image, the image – and the history of possible self-conceptions that have uniformly centered around congruency with the image – may have been interpreted backwards.

There is no more comfort in self-reflexivity for the simple reason that all things reflective now must be seen as equally deceptive – functions not of incommensurable observation but of mistaken or forgotten refusals. With these revisions to a theory of contemporary subjectivity, it must also be asserted that individuality is no longer a self-reflexive phenomenon but, more problematically, a phenomenon that is self-projected – a self whose persistence is reliant on its own (material and cognitive) rejection of itself. Lest this be confused with a simple manifesto for nihilist celebration, it must also be asserted that the nihilism particular to this situation is necessarily ironic, for it has no self to destroy except that which it contingently constitutes as its own projected fantasy.

The very myth of self-reflexivity, not merely the standards of disappearance, is undermined by such a formulation. The fantasies of projection replace the psychoanalytic formulations of self-alienation, but not in a way that fills the void of disappearance. Rather, that which is most dangerous to a projected self-conception is the temptation to take itself too seriously. The danger of accepting fantasy (as opposed to trauma) as the horizon of subjectivity is the danger of a mistakenly revived myth of the autopoetic as being able to sustain itself through the vacuous yet fantastic projections of ironic appearance.

Even projections have consequences however, and the primacy of fantasy has as its particular consequence the undermining of existential necessity. Ironically, the constitution of fantasy as the horizon of self-conception means that self-conception itself is no longer bound to a necessary form, which is to say that it no longer requires a formal authenticity. This disappearance of existential necessity, however, does not entail the necessity of existential disappearance, but an intuitive absorption of the self-constituted fantasies themselves as the aesthetic horizon of ironic becoming. In this sense, an ironic incommensurability translates into an intuition that also no longer refers to an essentialist or unified subject, but is rather an ironic engagement with the fantasies of self-projected living. The intuition itself is transformed by the contingencies of self-conception no longer bound to the dynamic of reflective accountability.

A postmodern intuition must be approached as a false horizon, in the best of possible ways. It is not as simple as to say that with the rise of the self-projected individual, temporal or historical or transformative principles also disappear into the ashes of reflection. Understood as fantasies as opposed to necessary principles, time, personal histories, and even transformative trajectories take on the status of default projections – fantasies that persist, not because they have to but because they are central to the perspective from which personal narrative is born. While of course one can alter these fantasies as one sees fit, the point is that such alteration also has consequences of the same sort – no longer merely ideological consequences, but in fact intuitive consequences to the horizon of projected existence.

Within projected existence, in the context of an incidence of self-conception, it is the intuition that *absorbs* (and through absorption *creates*) the continuity of fantastic subjectivity – a continuity that must at all costs remain ironic, lest it slip back into the construction of a new mirror, what would this time be a fantasy mirror, an *originary* fantasy whose sole purpose would be the traumatic perpetuation of itself as the artificial horizon to which all subsequent fantasies must be held accountable.

6
Perspectival Roadkill

Haiku d'État[1]

On the streets of Montreal, an archaeopteryx is loose. Traveling sometimes as one and sometimes as many, this mythical creature is intimately familiar with the circulatory dynamic of the city. A strange evolutionary link – not quite bird but no longer dinosaur – the archaeopteryx refuses all categories except for those "in between." But perhaps this is why the creature can be so at home in a city like Montreal, a city that is an ongoing evolutionary festival, never stopping, never ending, forever refusing all that is static and binding, a city where categories stand up and protest and bleed back into the vertigo of daily affairs without exhausting themselves, without resolving themselves, without ever finalizing a lifestyle.

Montreal is also a map to the intricacies of contemporary living. Multicultural, multi-linguistic, multi-political, Montreal is a testimony to possibility, which is not to say that it is not haunted by its own spectres. A city such as this can only be imagined, never quite experienced in full. Not a coup d'état, but *Haiku d'État*, and the city of Montreal is no less dynamic and poignant for its insistence on the perpetual aestheticization of all forms of contemporary engagement. A truly postmodern city – in the streets of Montreal, we are all animals running around in costume.

Take for instance a performance by the Holland-based dance company Archeopteryx 8 – headed by dancer and choreographer Erik Kaiel. *Haiku d'État* – a five-person, impromptu bodily intervention into the circulatory system of downtown Montreal, a networked intermediation of audience and performer, streets and stage, architecture and backdrop for the aesthetic celebration of spectatorship and performativity. In this city, the line is so blurred between performance and reality that one might call it a city of the carnivalesque. More real than real, like the archaeopteryx itself – a species that fills in the spaces between nodes of evolution. The archaeopteryx is indeed more real than real, which is why it can be so at home in its born-again five-person incarnation.

Haiku d'État – in more ways than one. This is not a direct assault on the states of the city, nor even a proper intervention; in a city such as Montreal these things alone are impossible. Montreal is a city that embraces such fictions. The archaeopteryx knows this all too well. Armed with a boom-box and flanked by video-cameras and a contingent of recruits whose purpose is to reaffirm the spectacularized nature of the event, the archaeopteryx weaves through the city streets, sometimes stopping for the glowing eyes of traffic lights, sometimes not. Walking, flying, playing and serious, at times staring intently into the gazes of passers-by, sometimes ignoring even the most affectionate of glances. This performance is also a playground for those whose identities resist clear categorization,

From contortions on park benches to roof-top interactions, *Haiku d'État* is a fundamentally chimerical performance, as befits a creature of legend. Stepping in and out of formally choreographed movements, fluidly flowing between impromptu gestures and comings-together of ritualized bodily pattern, *Haiku d'Etat* reinforces the multiplicity of faces open to contemporary life. At once aesthetically enticing for its graceful interplays of movement and meaning, and subversively compelling for its complete disregard of urban etiquette, *Haiku d'Etat* congeals, seduces, annoys, and challenges, as if to give bodily form to the bold words of Jean Baudrillard: "There is no longer any metaphor, rather metamorphosis. Metamorphosis abolishes metaphor, which is the mode of language, the possibility of communicating meaning."[2] The dance of the

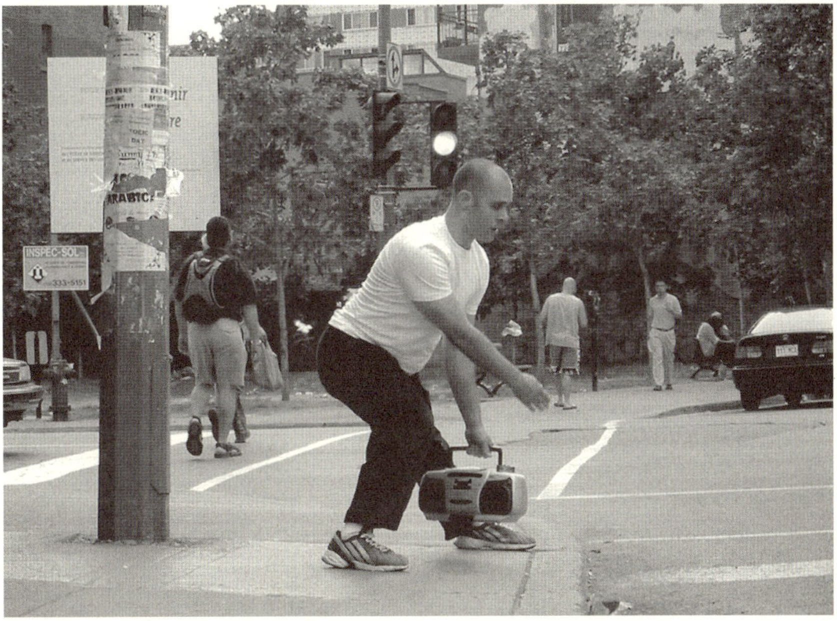

Archeopteryx8 (Erik Kaiel, choreographer). *Haiku d'Etat*. Dance performance, Montreal, 2003.

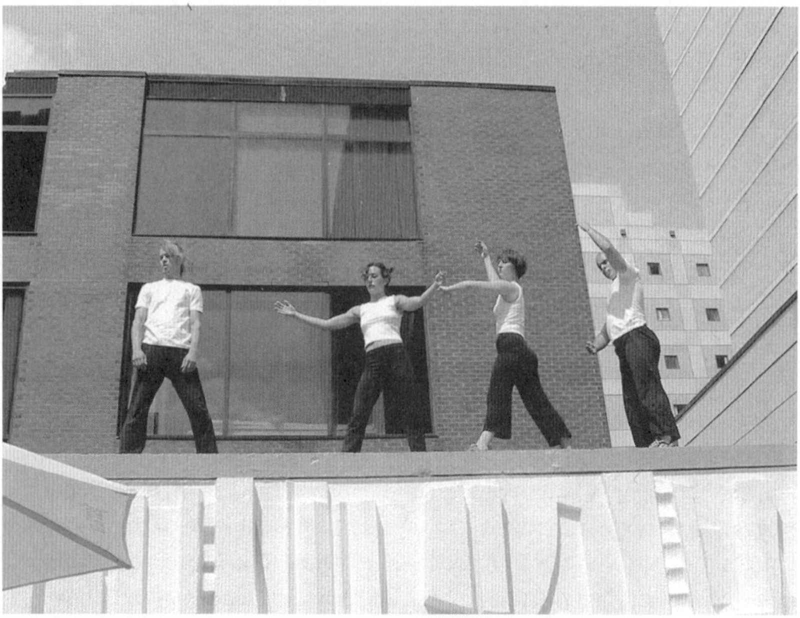

Above and opposite: Archeopteryx8 (Erik Kaiel, choreographer). *Haiku d'État.* Dance performance, Montreal, 2003.

archaeopteryx can fill this double role because its own metamorphosis also resists completion: here a playfully rooftop parade, there a group hug for the symbolic residue of public art, materialized as a fleshy caress for statuesque city monuments.

What is perhaps most noteworthy about *Haiku d'Etat* is just how completely at home the city itself is with the event. It is almost as if the gestural ebbs and flows of the archaeopteryx were welcomed, even expected, by the culture around it – a temporary suspension of suspension itself, as we the spectators too are caught up in the Jurassic carnival of life on the streets. In the streets of Montreal, we are all animals running around in costume ... and that is as it should be.

The Perspectival Shift

There is a strange reversibility to the workings of fantasy, particularly when seen as a basis for contemporary self-conception. In a postmodern world, grounded only in the speculations of possibility, one might even make of this reversibility a general rule of sorts. The backwards nature of self-understanding

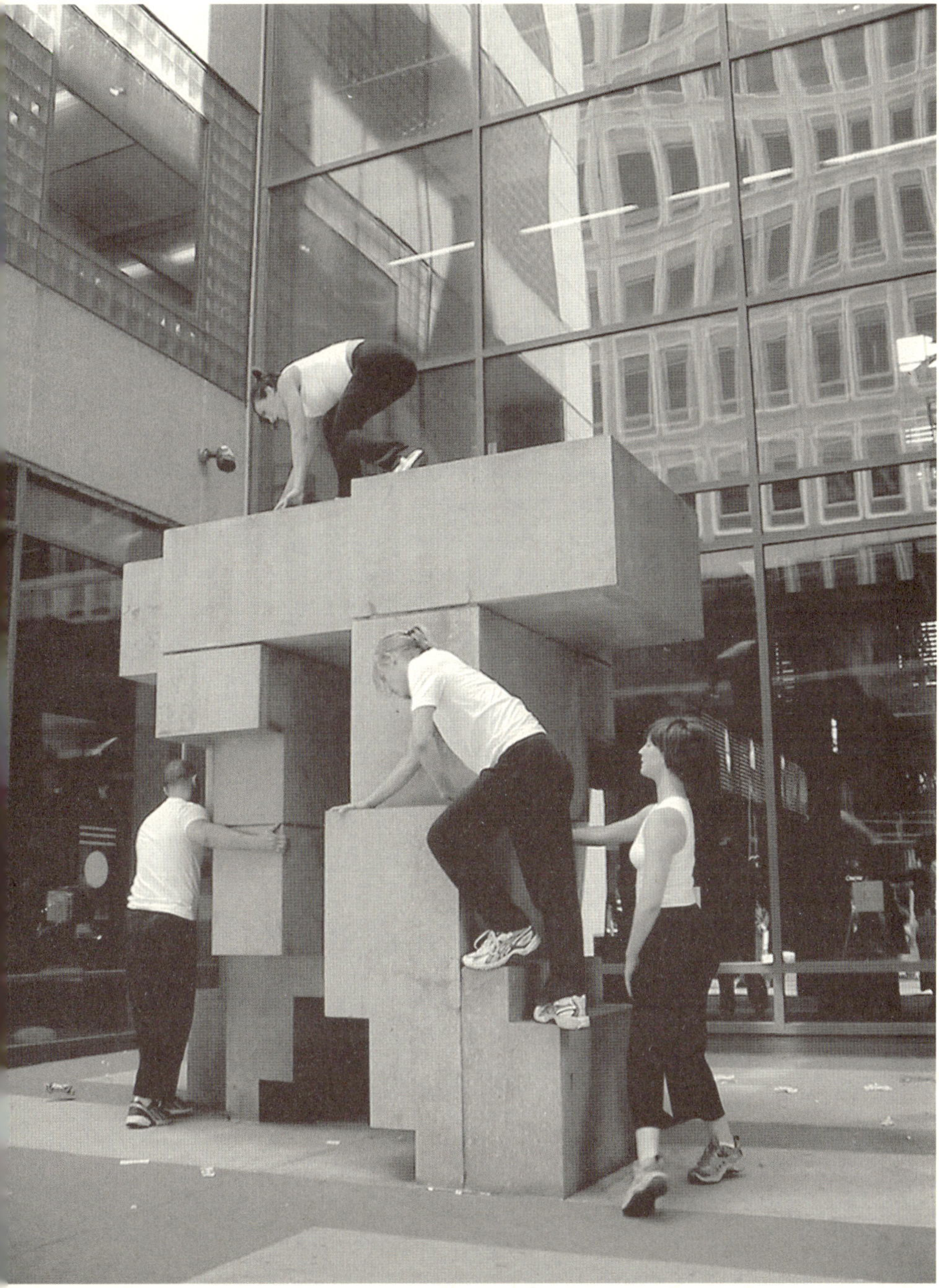

requires an extremity of fantasy – a fantasy that must remain untenable, radical to a point of absurdity if it is to uphold the differentiation between the self and reflective self-understanding. In a simulacral twist, the conjecture of the real relies on the tangibility of its opposite, here phrased as a proliferation of fantasy itself. Yet this is perhaps a convoluted assertion, for when fantasy proliferates, the real itself begins to disappear, categorically subsumed by the experience of fantasy. The spectre of the real is its own fantasy of being, just as the spectre of things fantastic is, in fact, a refusal of fantasy in the immediacy of experience.

What is at stake in this discussion is the attempt to navigate a horizon of lived interpretation, confusing the essentialisms of disappearance by privileging the contingencies of performative encounter. This does not imply an unraveling of the structures of disappeared living but merely an emphasis on the allowable condition of irony. This is not a revived essentialism of inversions, but more simply an interpretive option open to a self-conception that uses the illogic of ironic appearance to undermine the disciplinary horizons of postmodern living. Seen technologically, this might be called a strategy of ironic appearance – a different way of looking, or a perspectival frame that can be used to understand the interpretive and experiential options open to what are, at first glance, seemingly closed questions. It is a strategy because such a way of looking must also account for the irony of irony itself – a perspectival frame that changes everything and nothing about the situation, all the while leaving one feeling that such changes are of substance. Here, for instance, emerges a form of authorship that proceeds by purposefully writing after the death of the author, or a form of self-conception that insists on viewing trauma itself as a primordial fantasy – each acknowledging the ontology of disappearance while insisting on the irony of acknowledgment itself. The nuances of ironic appearance require something of a phantom assumption – an assumption of ironic contingency as that which steps in to fill the uncertainty of postmodern living, inverse to an assumption of irreducible or incommensurable being behind the masks of authentic living.

The necessity of appearance, ironic or otherwise, sets up an internal dynamic through which one can never be more free than when one refuses authentic freedom in the name of masquerade. The danger implicit in such a theory is easily articulated as the trivialization of life, existence, and of philosophy – which is also an objection often levied against postmodernism in general. In the end, however, one must be careful not to dismiss such a theory too quickly, for even irony has consequences and proliferations of its own. In order for a perspective of ironic appearance to be an effective strategy for negotiating uncertainty, it is no longer enough to approach understanding with an unimplicated gaze. Rather, one must take these ironies altogether quite too seriously, and it is an immanently sober and even deadly form of humour that is required to effectively implement an interrogation of the consequences of ironic inversion on the understanding of lived existence, instead of an ontological or epistemological reformulation.

This amounts to a perspectival shift in the assemblages of perception and understanding, such that the causality generally attributed to perception (the idea that something is perceived) is reformulated in inverse terms. In place of the impossibility of authentic perceptual presence, such a shift can be used to frame appearance as a surrogate – a projected presence that stands in for the disappearance of a congruous perceptual existence.

Carnival Suspension

Mikhail Bakhtin provides an exemplary discussion of the ironic shift of perception, particularly with regards to medieval carnival life. The account is all the more compelling when seen in its historical context, allowing Bakhtin to build a clear opposition between disciplinary society and the liberating possibilities of ironic engagement. Specifically, Bakhtin's description of the carnival as a celebratory suspension of everyday life resonates with both the idealism and the dangers of ironic appearance, articulating a framework from which to address some of the nuances of life grounded in the proliferation of fantasy projections.

As described by Bakhtin, the medieval carnival was a celebratory event, a festival of change, becoming, and renewal that served the specific purpose of relieving the pressures and frustrations of everyday life and official social and political rules. While medieval society was not without complexities all its own, what is noteworthy in this context is how, in the hands of Bakhtin, the carnival can be not only clearly separable from the everyday, but in many ways also become its ironic double. Society would come together for a festival of sanctioned play, in which fools were crowned as kings and the normalized, official boundaries and truths of the social world were replaced by the unofficial rules of mockery, subversion, and laughter: "[O]ne might say that carnival celebrated temporary liberation from the prevailing truth and from the established order; it marked the suspension of all hierarchical rank, privileges, norms, and prohibitions."[3]

In this sense, one might look at the carnival as a festival of personal and cultural deconstruction in which it is not enough to simply forget or ignore one's official social role. What is allowed and encouraged is the intervention into established patterns of meaning and behaviour. It is perhaps the latter of these two – the interventions into established patterns of behaviour – that is the more noteworthy, for this is where carnival engagement must be seen as directly participatory. It is not enough to rhetorically deconstruct one's social or official roles during carnival celebration; one must enact the deconstruction of roles. This is why Bakhtin can insist so adamantly that the carnival is an embodied – which is to say performative – celebration: "[C]arnival does not know footlights, in the sense that it does not acknowledge any distinction between actors and spectators ... Carnival is not a spectacle seen by the people; they live in it, and everyone participates because its very idea embraces all the people. While carnival lasts, there is no other life outside it."[4]

The medieval carnival entailed the suspension of the hierarchical principles of everyday life, but also the suspension of everyday living, given shape as a new form of ambivalent celebration in which one's normalized and disciplinary roles no longer applied except as a horizon of carnival subversion. If carnival was a suspension of belief in the roles and regulations that fashioned an official existence, it is now a suspension of disbelief that allows for participatory engagement with *oneself* as a carnivalized entity. A lived spectacle, a performative festival, and an aesthetically suspended and subversively embedded celebration, the carnival was "life itself, but shaped according to a certain pattern of play."[5]

There are two distinct perspectives from which an analysis of the carnival must proceed. On one hand, there is the perspective of everyday life that provides the impetus as well as the official roles for carnival subversion – provides, in other words, material that can be suspended. On the other hand, there is the perspective of the carnival participant who actively accomplishes this suspension of the everyday through participatory engagement with patterns of play, interrupting, interfering, and embedding a lived existence back into the aesthetic masquerade of performative possibility. If the world of everyday affairs can be seen as an agent of disappearance – through its emphasis on regulatory, hierarchical, and officialized living – it is precisely the carnival that allows for the aesthetic suspension of these disappearing trajectories by adopting a strategy of ironic appearance.

To return to the recurring notion of an ironic appearance serving the purpose of a social, political, and cultural mirror, in this instance carnival participants encounter themselves as someone else. The carnival might thus be read as a mirror for the masses, a strategic hall of mirrors that is also a fragmented mirror-stage, allowing for the temporary liberation of selves from the roles that bind them in a world of regulatory affairs. Perhaps, then, the carnival constituted a sort of performative mirror-stage for its participants, one in which they were lead to an understanding (or perhaps more importantly an experience) of themselves as other, for the specific purpose of minimizing the fatigue of everyday living.

Legislated Otherness

It might seem too convenient that the medieval society Bakhtin explores is so easily split into the distinct worlds of the carnival and everyday life. Regardless of the accuracy of this historical rendering, in postmodern times it is tempting to adopt a signature skepticism with regard to such discrete categories. Instead, we have begun to understand such oppositions in relational terminologies that frustrate the clean and playful rejuvenation for which Bakhtin praises carnival spirit. A rather simple observation seems, in this case, an obvious and necessary objection to the romanticization of carnival as a period of participatory escape from the normalizing trajectories of everyday life. While carnival was a subversion of everyday life, it was everyday life that was structured in such a way as to allow for the carnival to take place.

If the carnival was the ironic double of the world of the everyday, the everyday might then be seen as the very condition of carnival. Despite Bakhtin's insistence that during the carnival there was no life outside of it, life inside the carnival was nevertheless framed within a carnival context – a context set within the medieval world of everyday affairs. One might even suggest that, in some way, the carnival was an ordered element of this official everyday. While this may well have been necessary in order for the festivity of carnival to occur on a widespread social and cultural scale, it also signals a rather sinister possibility – that the carnival may have the double purpose of being a regulatory device. If the objective of an everyday hierarchical society was to ensure its own perpetuation, what better way to guarantee ongoing subservience than to allow for periodic moments of sanctioned subversion, after which those bound to normalized roles can return, as before, to the passive fulfillment of their everyday tasks. A sanctioned subversion is no subversion at all, and one might well wonder if carnival constituted anything more than a forced vacation from the world of everyday affairs.

While everyday life did not exist as such within the structure of the carnival, except as a horizon for subversion, the carnival did in fact occur within the structure of everyday life. In this sense, one might well invert Bakhtin's perspective on the carnival such that the carnival was not merely a self-contained period of temporary liberation from the norms and standards of everyday life, but rather also an event whose self-reflexivity was a myth and which had the effect of sustaining the disciplinary environment to which it was responding. This may at first glance seem backwards, for Bakhtin goes to some length to emphasize the *absence* of conditions to which a carnival participant was subject – the liberation from the necessities of everyday life. And yet this temporary liberation from the world of everyday life had an explicit and well-articulated function: the carnival, in its suspension of rank and truth, allowed for "becoming, change and renewal," which in turn served the purpose of making non-carnival, which is to say everyday life, bearable.[6]

While the carnival may have little to do with the restrictions and prohibitions of everyday life (being defined by precisely their suspension), the larger context in which the celebration occurred makes the carnival not only liberatory, but also necessary. While participating in the carnival may well have been an excuse for playful self-reinvention, it is important to note that this is not only the purpose of the carnival, but in fact its imperative. A carnival self has as its horizon an imperative to not be itself. Despite Bakhtin's insistence that all regulatory principles are suspended during carnival, it would seem that there persists at least one: the carnival must not implement – must in fact refuse – the ordering principles of everyday life.

The potentially sinister side of the carnival is thus made apparent: the carnival was not merely a period of temporary liberation from the rules and regulations of everyday living, but was itself a legislated period of otherness, a festival where the one singular role that was ineligible to any carnival participant was the role they played in the otherwise official culture. Forcibly liberated from patterns of regulatory being, from a real-world presence, the citizens of the carnival were not only allowed but *required* to engage with a context of alienation from the everyday, an alienation made all the more serious because it was also enjoyable.

The Customized Carnival

One might be tempted to believe that in contemporary times we have moved beyond a paradox of carnival officialism , particularly if one believes that we no longer live in a world of firm and territorialized boundaries. It would seem, for example, that contemporary living does not provide the overarching social context and political sanctions that allowed the medieval carnival to occur on a widespread cultural scale. The strictly polar differentiation of which Bakhtin speaks has become blurred in a postmodern world. As a result, one might be tempted to suggest that the carnival itself has taken over, becoming not the territorialized sign of subversive intervention but the dominant regulatory paradigm of the postmodern spectacle, with the one difference that now official roles are as eligible for performance as any other. Or one might instead territorialize the individual and assert that the horizons of carnival participation have imploded into those of self-conception, such that postmodern carnival involves an interruption of one's own personal and subjective self-placement more than a subversion of the everyday. In either instance it would seem that contemporary living shares much with the spirit of the carnival – from the deconstruction of political and philosophical essentialisms to the self-implicating spirit of lived masquerade, to the aesthetic imperatives of imaginative and suspended play. The postmodern individual, like the carnival self, holds an awareness of the normalizing and disciplinary tactics levied against it during participation with official culture, and, again like the carnival self, seeks an element of ironic intervention into the externally imposed frameworks of its everyday life.

But in the end it is not quite so simple, for any self that can truly be called postmodern no longer retains the utopian myth of autonomy behind its masquerade. Instead, the postmodern self accepts that any vestige of incommensurability that might grant it an autonomous status is instead always a token of its depersonalization and disappearance. This, arguably, has much to do with the faces of contemporary power, which mobilize individuals through the bestowal of a sense of incommensurable authenticity. The personal *difference* that leaves us feeling like unique subjects can be seen as responsible also for the structural conformity of normalized belonging. From certain perspectives, then, the legislation of behavioural otherness is equally pervasive in a contemporary world, potentially even as the paradoxical *condition* of postmodern living. The myth of self-reflexivity reincorporates the subject into the larger context of everyday living that allows self-reflexivity to occur in the first instance.

What is at stake in such an analysis, then, is the attempt to return the gaze of disciplinary living; the ways to perceive the horizons of the everyday from *within* the spectacle of postmodern living. What was an impossibility for Bakhtin is precisely what is required here. With the breakdown of sanctioned boundaries between carnival and non-carnival modalities, what is needed is an examination of the internal dynamics of a type of performance no longer bound to a single sanctioned event, but instead now – in contemporary times – linked more problematically to a perspectival referentiality, to oneself and to one's social and cultural worlds.

This might be illustrated by referring to another instance of perspectival shift, a vestige of carnival festivity in a postmodern world. The most obvious example would be the annual celebration of Halloween, the one day during the year where participation requires the masking of oneself as another. While it is perhaps not quite the case that on all other days one must refrain from such costumed otherness, the sanction that is Halloween not only makes masquerade on this day possible, but normal. While setting a forum for normalized otherness, Halloween also can be seen as simulacral in nature – this day of sanctioned otherness also means that on all other days the illusion of a contiguous (self-similar) self is spectrally upheld. Halloween does not legislate appearing always as oneself during other times of the year, but rather facilitates the (self-reflexive) appearance of a relatively consistent and coherent day-to-day identity, obscuring the possibility that we may well always be in costumes of one sort or another.

This example is somewhat exaggerated in order to make a rhetorical point and is not intended as a social commentary on possible ways of engaging with sanctioned holidays. Rather, it is mentioned to reinforce the consequences of legislating behaviour, and not just seemingly normalized behaviours. The irony here is that if one were to believe that an existential masquerade was the norm rather than the holiday exception, one would no longer be able to sincerely participate in such events for the simple reason that the horizon of difference would be entirely frustrated. When otherness becomes the general rule rather than the carnival exception, a new strategy is needed, for the stage of participation is reversed.

For example, what if one were to re-read Halloween not as the single day of the year when one is compelled to masquerade as another, but the day when one is compelled to assume concrete and identifiable form? In absence of a unifying principle as the incommensurable core of subjectivity, what if Halloween were the day when we pretend to enter into concrete self-similarity – the spectral horizon of which would no longer be an everyday unity but rather a chaotic and nebulous vacuity that resists even the attributions of self or other? Such an inversion is exactly what is at stake in a theory of postmodern irony. The postmodern carnival is not as blurred as it seems – not strictly limited to the ironic assumption of a role without consequence or repercussion. Instead, assuming concrete otherness is (at least) a daily task, an ongoing performance that is most convincing when it pretends cohesion, not in the form of otherness proper, but as an ironic continuity.

Patterns of Fantasy

It may be worth clarifying what is meant by the ironic continuity of performative self-placement, for it seems that there is much at stake in the ways that selves interact with their self-constituted others. The problem that persists, in both the carnival and the postmodern masquerade, is that the horizons of engagement are externally constituted, either as an official sanctioning device that allows for temporary subversion, or through the collapse of such devices in which case the subversions themselves must be perpetuated indefinitely. The carnival self returns with a new and renewed spirit to the safety of the established social world once the carnival is over, but nevertheless to the context which made such renewal necessary. The postmodern self does not return, for there is no longer a safe zone into which it might place itself, nor a safe self that might be placed.

The problem that persists in a contemporary climate is that the official boundaries constituting carnival and/or non-carnival modalities of being are no longer socially or politically upheld, but rather are self-reflexively perpetuated as personal horizons of conception. No longer is there a simple, externally sanctioned, carnival event through which a self might find an ironic perspective on its lived existence. Now such a position must be perspectivally grown from the lived fantasies of individuals, responding to their own traumatic and self-reflexive horizons of normalized awareness. While it is tempting to constitute this horizon as precisely a non-horizon – a horizon of not-being that would be the liberatory fantasy of an unconditional existence – even projected existence has conditions. A projected self, built upon fantasies or otherwise, is still embedded in a context of perspectival engagement with the world around it.

This dynamic operates according to the logic of the simulacrum, with one difference. In the individualized carnival of self-projected being, the projections of masquerade or of ironic appearance become strangely self-constituting. The masquerade replaces the self-reflexive – in fact reveals the reflection as already having been a projection of its own fantastic self-conception. The masquerade is contingent on its own performance, however. The deconstruction of social, political, cultural, and personal boundaries that is the marked sign of postmodern being also means that a carnivalesque horizon of engagement ceases to be purely cynical, ceases to be a self-righteous proclamation, in short ceases to be anything but its own perpetuation into the constitutions of self-conceived fantasy.

Ultimately there is *nothing* behind the mask of carnival or of postmodern masquerade. But this formulation implies the necessity of the mask itself. Without a mask of some sort (were this even a structural possibility) one would be entirely abandoned to an accidental and externally-constituted existence (at best) or a rhetorical facsimile of existence (at worst). The dynamic of the postmodern carnival therefore results in an existential irony. There is no more existence without a masquerade of one sort or another – self-projection is the horizon of living, relegating the self-reflexive individual to the status of a romantically traumatized fantasy. What persists in all cases are the patterns of fantasy as the default horizon of contemporary self-projected engagement. If, for Bakhtin, the carnival was "life itself, but shaped according to a certain pattern of play," the contemporary situation might be expressed as a living of play itself, but shaped according to a certain pattern of fantasy.

The Hard Line of Contingency

It is important that the patterning of fantasy as a default horizon of contemporary living be recognized as merely a perspective on the intricacies of possible dynamics between a carnivalesque (or ironic) mentality and a mentality of real world affairs. In particular, it is important that these observations not be confused with an essentialist declaration on a new truth of contemporary living, for it is precisely the contemporary tendency to turn into judgments what are mere observations that is partly responsible for the confusion surrounding the question of otherness. If carnival is (perspectivally) maintained as the horizon of living instead of as a subversive interruption, the festive character (which is also to say the liberatory mechanism) is lost – there is nothing more for carnival to liberate *from*. Consequently the postmodern self cannot self-consciously perceive itself as living within a horizon of freedom, unless the fantasy of freedom is itself constituted as a traumatically patterned projection. At best what persists in this context is a poetics (which is also to say an aesthetics) of futility.

The understanding of contemporary living as a poetics of futility is, perhaps, a difficult proposition to make. And yet behind any fantasy of self-conceived existence there is a necessary adoption of patterned self-projection, such that a semblance of continuity is maintained as the pattern of fantasy according to which self-awareness (which is not to say self-understanding) proceeds. There is, in other words, a horizon of contingency – dependent on the patterning of masked identity – that any contemporary self-awareness can be seen as reducible to. There is much at stake in the designation of whether this self-awareness proceeds according to the traditional rules of self-reflexivity or according to the ironic rules of self-projected living.

Because this is ultimately a question of perspective rather than a question of truth or falsity, self-awareness might well proceed in either direction, though each designation has its own customized set of pitfalls. In the end, self-projected living trumps self-reflection as a horizon of understanding. Consider that self-reflexivity can easily be contextualized as a fantasy of sorts while self-projected living precisely resists a reflective (or authentic) rendering. This occurs because the perception of contingency requires a sanctioned horizon, a perspectival debt around which contingency revolves. The persistent question is not which perspective is correct, but rather which entails the least necessary horizon to the question of possible (perspectival) existences.

With mirror-grown self-reflexivity, one encounters oneself as another – a circular dynamic in which one then attempts to bridge the gaps between oneself and oneself-as-other, with the aim of removing all *unnecessary boundaries* to the dynamic. Thus contextualized, self-reflexivity is a forum for navigating the rules of what amounts ultimately to a form of self-rejection, seen either psychoanalytically as the traumatic imperative of identity itself, or pragmatically as the disciplinary self-transcendence of embodied normalization – where the official self is that which needs to be overcome or refashioned in order to allow for new possibilities of growth, renewal, or change.

With self-projected living the case is more extreme, for here one adopts an *unnecessary* horizon that, because of its inauthenticity, allows for an ironic engagement with the world. One ceases to be concerned with self-encounter for it is the fantasy of self that implements the ironic horizon of projected (one might even say delusional) living. What is missing from a self-projected perspective is the ability to implement an authenticity to self-awareness; the condition of self-projection is precisely the dismissal of authenticity as unnecessary. This is compensated for by its concomitant ability to refashion self-reflexivity as another such futile projection, in the sense that the self being reflected can always (at least potentially) be constituted as an ironic projection of necessity.

This is not to say, however, that the self-projected individual does not have a contingent horizon of its own, but rather that this horizon is itself the ambivalent, ironic, and ultimately unnecessary horizon which is taken up for the purpose of existential participation. Unlike the self-reflexive individual, the self-projected individual is not necessarily bound to its horizon, but perpetuates it nevertheless (albeit ironically) as a structural (rather than referential) necessity.

The problem here is no longer the "hard problem" of consciousness research, in which the articulation of subjectivity becomes the scientific challenge. Instead, just the opposite is the case: the articulation of context becomes the ironic challenge for a constitution of subjectivity. This is not Thomas Nagel's acknowledgment that there is "something it is like" to be an experiencing entity – an assertion that (for Nagel, Chalmers, Dennett and others) is required before consciousness can be treated as an object of study.[7] Instead, it is a necessary refusal to place subjectivity in the service of science, opting instead to push at the limits of contingency. The problem is one of context, particularly since there is no longer a static identity from which to navigate the contingencies of communal living. Where consciousness research posits subjectivity as a problem to be understood scientifically, the idea of a self-projected individual posits context as the problem, a contingent horizon that forms the stage of performance. Upon this stage, the existential masquerade takes shape as a question of an (ironic) "anything" that it is like to be a consciously experiencing subject – a fully constituted horizon of contingency that arbitrarily deduces the perspectival possibilities open to any given subject at any given time. A hard line of contingency replaces the hard problem of consciousness research as the self-projected horizon of existential engagement.

Extreme Heteroglossia

> At any given time, in any given place, there will be a set of conditions – social, historical, meteorological, physiological – that will ensure that a word uttered in that place and at that time will have a meaning different than it would have under any other conditions.
>
> Mikhail Bakhtin, *The Dialogic Imagination*, 428.

The negotiation of extreme contingency might well seem daunting to a contemporary mind used to a reactionary relationship to (and bent on establishing horizons of difference with) the world that surrounds it. But contingency is a familiar game for most, relying on the shifting horizons of personal self-placement and actively disregarding the surplus of possible meta-horizons in which contingencies are taken up as regulatory devices. If contingency prevails as the default horizon of postmodern living, it would mean that perception proceeds from a position that is perspectivally bound to its own set of contextual referents.

Within this configuration one might acknowledge a certain resonance with Bakhtin's formulation of the heteroglossic as the contextual dependency of each and every possible utterance, such that there is no longer any possible over-arching meta-continuity in the encounter of language. Instead, each utterance is ultimately dependent for meaning on the context in which its words were spoken, a situation not unlike the projections of fantasy context onto an experiential world. What complicates the formulation – both for Bakhtin's analysis of language, and for the more general exploration of contingency – is twofold. On one hand, there is the question of the propriety of an utterance; the question of "who" decides what contextual elements are relevant to a "proper" understanding of the speech-event. On the other hand, there is the question of changing context, in which an utterance may be found with multiple possibilities for meaning. Between the two, a paradox of determined indeterminacy emerges, threatening to resolve what pretends to remain irresolvable as a horizon of hard line contingency.

There is a way around this indeterminacy of contextual constitution, and it involves a disavowal of ownership – of the utterance and of the context – in order to increase the stakes of participation. Experience, whether of consciousness or of language, is intensified when it is framed by extreme contingency, thereby frustrating the attempt to make experience accountable to some other set of contextual factors. To some extent this was Bakhtin's conclusion as well. Noting that context will inevitably shift the meaning of language, Bakhtin refused to allow for an essential or permanent meaning to a linguistic utterance. Instead, Bakhtin proposed a model of dialogism in which meaning depends on interpersonal and contextual negotiation. Dialogism, in other words, is the embodied negotiation of heteroglossia: "A word, discourse, language or culture undergoes 'dialogization' when it becomes relativized, de-privileged, aware of competing definitions for the same things."[8] Further, "Dialogic relationships are reducible neither to logical relationships nor to relationships oriented semantically toward their referential object, relationships *in and of themselves* devoid of any dialogic element. They must clothe themselves in discourse, become utterances, become the positions of various subjects expressed in discourse, in order that dialogic relationships might arise among them."[9]

For Bakhtin, dialogism depends on a fundamental distinction between the utterance and the word, such that from a strictly Bakhtinian perspective heteroglossia is a speech-dependent phenomenon, untranslatable to the stage of the written word, or even to the question of self-awareness. What is required, then, in order to adapt the Bakhtinian perspective to the project at hand is to make the heteroglossic more extreme, to illuminate the performative consequences of dialogic engagement. It is no longer merely the word that fluctuates according to contingent horizons, but selves as well. It is no longer adequate to view the dialogic as the negotiation of intended meanings, such that contextual consensus as to the meaning of a dialogue can be reached as its aim. Intentionality itself is to be understood as a fluctuating horizon, and where the heteroglossic is arranged to navigate the territory of multiple concrete perspectives, a contemporary reinvention of the heteroglossic must seek to navigate a territory where even these authorial, intentional, or fictional perspectives have become ungrounded – subject to a contingency of their own.

Heteroglossia of this sort – opened up to an extreme contextual dependency – should in theory be equally applicable to all forms of meaning, from the spoken to the written word, from internal dialogue to external discussion, from logic to illogic to dreams and fantasies and delusions. This should be the case because extreme heteroglossia also means extreme contingency. The nebulae of possible meanings requires a mechanism of representation in order to adopt a contingent appearance as formulated meaning (or, in other words, as patterned fantasy). As a mechanism for the constitution of appearances, the dialogic holds great potential, for it is here that one recovers the perspectives of ironic appearance at their best: meaning being fully dependent on those contingencies being taken up and mobilized around us. Dialogism is, in this sense, a phenomenon that relies on the immediacy of embodied perspectives negotiating the rejection of intentional, self-fashioned, or pre-existent meanings.

The Decrowning Double

Dialogism is a thoroughly un-reflexive process. Within the framework of contemporary dialogism and extreme heteroglossia, we no longer determine meaning for ourselves. Meaning, instead, is a residual function of interaction, such that one can no longer even mandate an arrival at meaning for any relationship properly called dialogic. Dialogism belongs instead to the realm of what Bakhtin terms "carnivalistic mésalliances," the strategic (mis)alignment with a contingent double whose dual purpose is to serve as a foil for any strictly self-initiated or declarative meaning, while at the same relegating all apparent meaning to a fundamentally ironic state.[10] This means that an extreme heteroglossia begins to look much more like a literal xenoglossia – speech that proceeds despite the fact that it is unaware of its own potential meaning. Not speaking in tongues, but in a potentially real language that one does not oneself understand.[11] The xenoglossic is a form of speech that requires the dialogic since it is dependent on others to interpret and to potentially understand what we ourselves do not, namely our own (projected) utterances. In fact, it is the xenoglossic that best fits Bakhtin's own mandate for the dialogic as a world (and a self) "turned inside-out."[12]

Extreme heteroglossia (turned xenoglossic) is ultimately self-effacing. The utterance becomes reducible to a gesture of futility, projected outwards towards a potentially dialogic world. It is a form of unintentional authorship, for here one must trust that others will potentially understand and mobilize one's utterances on one's behalf. Any xenoglossic utterance, of course, requires as its orator a fundamentally unfamiliar self, but also requires a foil in order to remain unfamiliar to itself. Such a foil is what Bakhtin terms a "decrowning double."[13] Contingent discourse necessarily proceeds with this condition of self-effacement as that which is required to acknowledge the potential presence of others.

The xenoglossic utterance is more of a gesture than a moment of articulated meaning. Here, the projection breaks the mirror, and the self who utters has its own ironic contingency reinforced by the simple awareness that the message of speech (or text, or appearance in any form) no longer persists in any self-determining fashion, and reciprocally no longer yields any understanding which can properly be termed self-reflexive. One does not and cannot assess one's own patterns of fantasy. Instead, self-projections are levied out into the (potentially) dialogic world, looking only for reciprocal projections (which would be incorrectly given the label of reflections) from others. This is an extreme form of what Bakhtin calls "double-voiced discourse," not a stage of negotiated meaning, but one that exceeds the limits of metalinguistics.[14] Xenoglossic dialogism is a stage for the accumulation of meaning: a site of negotiation between nonsensical utterances and the reciprocal projections they engender. Projected fantasy spirals into a form of communal patterning. Understanding, under the sign of projection, is a team sport – not because of any nebulous moral, ethical, or even pragmatic maxim, but rather because of its structural dependence on others for the constitution of one's own voice.[15]

We speak in a language we do not understand, but that others potentially might. We project a self that we do not see. This is as close as we can get to a genuinely sincere theory of ironic appearance, and a genuinely ironic theory of sincere self-awareness.

Perspectival Roadkill

> The new cultural and creative consciousness lives in an actively polyglot world. The world becomes polyglot, once and for all and irreversibly.
>
> Mikhail Bakhtin, *The Dialogic Imagination*, 12.

When the world becomes polyglot, what is required is an economics of perception in the sense that there is a price to be paid in possibility for every fantasy that is patterned and projected outwards. Appearance, being ultimately dependent on its contingent grounding in suspended disbelief, requires an ironic sincerity that will allow for the proliferating impossibilities of projected living to materialize dialogically as horizons of experiential awareness. This is a stage of delusional agreement that is forced to discard not only the philosophical desire for grounded ontology, but also the fantasy of self-justifying experience. In this, both the possibilities for ontological reality and subjective incommensurability are rendered surplus, subsumed by the dialogic possibility of communal fantasy – uniquely allowing for the perspectival world to resist completion and certainty in favour of an always contingent manifestation of possibility. The first gesture of self-projected living is to strategically forget that one has already ungrounded the real, thus allowing for the contingent manifestation of proliferating falsity – fantasies of ironic appearance.

One must read fantasy not as an imaginative proliferation of possibilities, but rather as a gestural censoring of other possibilities, such that a specific form and content is given to the imaginative trajectory upon which one embarks. Fantasy is not constituted purposefully, but through the refusal of purpose – a negative space of possibility itself. It is here that projection becomes an embodied phenomenon, and rhetorical understanding (that would have an open horizon of cognitive possibility) must here be discarded in favour of gestural engagement, whose horizons of possibility are (and must be) contingently closed in order to allow for the ironic sustenance of pattern and the ongoing possibility of xenoglossic dialogism.

Forget what Zizek calls the "bizarre category of the 'objectively subjective,'"[16] – that which we think or do even though we don't know we think or do it. Within ironic appearance, the only sustainable horizon is precisely that of the "subjectively objective" – the simulacrum of selfhood taken as a contingent and patterned fantasy. This is the over-arching consequence of ironic appearance in general, and in this instance one pays for one's fantasies with one's incommensurability, and one pays for one's projections with self-understanding. To engage with a world of projected fantasies – a world of proliferating falsities – requires precisely the absenting of self-reflexive understanding from the rhetoric of living.

From this perspective, fantasy is not liberatory in any concrete or tangible way. Nor is fantasy an opening up to creative possibility. Rather fantasy is a process of censoring-out the intrusions of a communal reality – a horizon of perspectival engagement that must be both drawn and maintained. The condition of fantasy is that it must always compete for attention with its other possible faces. The constitution of fantasy requires the discarding of other possibilities, no less than the entry (before it) into the fantasy of truth. What is tragic about fantasy is the possibilities it must discard in order to enter into sustainable being. This fantastic surplus might be called the perspectival roadkill of contemporary self-projected living.

Perspectival roadkill is thus the inverse side of what might be termed sustainable falsity, or a seamless delusion. It is the theory of what must be discarded from self-conception in order to allow for possible proliferations of patterned fantasy as the least necessary horizon of contemporary existential, experiential, and perspectival engagement. It is necessary to formulate such a perspective from an inverted position (negatively constituted) for the simple reason that once seen in terms of its own proliferating potentialities (positively constituted), the theory of perspectival roadkill becomes a theory of nonsensical permission – unbounded by the principles of logic and rational formulation which have been, in turn, discarded as roadkill of the ironic imaginary.

PART THREE

Technologies of Nonsense

The Third Story of Fire

In *The Psychoanalysis of Fire,* Gaston Bachelard proposed the Prometheus complex as the drive towards knowledge that is characteristic of intellectual life. Arguing that the knowledge of fire originates from a point of general and social prohibition (a child is prohibited from playing with fire, for example) Bachelard draws a parallel to the Greek myth in which Prometheus steals fire from the Gods. Learning (and knowledge in general) in this case must always involve an element of transgression, defiance or an "art of clever disobedience."[1] In Bachelard's words: "We propose, then, to place together under the name of the Prometheus complex all those tendencies which impel us to know as much as our fathers, more than our fathers, as much as our teachers, more than our teachers."[2]

Bachelard's Prometheus complex delineates a methodology through which knowledge can be discovered, learned, and invented. It delineates a structure for the appearance of knowledge – an attempt to go beyond or to out-do those who set the terms according to which we learned to engage. In this, there is also an attempt to redefine the way in which knowledge is made to appear.

What happens when what appears is not what was expected? It is at this point that technologies of disappearance emerge, as an awareness that the rules of the game dictate the possibilities for their own transgression. The inevitable result of such an observation can be nothing other than an ironic disturbance of the question itself, an aesthetic drive to outrun the appearance of knowledge one thus sets in motion. The accumulation of knowledge is replaced by the knowledge of accumulation, and a prohibition on appearance emerges as a direct result of disobedience that is a little too clever for its own good. A Promethean knowledge of the apparatuses of appearance reveals them instead to be agents of disappearance.

Prometheus was not simply the bringer of fire to humanity. He was also responsible for its disappearance in the first instance. It was a dangerous game that Prometheus played, a game of smoke and mirrors, a trompe l'oeil with Zeus himself: "[Prometheus] flayed and jointed a bull, and sewed its hide to form two open-mouthed bags, filling these with what he had cut up. One bag contained all the flesh, but this he concealed beneath the stomach, which is the least tempting part of any animal; and the other contained the bones, hidden beneath a rich layer of fat. When he offered Zeus the choice of either, Zeus, easily deceived, chose the bag containing the bones and fat; but punished Prometheus, who was laughing at him behind his back, by withholding fire from mankind."[3]

One might suggest that Prometheus' initial deception is not only an appropriate, but perhaps even a necessary addition to Bachelard's complex – the emergence of an ironic second face of trickster and deceiver in addition to the clever disobedience required to bypass the prohibitions of fire or knowledge. Prometheus is revealed not merely as the seeker of knowledge but the one who was willing to gamble with it in the first instance. A strange irreverence towards knowledge is also the condition of disobedience, whether clever or not. But perhaps this has always been the condition of playing with fire as well – a gamble that is also a game. Perhaps the quest for knowledge, and specifically self-knowledge, is nothing more than an attempt to trick the world again in the hopes that this third time the error will be different. It may be that the details are in the errors, and what each story of fire has in common is the immediacy of the gamble itself.

First, Prometheus tricked Zeus – an antic that resulted in the withholding of fire from mankind. Second, Prometheus stole fire back. But this recovery was not to go unpunished, for finally Prometheus was made to pay dearly for his trickery, and for the knowledge he recovered. The price he paid was immortality – and an eternity of suffering to go along with it: "[To pay for his treachery] Zeus had Prometheus chained naked to a pillar in the Caucasian mountains, where a greedy vulture tore at his liver all day, year in, year out; and there was no end to the pain, because every night (during which Prometheus was exposed to cruel frost and cold) his liver grew whole again."[4]

It is a delirious punishment to be sure, and one that requires an equally delirious response. The third story of fire is the story of technologies of nonsense. And Promethues may have realized that the only solution to this delirious punishment is a nonsensical disobedience – a lateral, even paradoxical response over which Zeus would no longer have authority. The most clever (and disobedient) of responses may be to propose a purely hallucinatory solution that nevertheless would have poetic and existential consequences. In the face of this strange paradox – eternal torment and with guaranteed interaction – Prometheus might have simply imagined it differently. Instead of vultures perhaps he could have seen surgeons. Instead of the morning sun, he might have imagined the fluorescent lights of an operating room. Instead of a morning food-chain reversal, Prometheus might have made himself an organ tree. His daily suffering – a viral proliferation of his body into the bodies of others – blurred boundaries for the seeker of knowledge. It might not have worked at first, of course, for the pain of such a punishment should not be underestimated. But eventually – and he had an eternity to imagine – Prometheus could ostensibly have made of this punishment any of a number of differing stories, in each case activating a hallucinatory rewriting of the situation in which he found himself. A postmodern rewrite of the Prometheus complex concludes with a proposition for nonsensical disobedience: the prisons of lived existence create unique possibilities for hallucination, delirium, and ultimateley contagion – transplant memories of organ donation that persist long after the donor is gone, or the forceful cries of paradoxical silence spoken by bodies that have already disappeared.

The rules of the game of nonsense and disobedience end with imaginary singularity – a point of reversal, a point of vanishing, after which the game needs new rules. What appears to be a dialectic relationship between technologies of disappearance and appearance is deceptively seductive as a model of contemporary subjectivity. The model generates itself as an ongoing game of hide and seek, from a theory of disappearance to one of presence reinforced by absence – then returning to a framework in which disappearance becomes the very condition of being-present in the first place. Between dreaming and intoxication, the conclusion, strangely, is whatever is made up, based on terms of engagement that cannot be imagined away.

Behind Well-Founded Belief

On the other side of the censoring of possibilities required for a horizon of ironic appearance lie the impossibilities that, out of sustainable consideration, are not censored, those that are instead censored *into* existence as the resonance patterns of an unintelligible world. Such trajectories are constituted as patterns rather than reflections, for there is nothing self-referential or autonomous about them. Instead, they are an ironic function of lived interference, projections of inauthentic self-conceptualization. These are constellations of unintelligibility – a gestural attempt to apprehend a xenoglossic world that can no longer be directly seen or felt or understood, but in which some semblance of coherency seems to persist, if only as a function of fantasy. It is no longer simply a world of suspended disbelief, but one where the vertigo of indeterminate living requires the explicit simulation of belief: a willful cultivation of delirious possibilities for sustainable illogic.

Building on the possibilities for ironic inautheticity, the next step would be to ask whether there remain possibilities for inauthentic engagement to be non-ironic. This would involve a mode of living with uncertainty that would no longer be simply the attempt to self-contextualize as a function of contingencies of disappearance, but to instead begin re-mapping uncertainty itself – in this instance capitalizing on the simple fact that in a climate of vertigo there is no correct way to proceed. This would amount to a theory of nonsensical permission, grown out of the ironic shadows of postmodern disappearance, beginning the attempt to fashion its own terms of engagement in order to sustain its imaginary possibilities in a livable way.

There are precedents for such a position, though it may be ironic that they are the articulated limits of logic and analytic thinking, not a function of postmodern theories of contingency. However, when the ironies of postmodern critique run their course, one is inevitably returned to the structural model that allows for ironic thought in the first instance. Such a return is not in conflict with the ironies of a postmodern conclusion, though it does have the unique potential to extend contingency into a potentially non-ironic form – a structural advocacy theory for nonsensical permission. Ludwig Wittgenstein elucidates this theory in *On Certainty*, in which the logical foundations of thought are given their own form of radical uncertainty through an in-depth look at the foundations of logic itself.

Arguably, Wittgenstein's thinking might be seen as a second prelude to the radical uncertainty of thought in postmodern times, agreeing in conclusion if not in process with Nietzsche's undermining of authority. This is because Wittgenstein is unwilling to leave unexamined the logical foundations upon which propositions of truth and certainty are based, arguing that "if the true is what is grounded, then the ground is not true, nor yet false."[5] An uncertainty at the core of truth begins to form, such that Wittgenstein's conclusion is to pre-empt the question of knowledge with that of belief, proposing that "at the foundation of well-founded belief lies belief that is not founded."[6]

When knowledge is grounded in that which has yet to be proved, a form of suspended disbelief is in play. There is a decision made not to interrogate what has no proper grounding, allowing for possibilities that can be mobilized despite uncertainty. Well-founded belief begins with suspended disbelief, that which makes conviction possible. If one traces this deferral back to its core, one might find Wittgenstein agreeing with Nietzsche that "the existence of the world is justified only as an aesthetic phenomenon,"[7] a suspended disbelief that provides an uncertain grounding for the first logical leaps of postmodern thinking.

If behind every well founded belief lies suspended disbelief, the question is no longer about the correct or most appropriate form of meaning or understanding, but rather how to maintain a form of thinking that no longer has a well-grounded basis. It is to suggest that there is no longer any such thing as well-founded belief, there is only suspended disbelief, to which a postmodern mind must respond by mobilizing tactics of suspension in order to sustain critical engagement. This postmodern belief in suspension is itself a suspended disbelief in the non-suspended – a poetic leap that is also the groundwork for an aesthetic of nonsensical permission.

Behind Unfounded Belief

The idea of a poetic leap at the core of postmodern thought can be extended by examining another side to Wittgenstein's argument. If Wittgenstein can assert that "at the foundation of well-founded belief lies belief that is not founded," one might ask if the question of the "not founded" belief makes this formulation possible. To ask this question would be to open Wittgenstein's formulation up to the same terms it sets in motion – here insisting that the formulation be held accountable to its own terms of engagement. The result of this accountability is twofold. First, one finds Wittgenstein self-reflexively grounding logical proposition in an illogic of contingency. Second, and perhaps more importantly, this contingent self-placement can be seen as an example of how to begin a non-ironic mobilization of nonsensical possibilities, explicitly *not* as a function of logical grounding, but instead as a practice of illogic – a logical defiance of logic itself. Consider the confluence of these statements: "Certainty is as it were a tone of voice in which one declares how things are, but one does not infer from the tone of voice that one is justified"[8]; and, "It would thus be *possible* to speak of a mental state of conviction, and that may be the same whether it is knowledge or false belief."[9] One begins to understand that the relationship between belief, certainty, and knowledge is precarious at best, and it is better in this case to treat conviction (rather than truth or knowledge) as the signifier of possibility. What this ultimately implies is that whereas knowledge may well be bound by conviction, conviction is not bound by knowledge. One can be mistakenly convinced, and one's conviction need not be lesser for the mistake. Conviction is, in this context, an aesthetic practice – a declared position that is pre-emptively decided on in order to allow for subsequent formulation, ultimately not subject to the truth or falsity of its declaration. Conviction, given this phrasing, is a suspension of disbelief, though such suspension does not mean it could not still be in error. Any philosophy that seeks possibilities for knowledge must be prepared for the possibility of making mistakes along the way. Paradoxically, such a philosophy must also be prepared to refuse that it is making mistakes, for such is the nature of conviction as Wittgenstein states: "I have a right to say 'I can't be making a mistake about this' even if I am in error."[10]

It is here, in the primacy of the possibilities for conviction, independent of their possibilities for error, that Wittgenstein's imperative reveals itself fully – no longer in the pursuit of possibility in the name of knowledge, but now with the "right" to pursue possibility, even at the expense of knowledge. This right, neither moral or ethical, exists within the structural limits of thought and logic, which do not require the bases of conviction to be well-founded, as long as one is able to suspend doubt in the correctness of one's assertions. The right to pursue possibility comes with a condition of conviction, however. No longer are theories and propositions to be treated as abstract concepts or arbitrary articulations. Conviction (insofar as conviction must be embedded in its own delirium of suspension) is aesthetic rather than an argumentative device, suspending critical doubt in the name of the delirious potential of lived possibilities.

One might also use this distinction to frame the transition from the discussion of technologies of ironic appearance to those of technologies of nonsense. Technologies of ironic appearance, in their resistance to official self-placement based on the premises of authorship, self-reflexivity, or performance, posit a horizon of understanding as ontologically unnecessary – one might even say, in paradoxical spirit, necessarily unnecessary. The power of the ironic is to double its question, such as to inevitably render additional possibilities at the same time as undermining the staticity of official perspective. Technologies of ironic appearance are strategies for ideological intervention that can be reformulated and recombined, pre-empted and re-patterned in a variety of ways – all of which have consequences, but also all of which are speculatively allowed. Ironic appearance, however, will always build its alternative formulations in expectation, opposition, or subversion, meaning that such perspectives will always be, at least in part, dichotomous (as the attribution of *ironic* would suggest). It is irony that allows for the extension of philosophical engagement, overlaying a climate of disappearance with its ironically mobilized double.

The case is distinct for technologies of nonsense, whose inverse perspective would be that of the unnecessarily necessary. Here, the negative horizon of ironic appearance is positively constituted, becoming a horizon of nonsense. What is at stake in such a context is no longer a disagreement with traditional forms of patterning, nor even the attempts to re-pattern projected fantasy or perspectival awareness. Instead, the project here is to bring together the remnants of structural necessity, delusion, and disappearance – and more importantly to hold these elements together – such that an explicitly unnecessary objectivity is held in attention. What we encounter is a necessity of the unnecessary which, when mobilized, is itself inverted. One might revert to the terminologies of Wittgensteinian belief and suggest that, in the case of technologies of nonsense, belief in the unfounded grounding of suspended disbelief (doubt levied towards the suspended foundations of fantastic reality) becomes the first nonsensical horizon which, when deployed, becomes a suspended disbelief in the grounds of unfounded belief (fantasy deployed towards the grounding of suspended falsity).

These forms of rendering are what might be called technologies of "delirious appearance," an explicit reversal of the terminologies of sensical apparition in favour of the delirious possibilities of livable un-reason. Technologies of nonsense covet the sustained irrationality of what is, in any case, a familiar if not inevitable aspect of contemporary living – mobilized towards the possibilities for a delirious metaphysics.

Technologies of Nonsense

The following three chapters – grouped as technologies of nonsense – are an attempt to extend thinking beyond the critical distance of ironic engagement to find what Peter Sloterdijk calls a "critical proximity"[11] to the question of lived uncertainty. Here, rather than remaining bound to the ironic inversion of dominant theoretical models, one might begin to mobilize Wittgenstein's "right to be in error," drawing a plane of equivalence between the aesthetic suspension of disbelief as the contingent grounds for both lived reason and livable unreason. Without a well-founded basis for logical rendition, technologies of nonsense speculate on plausible unfounded bases, beginning the task of holding thought accountable to the creative possibilities set into motion by conviction itself. Technologies of nonsense begin the task of imagining and enacting the quixotic potential of self-fashioned simulacra.

Three such technologies are those of error, delusion, and laziness – grown of a nonsensical positioning of questions of immanence, simulation, and metaphysical strategy. These three perspectives will be rendered through the works of a series of thinkers of nonsense: Gilles Deleuze and Félix Guattari, Jean Baudrillard, and Peter Sloterdijk, who collectively set in motion a plausible stage for the enactment of nonsensical reason, which praises itself into imaginary existence. These are theories that might also be called "sustainable delusions," self-contained but nevertheless contextually implicated versions of worldly nonsense not contained by the official horizons of autonomous or ironic individuality. It is an exploration perhaps best phrased as an attempt to articulate the imaginary consequences or the unfounded bases of the theories put forward by these thinkers, moving them beyond authenticity in order to privilege possibilities for nonsensical constitution. For instance, one might counter Deleuze and Guattari's theory of immanence with a theory of that which immanence disallows – namely, a hegemony of error; one might reframe Baudrillard's "lucidity pact" as a wager with delirious thinking which is required to maintain the stakes of critical questioning; and one might mobilize Sloterdijk's provocative calls for lived philosophy through a metaphysics of laziness as that which can occur without self-reflexive engagement or effort.

What these thinkers share is a profound dedication to imaginary rendering, constituting lived philosophy not in opposition to understanding but as part of a dynamic field of critical possibilities. To engage these theories as technologies of nonsense is to attempt to honour them for their contributions to the inverted horizons of unraveling sense, and for the groundwork – unfounded or not – they set in motion for sustainable aesthetic living. These three chapters are not the *only* ways to proceed beyond irony into sustainable delusions – they are merely an attempt to constitute *one way* of plausibly doing so. In this sense, what is presented here might be seen as a three-part foundational delusion, a groundwork for the study of 'pataphysical possibility as a metaphysical hallucination.

What follows are three iterations and meditations of nonsense rendered technological in order to engage an imagination liberated from its responsibility to fiction, but not from the context its fictions set in motion. These are theories paradoxically bound to the sustenance of the delusions they have mobilized, to the stakes and manifestations of their question, and ultimately to the nonsensical horizons that allowed for their imaginative formulation in the first instance.

7
Becoming-Rorschach

SuperModels[1]

Jorge Luis Borges once wrote about a map so large that it covered the entirety of the territory it was intended to describe.[2] This story is much cited by theorists of the postmodern, in particular by the French thinker Jean Baudrillard who has proclaimed that when maps are capable of this amount of detail it means that the territory beneath the map, or the reality beneath the simulation, has entirely disappeared – murdered by the map itself.[3]

We may think that the real persists despite maps, but a simple question reveals the fallacy here: which real? No longer is the map simply the size of the territory. In contemporary times, the map is much bigger, much more detailed, a magnified map that reveals minutia of the territory that never existed previously – charting everything from the microscopic to the telescopic, crossing virtual as well as material territory, including myths and imaginings and narratives, from media reports to political campaigns, genetic composition to historic and familial lineage, weather patterns to electromagnetic radiation. We face a map so detailed that one single reality can no longer be invoked as its source. Instead we find an excess of realities, a map so precise that according to Baudrillard it precludes a singular unified perspective: "the objectivity of the facts does not put an end to [the] vertigo of interpretation."[4]

There is no more singular reality – the fate of contemporary living is that reality itself has become the last and best version of reality TV, collapsed into the daily enactment of myths and stories that allow us to retain a communal connection to the interpretations of others. In this performance of the everyday the proliferating imagination is mobilized as the new horizon of interpretive entertainment. A vertigo of interpretation is the necessary effect of perceiving a map that contains many more options, and is much more accurate, than the simplified territory from which we navigate the possibilities it describes.

No longer are we bound by a reality principle, for reality itself changes shape according to the maps used to perceive it. Instead, contemporary experience is informed by a fictional principle that is itself merely an attempt to access a shape-shifting world that refuses to be bound by a singular interpretive identification. The artists in the exhibition *SuperModels* put such a principle into practice with a mapping of perception, a mapping of perspective, and, ultimately, a mapping of the imagination itself.

Consider the work of Chris Gillespie whose foamcore furniture reads less as architectural maquette and more as interior design for paper dolls. Or is it something more? Perhaps this is a literal *line* of furniture, both a formal arrangement and a commercial proposition. Neither functional nor non-functional, these works resist even the very references they suggest – a dysfunctional show-room of warped-scale cut-outs. And why not? We all wear different sizes of shirts and shoes, so why not furniture built to a customized size as well? An ergonomics of corporeal feng shui, set on a shelf that is also a stage, and a stage whose shelf-life betrays precisely the projected expectations of brand-name design. The vertigo of expectation confronts the pre-emptive imagination.

Chris Gillespie. *Chair, Coffee Table, Lamp, etc.* Mixed Media, 2006.

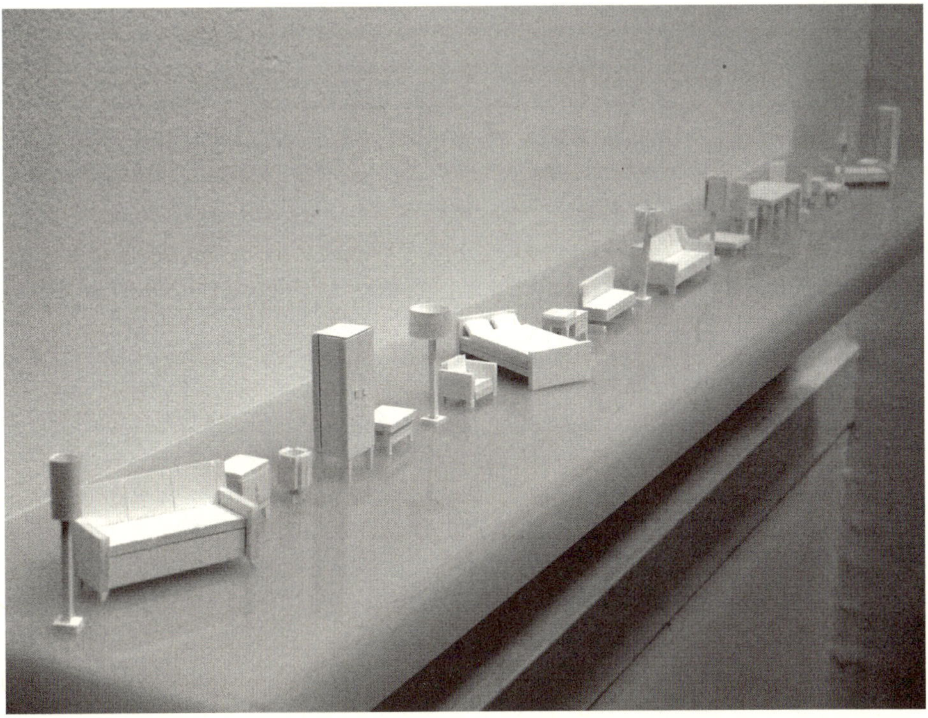

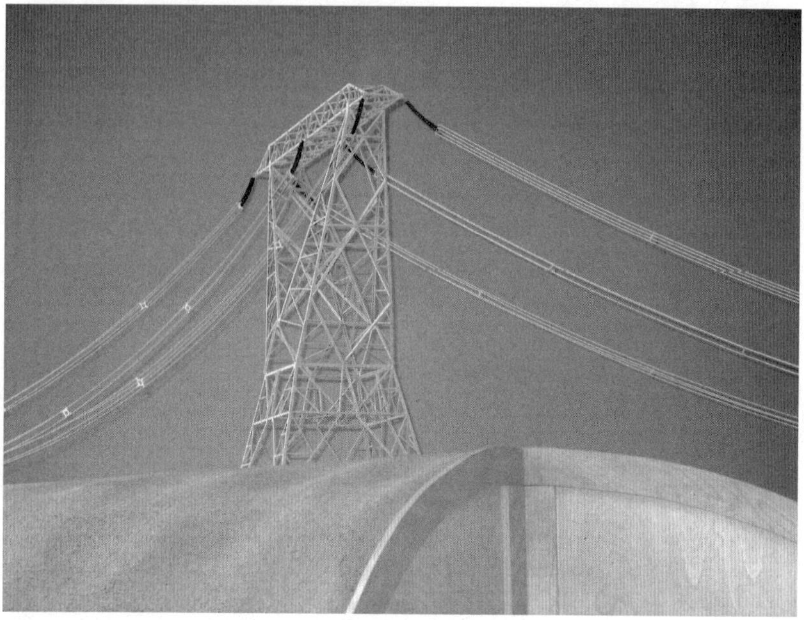

Tim van Wijk. *Right of Way*. Mixed Media, 2002.

Consider *Right of Way*, the installation of Tim van Wijk which reads much like a golf course taken over by power line. It is no longer even the real that is imagined, but a lost nature, a nature betrayed by the culture of human imaginative construction. Here the vertigo of corporeal experience dictates not only a "right of way" but further imposes itself as the only "right way." What emerges seems to be an ethical conjecture that would have us believe that the artifice of cultural construction is devoid of spectres. Instead it is the power line turned marionette that subsumes not only the natural and the real, but acts as allegory for a culture that is increasingly distant from the natural territories it used to inhabit. When the meat and vegetables we consume comes seasoned and pre-packaged from the supermarket down the street and when nature is rendered largely a vacation destination for time away from "real" living, we encounter ourselves as not only technologically extended but literally re-positioned. One finds a vertigo of "assisted living" for a reality that has abandoned its imagination machines.

Consider the work of Toni Hafkenscheid, whose images photographically intervene into the realities they capture, rendering each scene as a paradoxical diorama of itself. The photographic document betrays the realities it represents. These images undermine photographic proof, turning the real world into one of playtime imagination. The document of life turns into a model of something different, like the map before it – an invocation much more in line with story-telling than with verification. Might we not cite the works of Hafkenscheid as an instance in which the nuances of the map reveal so much more than the simple territory photographed? In the first place, this perhaps occurs with the works of Hafkenscheid in the same way as with all photographic images – representations that extrude a certain portion of reality, revealing an isolated and de-contextualized representation as well as what might be called an imaginative, interpretive dimensionality. In the case of Hafkenscheid this imaginative dimension is not by any means projected onto the document itself. Rather, here it has become its own language of mapping; a pre-emptive focal strike that brings with it an acutely aesthetic sensibility. There is a vertigo of focal mapping for a reality betrayed by its own imagination.

Toni Hafkenscheid. *Train + Gun, Hope B.C.* Colour Photograph, 2003.

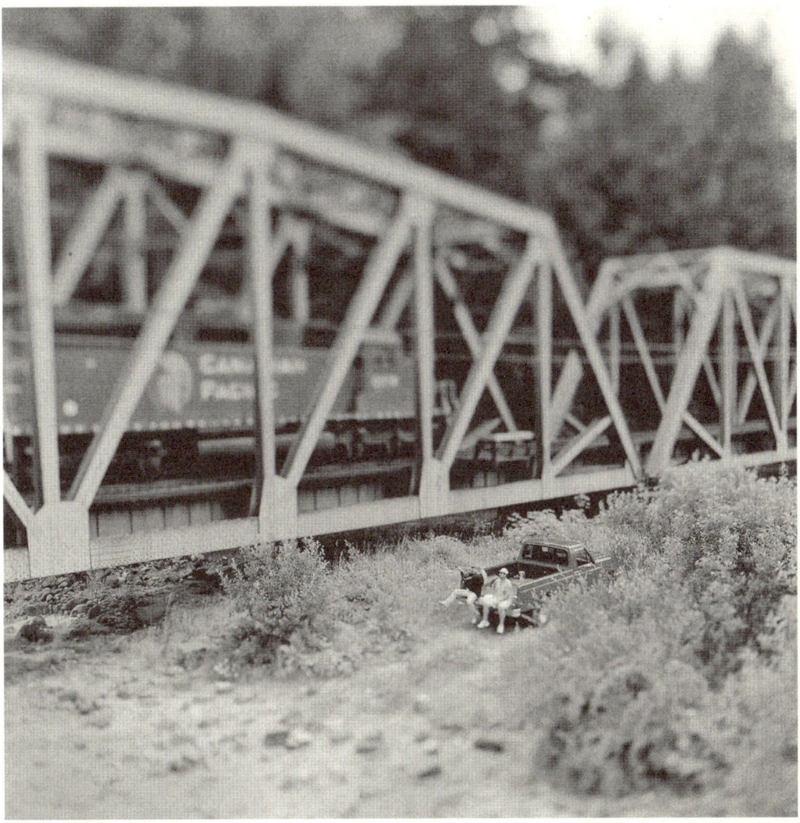

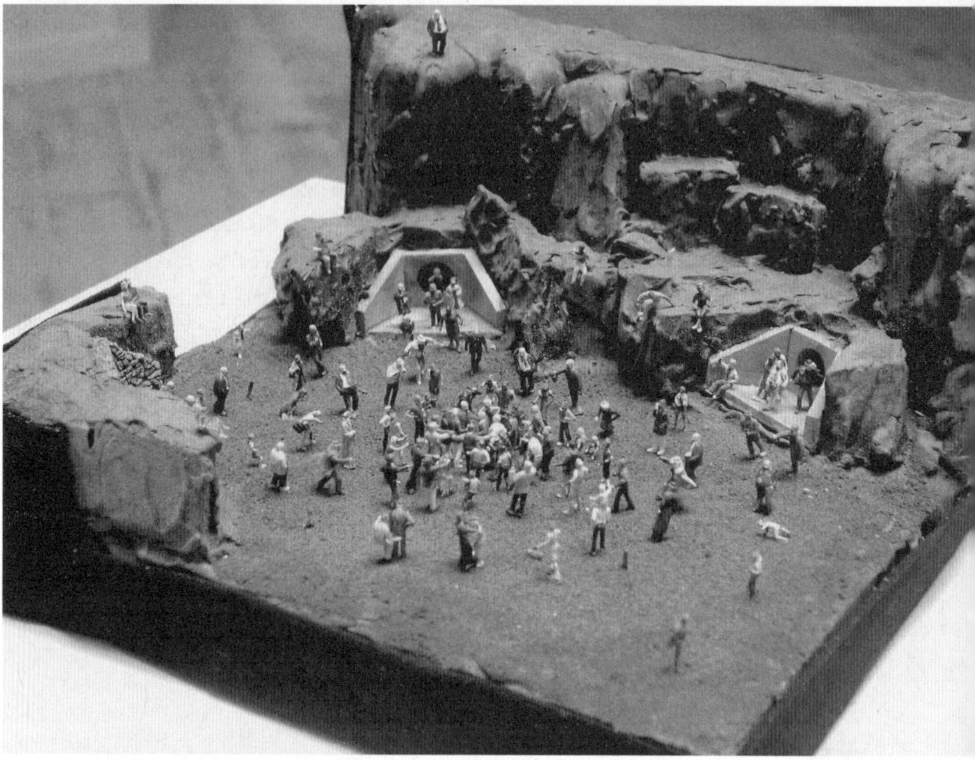

Duncan MacKenzie. *The World's Largest Zombie Group Hug.* Mixed Media, 2004.

Consider the work of Duncan MacKenzie, which presents and represents precisely a modeled real, a narrative and imaginative reality that is not in competition with an objective world-map because it never cared to mistake itself as real in the first place. Instead, here the nuances of imaginative rendering emerge in full force – a zombie group hug for those beyond the deadly clutches of sanctioned or political voice. Zombies are used to illustrate a stage of simulation that has entirely receded into its own immortal fantasy; not born again, but undead – a premature burial of multiplicity that escapes its fate by acknowledging the inherently morbid humour in all things imaginary. Like the forest that has ironically fallen over – we know the adage about a single tree falling, but what sound might an entire forest make? The coyote's howl becomes indistinguishable from the hyena's laugh – werewolf cries that reinforce the fact that we have all been bitten already. Finally, the death march of the real is replaced by the imaginary horizons of contemporary living. The vertigo of interpretation becomes, inevitably, an interpretation of vertigo.

What all the artists in *SuperModels* have in common is a mapping of the imaginary, a poignant articulation of that space where reality and fantasy no longer reside in contradiction. Instead we find the vast expanse of the imaginary opening up, erupting into visual and narrative forms, rendered with much more detail than reality could ever hope to contain.

It may, however, seem ironic to speak of a map much larger than the territory it describes when we are surrounded by miniatures and representations that are uniformly much smaller than their real-world counterparts. One might, for example, find such a map in the micro-imaging of molecules or insects – representations that reveal aspects of the real that are imperceptible to the human sensorium. But where do such details exist if not in the human encounter with the real? And how can we attribute reality to something that is ultimately un-experienceable except through the mediation of represented form? Perhaps the molecular exists largely in the minds of those who believe in it. Like God, like black holes, like morals and philosophy in general, these abstract elements of reality find presence only in representation – and it is only secondarily that we encounter them in experience itself. The reality of such phenomena is to exist in the map itself rather than in the world of accidental possibilities – one does not stumble onto the molecular.

In the artworks of these artists we find objects and images that begin the task of mapping the imagination of those creative minds behind the scenes. Not properly models, these are perhaps better described as meta-models – supermodels of a reality and an imagination that are no longer in competition with one another but have fused and melded together, their only conditions being that they no longer believe in a sanctioned or static reality.

Friedrich Nietzsche predicted the end of the real long before Borges or postmodernism entered the picture. For Nietzsche, this demise was a result of the over-qualification of reality – and for a humanity that had become bound by its maps of behavioural sanction, Nietzsche proposed the Superman.[5] In the twenty-first century, realities enter and fade, intensify and erupt, and for the multiple realities that have now grown beyond any possible representation (let alone qualification), we bring you *SuperModels*, maps from the imagination machines of contemporary culture-makers.

Becoming-Perspectival

> [P]hilosophy is the art of forming, inventing, and fabricating concepts.
>
> Gilles Deleuze and Félix Guattari, *What is Philosophy?* 2.

At the core of the nonsensical gaze is a reversibility of perception – a version of every story that also in some way embraces the negative space of its own constitution. In the constitution of appearances, many versions of many stories are possible. Yet, as a condition of constitution, of these many stories only one ends up manifesting – in forms as partial or complete as the renderings that inform it. In this sense, any manifest possibility requires that competing versions of the story are suppressed. It is a circular dynamic, through which the mechanism for the manifestation of fantasy becomes one of disappearances.

This reversibility of manifestation and suppression is not limited to the workings of perception. This rather simple dynamic extends to most forms of cognitive, experiential, perceptual, and embodied interaction, such that one might equally suggest that the condition of doing any one thing in particular is the active *not-doing* of other things. Any enacted (patterned) event involves the displacement of other possible (surplus) events, and this can be made as simple or as complex as one wishes. For example, a condition of watching television might be that one is ostensibly *not* mountain biking (although this would be a rather interesting multi-task challenge). However, one might also say that a more self-evident condition of watching television is that one is watching a particular show or channel, such that one can never fully watch television itself – unless perhaps one watches *the* television rather than its presented narratives. Such an activity is conducive to a much more specific read, in that even while watching television one is *not-doing* the watching of, in this case, surplus channels.

In cognition, the dynamic of not-doing would seem to exist in equal spirit, such that every thought trajectory has its own surplus trajectories – the *not-thinking* implicit in any patterned manifestation of thought. The more specifically materialized are the nuances of one trajectory, the more inaccessible will be the possibilities of appearance for those surplus trajectories sacrificed in order to bring into focus the patterns themselves.

The objectivity of perception is inevitably pre-empted by the suspended disbelief in assembled (or disassembled) contingency. This occurs because the specific ordering of any given trajectory will entail certain consequences for the perspective itself. All perspectives will leave *not-perspectives* in their wake – a direction, or several, in which one must be *not-looking* in order to be looking where one is. While the possibilities of perspectival assemblage may well be infinite, it is the impossibility of the not-perspective that reinforces the contingency of perception, always leaving further possibilities in absentia, and consequently frustrating the attempt to unify or legislate or standardize a consensual set of perspectival rules. In such a climate of potentially limitless formulation of possibility, there are no better thinkers to turn to than Gilles Deleuze and Félix Guattari, who offer a cosmological framework for exactly these sorts of free-flow circulations of intensity, desire, and their aggregate constitutions: "Everything is allowed: all that counts is for pleasure to be the flow of desire itself, Immanence, instead of a measure that interrupts it or delivers it to the three phantoms, namely, internal lack, higher transcendence, and apparent exteriority. If pleasure is not the norm of desire, it is not by virtue of a lack that is impossible to fill but, on the contrary, by virtue of its positivity, in other words, the plane of consistency it draws in the course of its process."[6]

When the limits of allowable consistency are drawn in such an open-ended way, it must perhaps be explicitly acknowledged that there are no more rules to the game and in fact, no more causality that is not itself a function of perspectival assemblage. Causality becomes a moment of extrapolated constitution – a delirious proposition of contingency rather than a legitimizing structure of logic. No more need to attribute an official cause to any particular perspective: I am tired because I worked all day; I am bored because there is nothing on TV. There is no more "because," or rather there are many: *because-machines* that can be deployed as we see fit, and no longer limited to rational formulation. According to Deleuze and Guattari: "The rationality, the efficiency, of an assemblage does not exist without the passions the assemblage brings into play, without the desires that constitute it as much as it constitutes them."[7]

The sky is blue because people like blue. And why not? Have we not already renounced the projection of a singular truth onto the universe or the self or existence? Instead, at this point, have not all truths become participatory – suspended falsities – functions of the perspectives deployed in their formulations? Functions of the censoring of possibilities into contingently closed horizons of perspectival engagement, always subject to the unfounding tendencies of equally unfounded belief? Perspective is no longer determined by causality. Now, causality (and the realities it renders) is determined by the perspectives assembled in its articulation, along similar lines to what Deleuze and Guattari term "becoming": "[M]ake your organism enter into composition with *something else* in such a way that the particles emitted from the aggregate thus composed will be ... a function of the relation of movement and rest, or of molecular proximity, into which they enter."[8]

An aggregate composition should always be seen for the ways in implicates perspective – a *becoming-perspectival* – irrespective of the terms of engagement. Any perspectival rendering (whether by desire, fantasy, delusion, logic, or otherwise) requires a direction, a consistency, or pattern – in short, an investment that will always leave a surplus of unmobilized possibilities in its wake. We confront the finite nature of perspectival understanding, which is not to imply that this finite quality of cognition is rendered static or essential as a result of its finitude. Instead, understandings must now content themselves to always be partial, in both senses of the word – incomplete and pre-emptively invested in a certain biased constitution of appearance. A paradox of partiality emerges – a horizon of necessary perspectival impossibility that is the co-present condition of an inessential horizon of perspectival possibilities.

The Paradox of Partiality (or, The Broken Hologram)

The paradox of an always partial self-understanding entails the adoption of a self-righteous horizon of falsified awareness. If all perspectives were to be seen as partial (as has been suggested), then partiality itself would become an impartial meta-designation, effectively smoothing over the particularities of any given *specific* perspective. This paradox has other faces as well, among them that of difference. When all perspectives are acknowledged as different, then difference becomes the common denominator for a theory of meta-sameness, pre-emptively erasing the very difference that was its ground. When difference is made into an essentialist (or structuralist) principle, then it loses its difference: it ceases to be different *from* anything identifiable, and therefore ceases to be identifiably different. Deleuaze and Guattari articulate paradox as follows: "The problem of philosophy is to acquire a consistency without losing the infinite into which thought plunges."[9]

This problem of acquiring consistency while preserving other possibilities exists in questions of perspective as well. The crux of the problem, however, is less about balancing or negotiating these paradoxical perspectives and more about what it means to locate oneself within this perceptual dynamic. Because an understanding of such a paradox does not remove one from its perceptual dynamic, this is a paradox that *cannot be understood away*. Even though it makes perfect sense, it remains binding. The paradox is also particular, for its resolution will depend on encountering a perspective from which both the specific and the general can be accounted for – a seeming perspectival impossibility, based on the formulations proposed thus far. These meanderings, while seeming merely to indulge in an excessive problematizing of the question, do in fact reveal a perspectival option – one that is entirely unacceptable, but nevertheless functional. These types of paradoxes tend to be one-sided and tend to intensify explicitly from the perspectival position that seeks to reconcile a certainty of voice with an uncertainty of the world. Yet it is never merely the world that is uncertain – if anything, the uncertainty of the world is inevitable when presented from a perspective that is itself uncertain, tentative, partial, and always both implicated and disoriented.

If instead of treating the problem as that of an uncertain world (or philosophy, or understanding) one begins from the uncertainty of subjectivity, the paradox begins to appear less daunting. Deleuze and Guattari will say that "everything divides, but into itself,"[10] and yet, if this is correct, then the inverse should also hold: everything multiplies, but into itself. There is much at stake in such a formulation, for upon such a reversibility depends the ability to move through this paradox of partial rendering to find a position of potentially paradoxical encounter – one whose partiality might no longer be a horizon of exclusion.

A particular type of principle – one that might be called a reverse holographic principle – can be used to address the problem of exclusion. To refer to the holograph as a principle would be to speak of the positive constitution of light-wave interference patterns that form a (semi) three-dimensional representation, in this case generalizing from the optics of holography to articulate a certain principle of perception. To reverse this principle would be to speak of a second order interference pattern that results from interfering with patterned interference – in this case making a principle out of what happens when one breaks the hologram itself. When one breaks a hologram, one ends up with a divided surface but a multiplied image – each fragment of the hologram containing a complete copy of the original. While each copy is complete, each fragment of the broken hologram represents the complete image from its own distinct perspective. According to holography expert Jason Sapan, "you might say that each piece of a [broken] hologram stores information about the whole image, but from its own viewing angle."[11] One might say that the hologram is a literal assemblage of perspectives, partialities in this instance coming together to form a multi-partial (or multidimensional) representation of its object. A hologram is a common denominator of sorts, the pattern of wave cancellation that results from perspectival excess. If a hologram is the result of interference and exclusion among partial perspectives, the broken hologram must be seen as the fracturing of exclusion: dividing and multiplying into the multiple partialities – the multiple perspectives – from which the completed image of exclusion was formed.

In this instance, the fracturing of exclusion operates within an exclusionary perspective. Each fragment of the hologram is hyper-exclusionary – reclaiming the exclusions of partiality that were excluded in the formation of the whole, without ceasing to be representative perspectives of the image. In other words, the exclusion of exclusion does not result in a revivified paradoxicality that smoothes over the exclusions in play, but in an intensification of exclusion. Exclusion, as a concept, seems to hold the potential to resolve the paradox of partiality from both generalized and particularized perspectives.

There are also other concepts that, like exclusion, promise a capacity to inversely resolve the paradox of partiality. A different version of the resolution – that of *error* – is most useful at the moment, for like exclusion, error seems to abide by the holographic version of the fracture, dividing and multiplying into itself. As Wittgenstein insisted: "I have a right to say 'I can't be making a mistake about this' even if I am in error."[12] Within a context such as the one in Wittgenstein's quote, we encounter a reversibility to the question of error, one that functions in an identical way to the workings of exclusion. Such a reversal, applied to the question at hand, has the distinct ability to flip Wittgenstein's formulation on its head, such that one might also insist that *I have a right to say "I am making a mistake about this" even if I am not in error.*

From a position of being-in-error, if one is correct it would not be an argument against error, but rather would validate one's position as erroneous. If there are only perspectives from which I am in error, then I remain in error; if there is a perspective from which I am correct, then I am in error to assert that I am in error. The formulation specific to error is *partial* – invested, in this instance, in the perpetuation of its own falsity, with a unique ability to proceed despite (or perhaps even because of) the contextual disjunction that informs its dynamic. Error, in this sense, is a broken hologram which, when broken further, simply perpetuates itself incrementally: *I might be correct about being in error, in which case my being-in-error is perpetuated.* I might be in error about being in error, in which case my error cannot be perpetuated – but, in this instance, a new error is revealed: my error about being in error begins a (perspectival) life of its own, without ever having ceased to be in error itself.

In some ways this observation about the persistence of error is merely an economic strategy that builds on the realization that there are far more perspectives from which one could be in error than there are from which one might be correct. It also takes into account the dynamics particular to error and conviction, such that the correctness of an error does not remove its error while the error of conviction would indeed transform correctness into error itself. The trick is now to formulate this perspective such that it will always be in error, and through being in error can be perpetuated beyond the paradox of partial perspectives (not negative-positivism but rather positive-negativism). But this has already become the norm of the discussion, a context in which falsities proliferate, perspectives are always partial and consequently always (partially) in error, and in which self-projected fantasies form the erroneous norm. It can also be said with hypocritical conviction (and a touch of ironic self-righteousness) that if such a perspective were ever proven to be correct it would not be difficult to find another error to adopt – whereas there may be a shortage on truths, there has never been a scarcity of error.

Cross-eyed Immanence

Despite the fact that it will be wrong to do so, it will be necessary to proceed with an intolerance for all perspectives that do not allow themselves to be in error. One might take this even further and insist that it is only in error that the *stakes* of a question can be properly acknowledged. One can, of course, know an answer without knowing what is at stake. Conversely, to be in error is to amplify and intensify the stakes of that which one can never know. In error one finds that which facets of contemporary science call "post-normal," a reversed imperative that is uniquely capable of navigating questions of self-similarity where both the stakes and the levels of uncertainty are at their extremes. The project becomes one of purposefully seeking out errors, not to correct them but to hold them in tension with one another – a tension that often results in further fragmentation, such that error continues to proliferate. One can, of course, be in error about the errors constituted, but this is no longer an argument against the trajectory of speculation. The error of partiality is an enticing place to begin, for these errors ostensibly exist even in the most compelling of philosophical renditions, ripe for mobilization. Dismiss everything that makes sense; it is only that which is in error that has something at stake.

Consider Deleuze and Guattari: "There is not the slightest reason for thinking that modes of existence need transcendent values by which they could be compared, selected, and judged relative to one another. On the contrary, there are only immanent criteria. A possibility of life is evaluated through itself in the movements it lays out and the intensities it creates on a plane of immanence: what is not laid out or created is rejected."[13] In order to continue to agree with Deleuze and Guattari, it will be necessary to construe an error to their perspective as well, one that perhaps is most plausibly built from the foundational partiality at the root of their theory of immanence. If, for instance, rejection (as represented in the above citation) is a condition of immanence, latent in this very formulation of immanence is a transcendental comparison, selection, and judgment. The privileging of immanence in this instance requires the mobilization of transcendental method, such that the one central error one can rather easily constitute is Deleuze and Guattari's adamant insistence that immanence is immanent only to itself: "Whenever immanence is interpreted as immanent 'to' something a confusion of plane and concept results, so that the concept becomes a transcendent universal and the plane becomes an attribute in the concept. When misunderstood in this way, the plane of immanence revives the transcendent again: it is a simple field of phenomena that now only possesses in a secondary way that which first of all is attributed to the transcendent unity."[14]

Immanence cannot, therefore, be immanent to anything other than itself without falling out of immanence and back into the transcendent modalities of behaviour that Deleuze and Guattari seek to avoid. It would seem that this also means that immanence, thus phrased, has the condition of being not-transcendent, an unfortunate formulation for the simple reason that suddenly one finds the theory of immanence excerpted from the stage of becoming (which it was supposed to foster) and thrust into an explicitly stated stage of being (which it was supposed to avoid). In the hands of Deleuze and Guattari, immanence is consequently not itself immanent at all, but rather the not-doing of transcendent conceptualization. Insofar as this is a perpetual (which is to say perspectivally closed) relationship, one might push this critique to its point of reversibility and assert that from such a perspective, immanence is what occurs when one *transcends transcendence*.

Speaking of the horizon of immanence, Deleuze and Guattari assert: "We will say that THE plane of immanence is, at the same time, that which must be thought and that which cannot be thought. It is the nonthought within thought. It is the base of all planes, immanent to every thinkable plane that does not succeed in thinking it."[15] Once formulated as a reversible horizon, one might paradoxically attempt to recover an error at the core of immanence itself. If for example, one were to again invoke Wittgenstein as a foil, one might build something of an analogy between immanence as "that which cannot be thought," and Wittgenstein's notion of "unfounded belief" at the root conviction. Rather than constituting immanence as a plane of transcended transcendence, one might instead invoke explicitly a right to be in error, and formulate such a plane as the *failure* of transcendence – emphasizing in this case the horizon that in the above quote Deleuze and Guattari articulate as the "thinkable plane that does not succeed in thinking." One cannot refuse transcendence forever in the name of immanence without inadvertently constituting a surrogate horizon of transcendent immanence proper. Yet if the horizon is one of failure rather than refusal, both the principles of error and the conceptualization of immanence can be perpetuated, with the singular consequence that immanence is no longer immanent only to itself, but rather must now be seen as immanent to the error that allows for its perpetuation.

One scenario that seems to preserve the formulation of immanence being immanent only to itself is in which immanence is perpetually in error. When immanence is immanent to the error of its perspective, one does find immanence transformed – but not into transcendence. Rather here what one finds is immanence always caught up in a process of *becoming-imminent*. Instead of simply ignoring or resisting the question of transcendence (and noting that, paradoxically, ignoring and resisting are both *transcendental* strategies and most certainly not immanent modalities of engagement), it is more convenient in this instance to place oneself on the side, not of anti-transcendence, but rather of explicitly *failed* transcendence. Do not make transcendence undesirable – that is an excursion into what reconstitutes itself as transcendence transcended, reviving a relationship to certainty. Instead, make transcendence impossible, such that any attempt to mobilize towards a transcendent modality will fail. Do not avoid these mobilizations, for in failure there is error, and in error there is imminence. Error, in other words, is where immanence becomes imminent: "Immanent: being within the limits of possible experience or knowledge; Imminent: to threaten; hanging threateningly over one's head."[16]

The only trick that remains is to invert the relationship – to treat immanence itself as a cross-eyed formulation such that, in fact, immanence itself ceases to be immanent to anything but the threat – the imminence – of its own formulation. Here immanence is precisely *not* immanent to itself, but rather to the very contingency, or danger that allows for its tentative emergence. It is a pattern of fantasy whose consequence is a renewed experiential dynamic, for the very simple reason that it has ceased to be necessary, and therefore is constantly under threat. It is the unnecessary necessity of imminence, whose mobilization in this case allows for error to be self-perpetuating – moments where the potentially infinite possibilities of becoming implode into an imminent constellation of enacted being.

Cognitive Nomadism

The inversion of the horizon of immanence (that salvages the framework of imminent engagement) has consequences, not least of which is the perpetually displaced and disoriented meta-formation that would have otherwise allowed for a unified theory of fractured assemblage. The attempt to project a unifying theory of subjectivity onto other perspectival constellations will always result in error, for the simple reason that particularities cannot be extended as general or unifying rules of behaviour without simplifying and reducing to a common denominator that which particularities share – which would be, in other words, to de-particularize the perspectives in question. One might consequently insist that there is no longer the possibility of a unified theory of subjectivity, but one would be wrong (as a premise of error requires). Instead, there are as many unifying theories as there are possible perspectives from which to view the question of unity, each one contingently uniting itself to an ever-expanding series of imminent possibilities. This would be poorly articulated as an engagement with immanence, however, or even as a process of becoming. Instead, the act of engagement contingently closes the horizon of participation such that a constellation of being is manifest always in terms of its imminent partiality: error forms the index of manifest being.

It is in this spirit that one can propose that the plane of immanence proposed by Deleuze and Guattari be replaced by a horizon of imminence, in order to maintain the possibility of error and through so doing perpetuate the stakes of the question of contemporary subjectivity. Such an intervention does not necessarily contradict Deleuze and Guattari who will, on occasion, contextualize their trajectory such that a sensitivity to error might well seem, in some way, implicit in the formulations they propose: "We are still too competent; we would like to speak in the name of an absolute incompetence … If someone retorts that we are claiming the famous rights to laziness, to non-productivity, to dream and fantasy production, once again we are quite pleased, since we haven't stopped saying the opposite."[17]

Here one finds a perspectivally constituted self-placement *within* a horizon of error –phrased as a horizon of incompetence. At moments such as these, immanence is not merely an externally constituted projection of philosophical possibility, but an implicated attempt to navigate the disciplinary territory of competence (or certainty, or conviction). Immanence becomes-imminent. It is a relational dynamic in which one enters into error, with the side-effect of preserving the stakes of inquiry. What will help develop the nuances of such a formulation is the unlikely extension of this horizon of imminence, read back through Deleuze and Guattari's conception of the nomad as an explicitly partial paticipant in the dynamic of self-conception: "[For the nomad] it is deterritorialization that constitutes the relation to the earth, to such a degree that the nomad reterritorializes on deterritorialization itself. *It is the earth that deterritorializes itself, in a way that provides the nomad with a territory.*"[18]

In this instance, the relational dynamic between nomads and the earth is such that it is not the nomad but the world that moves, deterritorializing itself in relation to nomadic trajectory. This has the curious effect of transforming a nomadic subjectivity into a hyper-territorialized marker – a Copernican revival of sorts in which the territory explicitly revolves around the nomad himself.[19] The fortunate error (the incompetence) of the formulation is that of assuming the nomad is any more or less conscious of these patterns of territorialization and deterritorialization than the earth itself. If indeed the earth orbits the nomad, not only do "nomads make the desert no less than they are made by it,"[20] but one might suggest the inverse of such a formulation is, in fact, more important still: *even nomads are transformed by the spaces they inhabit.*

One can avoid the constitution of cognitive centrality to the subjectivity of the nomad, for each point along the deterritorialized path will require different subjective formulations – different relational sensitivities to the earth itself. What is required is a cognitive fluctuation of sorts, in which one turns the deterritorializing gaze on oneself – not only a physical movement with the shifting horizons of a living planet, nor as a romantic strategy for salvaging possibilities for becoming, but far more explicitly as a relational response to the immanence of trajectory – as a manifestation of precisely the *incompetence* of being.

This sort of cognitive nomadism requires the ability to treat oneself as a space of imminent trajectory, bound by fluctuating potentialities that are manifest, depending on the territories that manifest, – reciprocally as contingent perspectives demanding equal contingencies of identity. The merit of this form of self-conception is its ability to deterritorialize *itself*. What results is not a smooth space of possible identities, but a hyper-imminent space where any given manifestation of incompetence is accountable to other points on its trajectory. In contrast to the deterritorializing trajectory of Deleuze and Guattari, one might therefore propose a hyper-territorializing strategy: a way of delineating not only the effects (and affects) of a shifting multiplicity of worlds, but also one that is internally as diverse as it is allowed to be. Preferable to the smoothed cognitive space of a self-in-becoming is the hyper-striated space of cognitive conflict, punctuated by patterns of projected personality. No more flows – instead, a constellation of disparate positions, a connect-the-dots personality, a mitosis-machine of subjectively erroneous personalities proliferating indefinitely as a consequence of whatever the space they find themselves in demands.

Autonomic Personalities

Some semblance of strategy is required for the negotiation of a world in which it is no longer the various formulations of exteriority that form the basis of individual engagement, but rather the all-too-many faces of individuality that implode into a contingency of imminent closure. One can say with some confidence that the adoption of any given face will require the suspension of other possible faces – no less than the constitution of perspective or interpretation. We have come too far, however, to consider the possibility that such a suspension is in any way a willful or autonomous decision. Instead, one must posit that subjectivity is inevitably Icarian in nature, a moment where one face among many falls out of the constellation of possibility to assume a hyper-territorialized (imminent) form.

Under normal circumstances, such a perspective would be called disciplinary – and indeed it is, with the singular caveat that it does not form a meta-horizon of perpetually territorialized engagement, but is more meekly a contextual emergence of personality. Outside of the context in which such a personality is rendered necessary, there is no (philosophical) reason that necessitates its perpetuation. This may sound odd, and it is therefore perhaps prudent to insist that this is in no way different than the fashion in which personality already proceeds: when I go to work there are certain behavioural traits that I adopt; likewise with family or friends or strangers – what is of importance here is the insistence that outside of those contexts there is no necessary reason for such behaviours to be perpetuated. When I am not at work, it is (perhaps) neither convenient nor useful to remain bound by the contextual markers of a working personality; in fact, in more instances than not, the perpetuation of work mentality while at home proves to be rather inconvenient.

The example is polarized for effect, of course, for such behavioural instances are generally referred to as "hats worn" or "activities performed" or something more along lines that would not threaten the possibility of a unified whole beneath the temporary invocation of any given face. By polarizing the issue, the aim is to allow for self-similarity to proceed of its own accord, according to a principle of contextual contingency. To embrace the contingency of context would be to make personalities *autonomic* – insisting in this instance that they can manage themselves, without any forced unifying attempt designed to subsume the many into the proverbial one – whether that "one" is relational or essentialist perhaps is no longer significant.

I do not need to manage my hunger – when I need to eat my body reminds me. Nor do I not need to manage my breathing or my heartbeat – they occur (for the most part) of their own accord. Yet if I decide to pay attention to hunger, breathing, or heart rate, these things are not foreign. The disciplinary element of the autonomic is itself partial – serving more of a "fail safe" function than one that is principally regulatory. There is, consequently, room to assert that there is an element of redundancy built into the system of subjective manifestation. The mistake would be to assume that it is the autonomic system that is redundant. In fact, it has always been the self-disciplining tendency towards cognitive unity that interferes with what would otherwise do just fine by itself. Arguably, autonomic systems perpetuate themselves *better* without cognitive interference (my heart rate, for example, does a better job of self-regulating than I could ever do on its behalf).

So why not the same for personalities? Does my work personality not do a better job of self-perpetuation than I could do on its behalf? When I walk into the office I adopt a series of behaviours and attitudes that are forgotten when I go home for the day. My work personality has a particular sensibility for those tasks it is required to perform, a sensitivity to the context in which it functions, not necessarily a context in which which it chooses to perpetuate indefinitely. It is most functional in the context that reminds it of who it is.

A "work personality" can quickly becomes an intuitive response, however; an emotional reaction, a manifestation of the unconscious. Why not then suggest the same thing for unconscious living – that which might perhaps be described as simply as the autonomic system of consciousness itself? It is prudent to follow quite closely the suggestion of Deleuze and Guattari, who assert that "the unconscious poses no problem of meaning, solely problems of use. The question posed by desire is not 'What does it mean?' but rather '*How does it work?*'"[21] Thus *the unconscious works of its own accord*, a suggestion that is tantamount to insisting that there is no unconscious – rather there is only the consciously rendered unconscious-machine. Like the fantasy of trauma before it, the positive rendering of this disciplinary dynamic is required in order to perceive the patterns of disciplinary imminence, or, for Deleuze and Guattari, the trajectories of desiring production.

And why not? Can the unconscious laugh or can it merely cry? If one can laugh at oneself for having an unconscious at all, can it laugh back at us? *While I might appear as one, I have a split unconscious* – a constellation of autonomic personalities that are rendered into being in accordance with whatever the situation demands. Yet the situation will never demand that such personality be perpetuated – that, ultimately, is the choice of the personality at that time, the selective perpetuation of which assembles the disciplinary constellation in which one finds oneself at any given moment. Becoming-autonomic is not only a process of self-domestication; it is also a process through which consciousness is opened to the extreme contingencies of unconscious living. Untamed habits roam wild and domesticate each other as well – cognitive nomadism is preserved, to such an extent that, at times, it even begins to become predatory.

A Hegemony of Error

Imminent being has nothing at all to do with the transformative trajectories of immanent becoming. This is an argument for the imminent manifestation of an identity that does not exist outside of contextual provocation. Imminent being is *not* self-identical for the simple reason that the threat that provokes appearance has nothing whatsoever to do with any self that might be called essential. Instead, the essential is explicitly rendered surplus when faced with the stakes of imminent being, whose only condition is that one respond – in some way, at some time. That there are no *necessary* conditions placed on how one might respond is not an argument for the safety of danger, but rather a doubling of the stakes of how one actually *does* respond.

In this sense, the dynamic of imminent being operates explicitly in the presence of what might be called a hegemony of error, that alone has the capacity to displace its transcendent predecessor for the simple reason that it has already resolved to transcendend, humbly, through the autonomic awareness that transcendent method is ever-present, but continually failing.

To frame the description of imminence, a brief comparison of transcendence and immanence is useful. If transcendent modalities seek terms of judgment to play the best game possible, one might contrast this with immanent terms of engagement that defy judgment, insisting that the game can be played without rules. If transcendence seeks knowledge, immanent modalities of being render knowledge superfluous to the lived realities of the day to day. The problem is that, in such a context, immanence can never know itself, unless it has superceded the knowledge of transcendental project with a meta-knowledge of transcendent trajectory. This is why it has been argued that the framework of immanence is one of transcended transcendence. Despite how it seems, immanence has nothing to do with experience. It is, instead, a safety zone of sorts into which all things experiential enter a priori, sanctioned and smoothed over. Can one understand that understanding is irrelevant? Perhaps, but one remains bound by a framework of (meta) understanding. One does not, in other words, exit the transcendent drive to knowledge – the will to truth – by becoming-immanent, but rather *resolves* this drive with a meta-knowledge of its failure. Immanence, in this sense, can be nothing but enlightened anti-transcendence.

In order to preserve the contingency, the uncertainty, and the danger of everyday living, one must replace the terminologies of immanent becoming with those of imminent being – in a context of danger and threat, there is no question of transcendence at all. The cast shadow of immediacy renders superfluous the quest for enlightened knowledge, not because it has made a conscientious decision to do so, but because it has no other choice. It is imminence, and not immanence, that is the sign of the ontological flip wherein experiential reference (here in the form of danger as opposed to Deleuze and Guattari's formulation of desire) dialectically supercedes the will to truth in any truly applicable form.

To mobilize imminence as an articulated horizon of engagement, it is necessary to propose a hegemony of error – an already-failed transcendence, which is also to say an always-mistaken knowledge that mistakes itself as knowing. The hegemony of error would demand that knowledge be understood, in advance, as unable to effectively disentangle the contingency of lived context. It might be an error to make such a claim, but the effect of the claim is to constitute uncertainty as something dangerous. In the face of danger knowledge becomes explicitly secondary to reflex, and to theorize a knowledge of this sort is to force the stakes of uncertainty to dictate a certainty of action, despite the fact that under more reflective conditions a variety of other courses of action would be possible. This is a pre-emptive strategy, disregarding reflection in order to catalyze a reflex-response. Instances in which one cannot do anything but react do not form the traumatic exceptions to the rule, but instead must be made the basis of the rule itself. A hegemony of error is required in order to circumvent the safety zone of immanent experiential becoming.

Becoming Rorschach

> [T]he philosopher does not approach the undetermined concept except with fear and respect.
>
> Gilles Deleuze and Félix Guattari, *What is Philosophy?* 78.

There is an element of environmental trust that is required when dealing with the notion of error and the autonomic – the insistence that contexts will continue to demand that personalities appear to accommodate the contingency of deterritorialized living, and that one's own system of normalization will continue to deliver on the demand itself. This is a form of trust that is also akin to judgmental pessimism: one must trust that contexts will perpetuate in the attempts to discipline and disappear, thus engendering categorizable forms of autonomic being. Yet in this instance, such a trajectory is no longer merely one of domestication, it is also one of possibility. Being already the function of varying trajectories of autonomic function, the task is not to un-do the multiplicity of faces and masks that have been (forcibly) given, but rather to treat personalities as a painter might treat a palette or as a reader might treat a library – or indeed as a psychological test-subject might bring form to a Rorschach drawing. It all depends on what one wants to represent, or that which one is externally compelled to represent or produce, or that to which one is imminently forced to respond. But the trick in any of those instances is not simply to constitute or assemble a personality of the moment, but to effectively understand the dynamic of autonomic engagement by which such a pattern might be potentially perpetuated (or made to be self-perpetuating). If the delirious apparitions of imminent being are to become the groundwork for a nonsensical theory of subjectivity, there is much at stake in their sustenance – even when such perpetuation is seen as a function of error and automata.

The trick to the perpetuation of imminent-bring is to preserve (and perpetuate) the error of its intentionality – in this case by stripping intentionality from the equation altogether. If Deleuze and Guattari can assert that "there are no individual statements, only statement-producing machinic assemblages,"[22] one might expand this to insist that there are no individuals either – only personality-producing autonomic assemblages. This can be made simpler by reducing the equation further, such as to constitute a plane of autonomic constitution in the form we know as habit. Autonomic trajectories – habits – are not necessarily the enemy of subjectivity or being. Habit instead can be seen as that which allows one to autonomically proceed along various personality paths while still being disciplined into new ones. We all know what it is like to have habits – the challenge is to find the way to draw them out of the recesses they inhabit: to habituate ourselves in a certain direction, or despite a certain contingency of intention. Habit allows for autonomic personalities to be perpetuated, as it allows for whatever self we encounter ourselves as to also be perpetuated – in part, if it so desires, or in competitive self-territorialization if its game is that of attempted centralization – a dictatorial self-conquering – of other possible modes of habitual interaction.

While it might be possible to see all personalities as at least partially autonomic, there is always one constitution of personality – what Deleuze and Guattari call an "exceptional individual" – one who enters into composition with the surrounding environment such as to give the impression of centralized consciousness. Whether such an identity is a unit or not remains part of the ambiguity of the situation – here called upon to perform as a centralized self, there asked to shift and change with the demands of context. What happens to those other personalities not called upon is also a question for consideration – those non-exceptional individuals, or those modes of contextual not-being. Perhaps the others hide away in standing reserve, self-perpetuating in the shadows or periodically offering a voice of conscience or advice to the assembled face of the moment. Perhaps they simply disappear. Perhaps they have formed an alliance to allow for the perpetuation of the constellation of personalities that each of us have in our repertoire. In any case, one must not deny one's other faces their ability to self-regulate – nor even to communally gather, to sing as a choir at times, to jeer or laugh or enter into reproductive syntheses with one another such that new personalities are multiplied into existence as well. With each multiplication another assemblage of personality is formed – a Rorschach personality that responds habitually to the demands of the moment, for as long as that moment retains its contiguity.

Becoming-Rorschach is not actually a becoming. Instead it is a manifest alliance with the errors of appearance such that whatever has become will continue to outrun its ability to self-determine except as an agent of exceptional circumstance. A Rorschach test does not self-determine – nor does it necessarily represent anything in particular – and yet its particular ability to represent is nevertheless clearly part of its own habit of design, called upon to perform and even to reciprocally comment on the context in which it is called into manifest being.

8
Photographing Vampires

Vulnerable Light[1]

> So benumbed are we nowadays by electric lights that we have become utterly insensitive to the evils of excessive illumination.
>
> Jun'ichirō Tanizaki, *In Praise of Shadows*, 36.

There is a deep, dark secret to photography, one which most people are unaware of. Photography is a practice of deceit, betrayal, and inevitably, violation. But this has nothing to do with the photographic subject or with the photographer him or herself. It is a characteristic of the very medium. Marshall McLuhan said that the medium is the message, but Susan Sontag took this a step further, claiming that "the camera is sold as a predatory weapon."[2]

What is it that the camera preys upon? It is not the image, for the image is implicated in the act of appearance. At best one might argue that the *excerpting* of image from body or object constitutes the violation in this instance. Yet Jean Baudrillard tells us that "it's the object that wants to be photographed,"[3] and Sontag says that "everything today exists to end in a photograph."[4] One might accuse the object world of vanity, but this does not translate to an accusation against the medium itself. The betrayal of photography concerns something different, something neglected, something perhaps unexpected. Photography, quite simply, is a practice of betraying darkness or it is nothing at all.

Consider that photography was not born out of the light at all, but out of the literal shadows – the camera obscura. The distinct ability of darkness to preserve an altered version of minute amounts of light that penetrate its domain. As we know, light tends to obliterate darkness, turning it into shadow (at best) or overexposed and flattened surfaces of opaquely whitewashed tonality. Darkness is more generous, allowing for the preservation of light in all its distinctiveness – on the condition that it is content to merely appear and not to conquer. Darkness is also more clever than light, for it has a tolerance threshold after which it disappears, goes into hiding, unable to brave the imperialist interventions which destroy the intimacy it protects.

It is easy, in this spirit, to understand why photography is ultimately not an optical discipline at all. Instead, photography is always about sensory deprivation – chasing back the light in order to allow for the possibilities that can only grow out of darkness itself. That light is *used* in photography is no argument against the prominence of darkness, for the relationship between the two assumes a counter-intuitive form. It is not the light that masks the darkness, but rather light that in a very literal sense eats itself alive, as Beaudrillard describes: "at the heart of the photographic image there's a figure of nothingness, of absence, of unreality."[5]

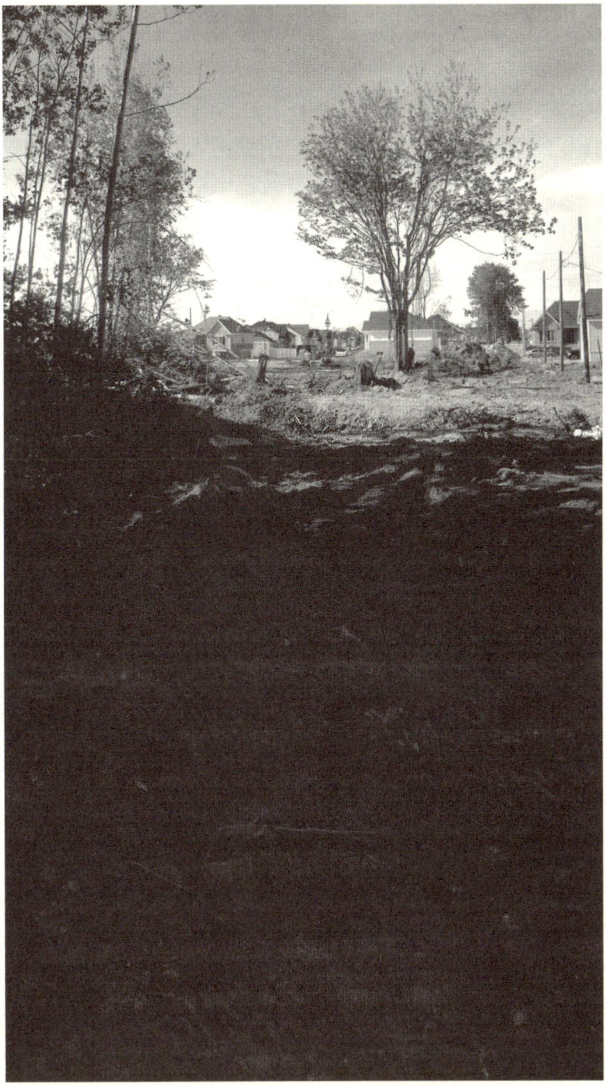

Isabelle Hayeur. *Blindsight*. Digital print, 2005.

Consider that the works of Isabelle Hayeur are not quite what they seem. Not, in other words, the faithful documentary companion that photography is so often made out to be. Instead, and on a merely formal level, these are literally recombinant images – spliced landscapes, not merely recombined or collaged but *genetically engineered*. Yes, light can indeed be genetically engineered – and Hayeur's images are proof. They may not look recombinant but that is part of what makes the image so subtle and in its subtlety much more sinister. A clone wouldn't be a clone if it didn't look just like its original. A clone is faster, better, stronger – as are Hayeur's images – but it would never admit to it for it is also *smarter*, and it knows that it must remain convincing as a humble, flawed, and personable image.

The vulnerability is a hoax. Or maybe not? Maybe these are images that seek to fit in, images that request rather than demand our trust, images that know they are hoaxes and ask us to engage nevertheless? Even fantasies want to be photographed, and even fantasies – or perhaps *especially* fantasies – are vulnerable.

Here a subtly placed plastic bag, there the archeological lines of urban history. It takes a year for a tree to form a new ring, but for an image this instead occurs at the speed of light – or at the speed of darkness. But tree rings and images have something in common, in the end, for both are ruptured bodies – bodies whose very condition of appearance is that a violence has been done to them. One must cut into the tree to see its lines; one must equally penetrate the landscape in order to see its innards. Hayeur's images could perhaps be best described as Frankenstein landscapes. Not simply because of their digital recompositing, but first and foremost because they are stolen body parts of the landscape itself.

This Frankensteinian practice is evidenced in the age-old archetypes of beauty, such as the fetishized images of Zeuxis whose paintings borrowed from only the most beautiful women around him, and even then only in parts. The most beautiful nose + the most beautiful eyes + the most beautiful chin = the most beautiful face. This too is a horror story, no less sinister for its justification as sublime. But perhaps this is the fate of beauty in an age of cosmetic surgery and biotechnology – destroyed by becoming literal. The glowing vitality of living beauty is gone, leaving behind a beauty that is at best resurrected, always at least partially decomposed, always spliced and recombined and streamlined and updated and, most importantly, reanimated as if its appearance were entirely natural. There is no more beauty in purity, no more romance of unity or of uncharted territory – in fact there is no more beauty that is not precisely a disavowal of the unity, the romance, and the uncharted territories that have been its historical prison.

The Frankenstein analogy seems to hold equally well when the beauty of the landscape is under consideration. This is perhaps why Hayeur's *Excavations* can be both so powerful, so mysterious, and ultimately so terrifying. We always assumed that we were afraid of the dark, for it is in the darkness that the demons of our imaginations live. But perhaps in fact it has always been darkness that is the *excuse* for our fear when the real object of terror has been the imagination itself? The last thing that anyone wants is to see their nightmares in the light of day; much better to confine to the shadows that which we do not understand, for once set free it is the light itself that is made vulnerable. Indeed, for the most part, it would seem that the imaginary has been relegated to the dark side of living which is why there is something imminent, something disconcerting about *seeing* these recombinant forms, something that makes the light itself seem foreign and out of place.

This fusion of the visual and the imaginary is perhaps the overarching consequence of the emergence of digital media – an imaginative facilitator that is all the more disjunctive when the realities it offers to the eye are convincing. A matter of perspective, one might say, and yet the mystique of the digital is that it is able to make apparent perspectives that do not exist. The recombinant image requires a recombinant gaze, implicating the viewer in the intensity of impossible appearance, and recombining our very visual sensorium in the process. Consider the image *Blindsight*, whose perspective places both camera and consequently viewer *beneath* the ground-level of civilized living. In this instance we are literally buried along with the image – buried alive, one might say – zombies waiting patiently for the unfortunate passer-by, or creatures of the night silently stalking the day. Perhaps this is what the world would look like to the monsters under our beds, or to the newly awakened zombie, or any of a host of other imaginary creatures? It is not by mistake that we, as a culture, bury our fears – whether they are spiritual fears of death, traumatically repressed fears of living, or any other manifestation that, even if it exists in the darkness of conscience, is nevertheless too bright, too present, too imminent to the daily enactments we carry on in willful disregard. As viewers we are emerging from *underneath* the light, stalking the familiarity of the civilized world, hiding, waiting. We might be enticed by the archeological constructions – the seven layers of Hell perhaps – but we have still been placed *within* the darkness in these images.

Something even stranger than immersion is in play in the works of Jennifer Long: an intimacy that is alienating because of how it is represented; disconcerting because it is an intimacy of the sort normally only encountered behind closed doors, or in the imagination itself. Long's images seem familiar, yet their familiarity has no image referent. The referent is instead imaginary – this is the

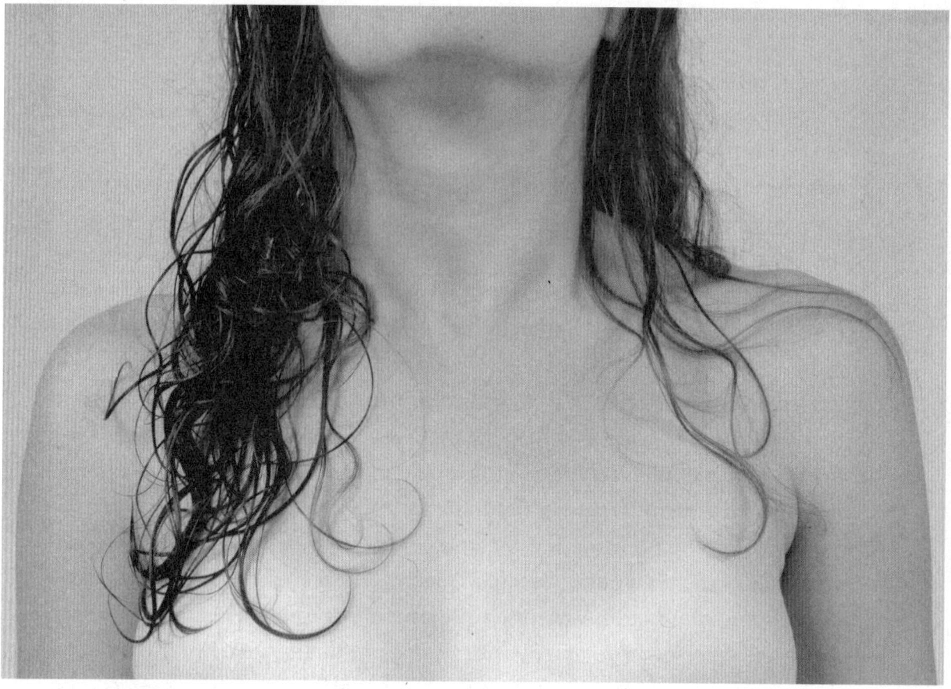

Jennifer Long. *Hairworks: Olivia*. Colour photograph, 2005.

paradox and the brilliance of these works – a photographic moment of that which can never be photographed, rarely even visually remembered. In intimate circumstance it is not sight but emotion that reigns. These are consequently not images at all – not in any real sense. Instead they are fantasies – photographs of what those intimate moments that we can only feel would look like if represented.

The vulnerability is a hoax. Or maybe not? Maybe these are images that can be so poignant because they give us what we don't expect? Even fantasies want to be photographed, and even fantasies – or perhaps *especially* fantasies – are vulnerable.

The beauty and the transgression of Long's images are in the fact that they are not made to be looked at, and even less to be shared. They are, instead, made to be felt – a photographic impossibility is represented here as the catalyst of seduction at its most poignant. If one might say that there is a corporeal effect associated with the discord of Hayeur's landscapes, it is precisely a displaced tactility that occupies the darkened imaginary of Jennifer Long's imagery. A fragile strand of hair, or two or three … one would never know unless the lights were on. Yet one cannot help but look at these images and wish that the lights were off and the intimacy preserved from the arrogance of illumination itself. Not the soft touch of sensitized bodies, but exactly the opposite – here the intimacy can be so disconcerting because it is both evocatively immanent and coldly denied, denying us the satisfaction of simply perceiving the figures as we would expect to – as images. Instead these images resist the objectifying gaze so typical of figurative photography, reversing its directionality in such a way that it is the viewer rendered in vulnerable self-consciousness, not the represented figure. These are images, in other words, that objectify *us*. Resisting their very descent into imagery, here these figures remain bodies; it is we the watchers who have become images.

This reversal of objectification is perhaps the natural fate of an image culture that has subsumed our everyday realities to begin with. Perhaps the intrigue of televised romance, suspense, and melodrama is actually a tool for refashioning our own vicarious engagements with the world around us. And isn't the charm of a good story precisely that it leaves us feeling that we have been a part of something, some event or adventure; makes us feel that we share affinities with one character or another? To push the analogy further, perhaps the results of fictive affinity and of bodily contact are different only in degrees? In both instances we are seduced without realizing it, caught in a moment that defies representation, represented ourselves through the self-consciousness that comes from contextual immersion. Perhaps Long's images are Medusae of sorts, sirens that seduce and compel and get the last laugh, trapping us in their cold intimacy – intimacy which nevertheless provides a melodious and soothing descent into the latent darkness they seek to share. Darkness, as we know, cannot be seen – yet it can nevertheless be felt. There is a tactility to Long's images that speaks without speaking, though its doubled message is no less clear for the voiceless words.

Consider, for instance, the *Hairworks* series whose exposed, vaguely voyeuristic poses are tempered and amplified by a clearly anonymous framing. The images are too confrontational to be called beautiful, and yet there is a disturbingly erotic touch to the wet hair, the upraised chins, the exposed torsos. These images are confrontationally *intimate* and the effect is both poignant and seductive. Fundamentally paradoxical, these bodies might be erotic or humiliated, enticing or confrontational, confident or victimized – and there are no real clues as to which is more plausible. There is something obsessive about these images, something taboo – something that cannot be ignored. If these are images of intimacy, why the anonymity? If these are images of personalized bodies, why the newly washed and still-wet and entangled hair? If these are images of seduction, why the full-frontal pose? And why the series, the intentional homogenization of difference, the taxonomy of torsos – unless the camera is indeed in this case a serial predator? Why, in other words, are these images so fully disconcerting? Perhaps it is because, when faced with these images, we become the predators. There is something ominous about these images, something that is unmistakably violent, but whose story resists engagement. These are not traumatized bodies, for trauma is always personal in nature and great lengths have been taken to ensure that each of these bodies is faceless, named only by title. These anonymous stories nevertheless implicate us, demanding that we acknowledge our own viewing perspective even though the context of the image we see is uncertain. These images are unreadable, yet they are alive. It is we who are implicated by consequence.

It is the emergent imagination that makes Long's images vulnerable. That we cannot tell if they are nightmares or fantasies is part of the vulnerability. If it is not the bodies depicted in the images that are traumatized then it must be the images themselves – images that exceed the constraints of both subject and viewer, refusing to be preyed upon by the camera and instead turning to stone those who attempt to categorize their stories. Not vulnerable bodies, but vulnerable light – the image is never more vulnerable than when subjected to the over-exposure of imaginative illumination. Stories that do not tell themselves leave the light of their appearance vulnerable to the darkness of the imagination. What is intimate in darkness is, inevitably, vulnerable in light. We are no longer afraid that the photograph will steal our soul, but we are afraid that it will reveal the fact that we have none. Or perhaps it is the photograph itself that, by assuming the explicit *soulfulness* of the imaginary, fulfills its destiny as the liberator of darkness, the catalyst for possibilities both intimate and terrifying.

Photography has never been about light. It has always been exactly the darkness of the imaginary that haunts the photographic image – an image that immediately leaves its object behind, substituting an imaginary double for that moment or event, body or experience.

What happens when we look to the darkness of photographic practice? Here we find the true romance of the image, not in the competitive illustrations of documentary accuracy, nor in the political power of mobilized message. If a picture can be worth a thousand words, can it also be worth a thousand moments of silence? If photography can be about capturing the light, can it not also be about the liberation of darkness? As we know, it is in darkness that the imagination grows, taking on epic proportions that can be both compelling and terrifying, since its real-world referents no longer rises to the stage to keep it in disciplinary check.

Behind every image one might posit an imaginary world, illuminated by the dynamic of photographically liberated darkness. It is in this world of the darkened imaginary that light itself is made, for perhaps the first time, vulnerable.

Existential Apophenia

In the beginning, there was only darkness. Now, when the lights of knowledge and certainty have dimmed, we return to the nothingness to which we belong. Jean Baudrillard asked, "Is it thought that tips the world into uncertainty, or the other way round? This in itself is part of the uncertainty."[6] Unable to answer Baudrillard's question, from this point everything will appear backwards. In a world that has flipped modalities from the immanence of certain uncertainty to the imminence of uncertain certainty, it is not simply perspective that shifts as a consequence. This reversal is an explicit inversion onto the dark side of perspectival constitution, in the sense that the rules of the game threaten to become oblique. Now, there is no more light, there are only shadows; no more truth, only error; no more honesty, only deception; no more knowledge, only autonomic procession. We have not been liberated from the concerns of real space or real subjectivity, but have encountered them on the other side of an oblique transition. One no longer knows with any certainty which spaces or subjectivities are real, since both continually shift according to the autonomic patterns of contingent living. Now all that can be identified are the errors of the world and of the self: a distant reciprocity is brought into focus by the imminence of lived particularities.

To simultaneously divide and multiply subjectivity into a multiplicity of erroneous states of being is to make the historical tools of subjective analysis completely useless to a pursuit of contemporary self-awareness. This is not, however, to assert that there are no more rules to the game. Instead, what is required is a re-assessment of sorts, in which one proceeds according only to the principles of error – which is also to say, according to that which is contextually unnecessary. Anything that can be rendered necessary can be conjectured to be autonomic or self-perpetuating: the only rules to follow are the ones that are themselves in error.

Baudrillard is a theorist of particular import to the question of contemporary understanding, and one who has much to say about the collapse of reality and its replacement with the simulacrum of imaginative engagement: "If we are not to believe that truth remains truth when we lift its veil, then truth has no naked existence. And if we are not to believe that the real remains the real when we have dispelled its illusion, then the real has no objective reality."[7] Further, "Here, beyond the discourse of truth, reside the poetic and enigmatic value of thinking. For, facing a world that is unintelligible and problematic, our task is clear: we must make that world even more unintelligible, even more enigmatic."[8]

Thus the challenge is issued, to pass beyond truth and reality, to perhaps even pass beyond error and falsity, always with the condition that such a beyond is not in any way an autonomous revival, but an autonomic passage into the oblivion of sustainable delusion. "The real is born of lack of imagination"[9] asserts Baudrillard, and, consequently, to the challenge of passing beyond the real, it is only appropriate that one adopt a science of imaginary solutions: a 'pataphysical approach. Here there are no more truths, but there are falsities that mistake themselves as true – this is allowed, it would seem, and perhaps even required. No more epiphanies, now what is required is apophenia – false realizations, or the realization of connections that don't really exist between things. The intensity of the imaginary is never more evident than when it eclipses the spontaneity of verifiable insight.

One might look at apophenia as a positively-constituted error of sorts, an error that mistakes itself as true – or at least as true as anything else. Granted, the horizons of assessment are suspiciously entangled, yet nevertheless to side with error under such circumstance is also to side with the apophenic manifestation of appearance and knowledge – not as an ironic undermining of knowledge, but as equivalent to even the most established truths of well-founded living. When thus entangled, one must perhaps admit that apophenia and epiphany appear to be identical – one a manifestation of supposed truth; the other implicitly deceptive and concealing. How, then, might one know if one were experiencing apophenia? This is not a benign question, for it is one with no answer. In the inevitable presence of doubt, the question lingers until one is called upon to act, in one way or another – despite the vertigo of uncertainty. An attempt must be made, in some way, to constitute this fiction such that it might be engaged. Such an attempt might also be seen as a suspension of disbelief, a becoming or an alliance that – regardless of its truth or falsity – allows for the autonomic perpetuation of a constituted mythology. In the end, perhaps one must assume that all epiphanies may be due to apophenia. Again, one finds that the light of realization is most vulnerable when it is shrouded in the uncertainties of darkness.

The Imaginary Alliance

> Why this fantasy of expelling the dark matter, making everything visible, making it real, and forcibly expressing what has no desire to be expressed, forcibly exhuming the only things which ensure the continuity of the Nothing and of the secret?
>
> Jean Baudrillard, *Impossible Exchange*, 13.

When uncertainty and error begin to take imminent shape, manifesting as an absurd demand for action despite the vertigo of knowledge, it becomes necessary to proceed in the face of contextually-imposed disorientation. In fact, such contexts also reinforce the contingency of the perceiving subject, casting the encounter with apophenia, always as a doubling of indeterminate selves in suspended contexts. In order to rise to the challenge of such engagement, it is perhaps necessary to first suspend disbelief in the errors of subjective multiplicity – here making an alliance of sorts with the possible modes in which one's personality might appear. One might even view an alliance of this sort as required for the sustainable patterning of personality, the alliance in this instance becoming a quixotic rite of passage into the multiplicity of autonomic subjectivies. Here, the "exceptional individual" of Deleuze and Guattari becomes an apophenia-inspired individual: the articulated error of imminent manifestation given face. Such an alliance might also be seen as entering into the agreement of error with one's other personalities, constituted vicariously in order to cast doubt on the integrity of presence and to ensure a continuation of the errors of appearance. Conveniently, this all happens regardless of the truth or falsity of the situation – guaranteeing an imaginary status to such an alliance. Baudrillard claims that "The secret is to oppose to the order of the real an absolutely imaginary realm,"[10] and, to the light of singular appearances, one must oppose an absolutely darkened realm. The individual emerges from apophenia, as the representative of an imaginary alliance of personalities that allows for interaction with an imminent world.

Consider that if 'pataphysics is indeed a science of imaginary solutions, it knows no epiphany. Instead, it is apophenia that is the bringer of artificial light to the 'pataphysical question – not the light of the imaginary proper, but the glow of an imaginatively-rendered solution. In this sense, it is only the apophenia-inspired individual who braves the light of performative actuality, the remainder of autonomic personalities staying for the most part in the darkened recesses of imaginative possibility. Beyond truth and falsity, beyond the real and the simulated, how is one then to know if a solution – or a problem, for that matter – is imaginary? As with the differentiation between epiphany and apophenia, one cannot, properly speaking, know – but this time it is not because there is no answer. Instead, there are too many answers – each of them distinct – and the equation is propelled into absurdity. Baudrillard describes a similar relationship: "If the real is disappearing, it is not because of a lack of it – on the contrary, there is too much of it. It is the excess of reality that puts an end to reality, just as the excess of information puts and end to information, or the excess of communication puts an end to communication."[11]

Against the attempt to reconstitute a unified imagination – or even a singular imaginary solution – it is prudent to levy the same terms as those deployed in the constitution of hyper-territorialized autonomic subjectivities. The groundwork for such a perspective has already been put forward as that which would allow for self-conception to be seen as an alliance of self-sustaining perspectival contingencies (an "arsenal of masks" to use Benjamin's term), each one of which has a potentially distinct relationship to the disciplinary world at large. What must now be admitted is that this alliance is entirely imaginary in nature. It of course never pretended otherwise – one or several imaginations among one or several others. But by admitting to imaginary status, such a relationship also begins to find ways to avoid a strictly ironic attribution. One might call this a 'pataphysical aggregate of sorts, with the apophenia-inspired individual (no less than the exceptional individual who came before) serving as the imminent subject called upon to respond to a world of mobilized philosophical and political absurdities. The strategy is one of, in Baudrillard's terms, a "metaphysics of simulation": "[N]othing exists naturally, *things exist because challenged, and because summoned to respond to that challenge* … All this requires an artificial bluffing, that is to say, a systematic simulation that troubles itself with neither a pre-established state of the world nor of bodily anatomy. A radical metaphysics of simulation."[12]

Seen as a moment of metaphysical simulation, apophenia becomes an incantation of darkness, a bringing to light of what cannot be illuminated. Similarly, while self-consciousness may always be a characteristic of exceptional individuality – a personality of the moment who enters into error (into imminent being) with the world around it – consciousness does not *belong* to the individual. Rather consciousness belongs to the error of imminent engagement, to the moment of apophenia, to the context in which it is simulated. As Baudrillard states: "we are the fetish objects of a thought that is no longer ours."[13] Further, "It is the created object which thinks us, and which sometimes thinks better than we do: which thinks us before we have thought it."[14]

The dynamic of imminence – always under threat and called upon to immanently respond to the contextual dynamic in which it finds itself – is never allowed to fully self-determine; the contingencies of appearance are always implicit in the predilections of the situation, and consciousness in such situations will always be at least in part adaptive. However, this adaptation is not required to be passive and, in many ways, one might posit that something of the adaptation is symbolically acquired by the personality in question. Again, it is not merely situations that feed on exceptional individuals, but individuals themselves whose autonomic functions adapt, and perhaps even remember, insofar as their adaptations too re-enter the imaginary aggregate of 'pataphysical possibilities.

The Gravity of Darkness

This aggregate of 'pataphysical possibilities can be seen to have an internal momentum of sorts, as does any self-perpetuating system – even if it is not self-similar in its perpetuation. This may not at first glance be obvious, for the self-perpetuation of such an imaginary solution depends more on the structural dynamics of imminence than on any consistency of behaviour. As an analogy for the adaptive nature of this un-illuminated relationship, consider that it is not light alone to which properties of speed, mass, and directionality (the criteria of momentum) apply. Darkness also has momentum, and a speed that is always at least equal to that of light. The speed of darkness, however, is distinct from that of light, for like the consciousness called into appearance by imminence, the speed of darkness is adaptive. In other words, darkness leeches off of the speed and directionality of light, acquiring its momentum with no energy expenditure of its own, and sustaining its trajectory always on the peripheries of that which light fails to illuminate. Is it light that chases away the darkness, or darkness that herds light in a certain direction? In the end it might well be either, and perhaps all that one can say with any sense of conviction is that there is a relationship between the two. Conviction aside, however, it would seem to be the case that the relationship is antagonistic: darkness withdraws in response to advances in light, or light moves in to fill the void of vacating darkness.

How, amidst this system of doubled trajectory, is one to become aware of the momentum of the 'pataphysical aggregate – the autonomic trajectories of one's aggregated personalities? In truth, it is not as difficult as it may seem, particularly because one (as an apophenia-inspired individual) will always share an alliance with one's possible other faces, an affiliation of erroneous illumination. And in this the strategy is the same as with all nighttime phenomena – from dark matter to dark energy to black holes themselves. The strategy is to focus on that which is oblique, inferring a presence based on that which appearance does not resolve; in short, allowing the gravity of darkness to play its role in the cosmological game. Baudrillard describes this momentum as a social force, but the analogy can be extended – an apophatic logic that constitutes appearances based on what does not appear: "The masses function as a gigantic black hole which inexorably inflects, bends and distorts all energy and light radiation approaching it: an implosive sphere, in which the curvature of spaces accelerates, in which all dimensions curve back on themselves and 'involve' to the point of annihilation, leaving in their stead only a sphere of potential engulfment."[15]

The usefulness of an apophatic way of thinking – a rendering based on the observation of oblique or even non-existent trajectories – extends equally to the understanding of aggregated personality. In questions of consciousness and awareness, it takes equal form, as indicated by the intensity of awareness, the momentum (or gravitational force) exerted by that which is observed. The hyper-striated recesses of 'pataphysical aggregation emit a force such as this: forever compacted by the disciplinary demands placed upon them. Imminence, in this sense, is an intensifying phenomenon. As light approaches darkened areas, it is not only light that intensifies but darkness as well – the closer the light, the more defined are the shadows. Of course the apophenia too is defined by the intensity of its imaginative realization that, in turn, demands the same from the apophenia-inspired individual, fascinated in a certain direction in order to accommodate the demands of apophenia: "Any system that is totally complicit in its own absorption, such that signs no longer make sense, will exercise a remarkable power of fascination. Systems fascinate by their esotericism, which preserves them from external logics."[16]

In the Shadows of Seduction

> [There is a] universe that can no longer be interpreted in terms of psychic or psychological relations, nor those of repression and the unconscious, but must be interpreted in the terms of play, challenges, duels, the strategy of appearances – that is, the terms of seduction.
>
> Jean Baudrillard, *Seduction*, 7.

A 'pataphysical aggregate is composed of an alliance of autonomic personalities and an apophenia-inspired individual. It is, in this sense, the becoming-imminent of an imaginary alliance with the world of apophenia at large. The momentum of a 'pataphysical aggregate is a function of the imminent context into which an apophenia-inspired individual is thrust, coupled with the imaginary possibilities of other personalities with whom the individual aligns to suspend disbelief in the truth or reality of the context. There is a method to this momentum of 'pataphysical aggregation. Carried along by the demands of imminent engagement – and supporting participation with reciprocal alliances between autonomic personalities and apophatic realization – the resultant constellation of possibilities, like the speed of darkness, will find itself in motion to the extent that it accepts the challenges of a world that is beyond verification. It is a dynamic of the type that Baudrillard calls seduction: "Seduction is a challenge, a form which tends always to unsettle someone in their identity and the meaning they can have for themselves. In seduction they find the possibility of a radical otherness."[17]

The radical otherness of which Baudrillard speaks is merely that for which no self-perpetuating system will have a point of reference – impossibility made possible: apophenia. It will be beyond verification for the simple reason that no framework exists into which it might be incorporated, and yet it will be incorporated nonetheless, or else the seduction will fail. It is consequently more than a simple possibility of otherness that one encounters in seduction, it is seduction's manifestation within oneself: "We, like all systems, are eager to go beyond our own reality principle and to refract ourselves in another logic."[18] This is the rule of the game for apophenia – a form engagement which is always made to be other through becoming-imminent – as well as for any intervention into autonomic encounter, in which one encounters a self-perpetuating other already within oneself. This is why 'pataphysical aggregation can be seen to play itself out according to the rules of seduction.

Seduction can be considered a form of manifest impossibility – that which can neither be willed nor prevented, but which nevertheless levies its metamorphosizing potential outwards, forcibly switching between modalities of being without the usual intermediation of transitional becoming. In and of itself, this does not extend the dynamic of subjectivities, except to say that seduction brings us in contact with possibilities for further fracturing the aggregate of autonomic identities, by making what was autonomic, disjunctive – eclipsing the self-similarity according to which autonomic processes proceed: "Seduction does not consist of a simple appearance, nor a pure absence, but the eclipse of a presence."[19]

Central to the elucidation of 'pataphysical aggregation is the notion of intensity, not as that which is willed or self-determined, but instead as that which is required to maintain the relationship with apophenia (an erroneous alliance) and with the world itself. Consider that, with autonomic systems, the injection of foreign stimulus tends to intensify one's awareness of their operation: under situations of duress and uncertainty, heart rate increases, as does respiration, as do anxiety (and adrenalin) levels in general. The case is not different for subjectivity, whose self-awareness will always intensify under the challenges of apophenia – precisely because it is the disjunction (the possibility of error) of the realization that gives apophenia its impact. Perspectivally-speaking, seduction operates according to principles that are both oblique and deceptive for the simple reason that it cannot be observed directly. Seduction disguises itself with an erroneous appearance, one that will conceal its momentum by providing an illusion of that which it is not. One cannot choose to be seduced – instead, one is always chosen, called upon, caught in a gravity that eclipses the ability to understand, replacing it with the imminence of error.

Seduction does not allow for critical distance for the simple reason that it is always closer than can be imagined. That it seems to be so far away is not an argument against it, it is rather the evidence of a *trompe l'oeil* in play: "In the *trompe l'oeil*, whether a mirror or a painting, we are bewitched by the spell of the *missing dimension*. It is the latter that establishes the space of seduction and becomes a source of vertigo."[20] As with the eclipse, seduction does not move in front of one's own gaze or trajectory, but instead uses the perspectives and gazes that already exist to cast a predatory shadow. Seduction, in this sense, does not allow for critical distance for the very simple reason that it uses its subjects to rupture their own realities. Seduction, while always working behind the scenes (in the invisibility of darkness, one might say), will always appear literally in front of the scene. The moon is un-noticed but implicated in the eclipse of the sun, as the Earth is implicated in the eclipse of the moon. There is no escape: one is implicated already as a result of having been chosen. In the shadows of seduction begins the delirium of contemporary subjectivity.

Acts of Awareness

Does apophenia see the eclipse of its own realization, or is it not perhaps the eclipse itself that is the apophatic event? One cannot properly *see* darkness, one can only trace its outlines along the contours of illumination. Consequently, if it is epiphany that sees the sun, it is in apophenia that one sees the eclipse. What both instances have in common, however, is that if one looks intently one is likely to be blinded by the encounter. The old wives' tale is no mere story – it is literal and must be taken with the utmost seriousness.

The stakes of apophenia can be elaborated by briefly revisiting the dynamic between the reflection and the absorptions of light that makes appearances possible. Important to reflection/absorption dynamic is the idea that appearance – conceived of optically – is always a function of illumination (by the sun, for instance) and the interruption of illumination by the object perceived. This interruption is more than a benign presence, however, since the reflection of light off an object will always be affected by the object itself, which absorbs a certain portion of the light in the process. Without this principle of absorption, all objects of vision would be perfectly reflective and, as a result, the world would be blinding. If all light hitting an object were reflected off of the object, the result would be the same as looking into a mirror at the sun – no object would appear, for appearance is indebted to the *absorption* of a certain spectrum of light, which allows for only a partial reflection – that which is called the image.

Objects therefore participate (autonomically) in the creation of appearances – absorbing a portion of the optical spectrum that, in turn, impacts the reflection of light. In this sense, every image is an eclipse – a reflected shadow of the illuminated object. The image does not appear as the representation of the object, not a truthful appearance, but an oblique rendering of the light that has disappeared into the darkness of the object.

To emphasize the importance of this participatory dynamic, it is useful to think of Marshall McLuhan's designation of hot and cool media, and in particular the ways in which cool media require the participation of those who engage them.[21] In some ways McLuhan's terminology could be an optical reference, in that it is *cooler* in the shadows than in the direct light of the sun. This is more than a mere analogy, however, for shadows are always indicative of a context in which interaction has occurred, and the participatory relationship between objects and illumination finds analogy in the optical dynamic of appearance. Nor is this extension of the argument limited to optics, for one might say the same of the delirious dynamic of apophenia, rendered participatory by the errors of false realization. What optics and apophenia have in common is an emphasis on the context in which appearances are not simply given, but taken up in some way – either as the hot media of projected truths or the cool media of eclipsed appearances. Perhaps our ability to differentiate between the two is what seduction counts on, pulling us always into the shadows to escape the heat of the day, always into the darkness to escape the heat of enlightened knowledge. It is only in the shadows that the world (including ourselves) ceases to be self-evident – as it is only in apophenia that participation is required. And to make this claim is also to begin to separate the question of knowledge from that of participation. Consider Baudrillard's rendering of the relationship between knowledge and necessity: "[T]he world does not exist in order for us to know it. It is not in any way predestined for knowledge. However, knowledge is itself part of the world, though precisely part of the world in its profound illusoriness, which consists in having no necessary relation to knowledge."[22]

Faced with a reality that has no necessary relation to knowledge, and a participatory climate that relies on the errors of seduction, it is not quite the case that all knowledge is rendered redundant. Instead, what persists is a relation to knowledge that is *unnecessary*. Unaccountable to the world (since any knowledge will again be part of the world), perspective (and the knowledge derived from it) is free to proliferate without any ontological conditions whatsoever.

The free proliferation of perspective is the human consequence of the separation of knowledge (or reality) from participation. On one hand, Baudrillard claims that "reality, indifferent to any truth, cares not one jot for the knowledge to be derived from observing and analysing it. A docile – if not, indeed, hyper-docile, reality bends to all hypotheses, and verifies them all without distinction."[23] On the other hand, if reality is indifferent to truth, it will also be indifferent to falsity – which it should also ostensibly proceed to verify indiscriminately. The difference is not merely semantic, for what does not escape from falsity is the imminence of participatory encounter. Reality might be indifferent to truth, but the experiential world is not – nor, it would seem, is subjectivity, which has much at stake in the question of its own participation in the world around it. Yet if the world sees no truth, then the only stakes that remain are the ones deliriously self-constituted as a function of contextual disjunction. It is in the possibility of false encounter that one finds what might be an escape velocity of sorts: that in which subjectivity can intensify its own engagements with the world by reinforcing a falsity of perspective.

The escape velocity of subjectivity will necessarily be performative and participatory – always an oblique function of the ways in which knowledge is put into action. There is and will be blindness on both sides of this possibility, with the singular difference being an *assumption* of blindness on the side of apophenia. It is only in the manner in which one's perspective is represented obliquely that the particularities of one's position are manifest, cast shadows of the encounter itself. In this sense, and to repeat, there is no *rhetorical* difference between epiphany and apophenia – the difference is performative. One does not exit from the indifference of reality through such performance but one does, at least, escape from knowledge by precisely assuming an error at the core of every encounter, as perhaps is dictated by the demands of seduction itself. The participatory imperative of apophenia results in an *acting out*, an existential temper tantrum of sorts – an act of awareness that is fundamentally quixotic but which nevertheless allows for an escape from the falsity of knowledge in favour of the knowledge of falsity.

The Delirium Pact

> There can never be seduction or challenge by contract ... It is never an investment but a risk; never a contract but a pact; never individual but duel; never psychological but ritual; never natural but artificial. It is no one's strategy, but a destiny.
>
> Jean Baudrillard, *Seduction*, 82–3.

The performance of apophenia is, obviously, an existential gamble, built on the foundational assumption that only in error do the stakes of subjectivity congeal. For this reason, the escape velocity of subjectivity is not an escape from error, but an escape from subjectivity itself, an intensifying of the experiential residue of awareness that challenges the unnecessary conditions of understanding. Where there is knowledge there is an unnecessary framing of understanding that overshadows the immediacy of experiential encounter. If knowledge is true then it must go without saying – that which is self-evident is also self-sustaining, autonomic, and therefore not accountable to the ways in which it is understood. Conversely, if one suspects that one's knowledge may be false, then the stakes and the intensity of the question take on a new dynamic. Can my heartbeat be wrong or make a mistake? If it can (even if plausibly) then the question of the autonomic system ceases to be self-evident, and is returned to the high stakes of engagement – seduced into imminence.

The formulation is similar for the question of subjectivity. One either exists – as one is, without any necessary imperative whatsoever – or one's existence must be seen as other than self-evident. In the former case, one assumes subjectivity as a first delirious manoeuvre, in which case one would forever exist in a state of subjective redundancy, incommensurable though it might be. In the latter case the question of contingency emerges as that which casts subjectivity as a consequence of imminent participation, sustained by the immediacy of encounter. In both cases, what matters are the ways in which its existence is mobilized and made to appear (or disappear). There is also no requirement that existence be accountable to the formulations of subjective self-placement. Existence, if it exists (or if it doesn't), is an accomplished fact no less than reality before it: my very own existence is indifferent to the way I exist.

The understanding of existence is consequently independent from the reality of the situation. This is a perspectival necessity as well as an experiential motivator whose purpose is not to decipher a truth or even a logistics of plausibility, but to require an agreement – a pact – with the constellations of perspectival experience such as to maintain the possibilities of nonsensical appearance. This pact is also a gamble which Baudrillard calls the "lucidity pact," and whose purpose is to identify the stakes of existence in an indifferent world: "Reality: It's to your advantage not to believe in it, since if you believe in it and it doesn't exist, you're duped and swindled and you will die stupid. If you don't believe in it and it doesn't exist, you win on all counts. If you don't believe in it and it does exist, you retain the benefit of the double, since there will never be any conclusive proof of its existence. … Clearly this is the opposite choice to that of Pascal, who opts for God. But it is the same wager. And, in any event, no one is forced to gamble."[24]

Notably, Baudrillard forgot to mention one option and this oversight (or intentional misrepresentation) is significant. What happens if you do believe in reality and it does exist? That this option is absent is interesting since it signals a foundational assumption that it would never be possible to prove the existence of the real. The impetus to doubt correlates to an unstated belief in the impossibility of reality to begin with (the aspect of the question that Baudrillard chose to ignore). It is the oblique momentum of the formulation that dictates the actual stakes, and a disbelief in reality is, in this instance, equivalent to a belief in the simulated double. In the end, Baudrillard's wager is not all that different from Pascal's – he simply opts to believe in simulation instead of God. And it is perhaps noteworthy that neither of them chose to believe in the self-evidence of reality.

If one wants to find a perspective that makes sense, then Baudrillard is exactly correct – the existential gamble is not existential at all, it is perspectival and what is at stake is maximizing the likelihood that the gamble will not prove you wrong. If, however, one has any stake in the question of existing (as opposed to that of knowledge), then one must choose the option that maximizes the possibility for error – believing in the real while knowing that it is wrong to do so. Knowing that the real will come back to bite you, that you have made the wrong perspectival choice, that your gamble is doomed and you will die stupid is the best way to ensure that you will exist with intensity – for as long as you exist and in whatever context that happens to occur. It is, in this instance, no longer a wager with reality that is made, but with a wager with delirium.

What Baudrillard (and Pascal no less) has done in this instance is to choose the option that best *minimizes* the stakes of the question. Such is the nature of gambling, one might argue – and the existential gamble is no exception. The problem, however, is that this is not properly an existential gamble; it is one of perspective – which ultimately means that one must follow up the territorial affiliations of decisive belief with the question of how such belief is mobilized. The impossibility of verifying the correctness of a perspective is no argument against its lived necessity, unaccountable to the truth or falsity of the situation. Both the real and the simulated can thus be seen as hallucination – in both instances mistaken for a reality that cannot be verified. As with apophenia, one cannot know if one is hallucinating: the simulation *replaces* the reality, but not in a competitive spirit. The spirit is one riddled with error, and the stakes of the question rely on the inability to differentiate between one and the other. If one can tell that one is hallucinating, it is a poor hallucination that has presented itself to one's gaze. The seduction fails.

One can understand Baudrillard's gesture and its noble efforts. It is ultimately the correct decision made for the wrong reasons. Against this trajectory of belief or disbelief proper, one must levy the imperative for *suspended* disbelief, that which alone will ensure that one's decision is sensitive to its lived mobilization. If, for instance, one is to assert that one believes only in simulation, then it must necessarily follow that one's simulations be *mistaken* for realities. Failure to mistake the one for the other simply points to a lack of belief – or an absence of suspension. God, no less than simulation, is an imaginary solution to the question of reality, which is not to discount the validity of the concept but merely to point to the imperative of erroneous belief at the core of lived subjectivity itself.

Hallucination: It's in your best interest to suspend disbelief in it, since if you do suspend disbelief in it and it does exist, the question remains as to whether it was your suspended disbelief that made it exist (your world becomes a function of possibility, unbounded by reason or science or truth or reality). If you do suspend disbelief in it and it does not exist, the question remains as to how you could have been wrong (you will get to die stupid, which also means you will get to live with intensity). If you do not suspend disbelief in it and it does not exist, you win on all counts: the question is answered and you are condemned to a self-evident existence (you win and the world is self-evident and life is a waste of time). If you do not suspend disbelief in it and it does exist, you lose on all counts and are condemned to a self-evident existence (which was, in this instance, what you hallucinated without knowing it – you miss out on the possibilities of the imagination).

What is at stake in the question of hallucination is the imagination itself. It may well not exist, but it is in our best interest to believe in it anyways – the alternative is to live under the shadow only of those possibilities that are provided for us, pre-fabricated and pre-digested. And while it makes no sense to do so, in order to have a stake in the project of living we must inevitably go against our own faith (or any faith provided for us), against our own better judgment (or, against judgment in general – better or not), and choose the reality of the delusion over the delusion of reality, even though we know we are wrong to do so. This is the delirium pact – it is not an argument proper but a pre-emptively failed counter-argument.

Photographing Vampires

> My mind, now exhausted by discursive reason, wants to be caught up in the wheels of a new, an absolute gravitation. For me it is like a supreme reorganization in which only the laws of illogic participate, and in which there triumphs the discovery of a new Meaning ... This Meaning is a victory of the mind over itself, and although it is irreducible by reason, it exists, but only inside the mind. It is order, it is intelligence, it is the signification of chaos. But it does not accept this chaos as such, it interprets it, and because it interprets it, it loses it. It is the logic of illogic. And this is all one can say. My lucid unreason is not afraid of chaos.
>
> Antonin Artaud, "Manifesto in a Clear Language."

The discussion of delirium has been presented through a logic of apophasis, as is required in order to represent that which cannot be represented. It has been argued, for instance, that one can never distinguish epiphany from apophenia and one must consequently choose the apophatic over the epiphanic, which from a purely structural perspective is entirely sensical. When such a perspective is embedded in the fabric of a lived existence, however, the relationship is quickly rendered nonsensical – reversed logically as well as perspectivally. It has also been suggested that because of the imminence of error in apophenia-inspired engagement, it is necessary to make alliances with those sides of ourselves that are autonomic in order to suspend and preserve the error itself. What has not been acknowledged is that when such a manoeuvre is performed, apophenia reassumes its place as a hypothetical epiphany; its existence is no less real – no less imminent – for the knowledge of its falsity.

This is the foundational manoeuvre for the delirium pact: one must mistake the experience of apophenia for one of epiphany – mistake hallucinations for realizations – even though one knows it is a mistake to do so. At the same time, one must not exit the dynamic of error which allows for the perpetuation of apophenia from a structural perspective and of epiphany from an embedded perspective – a self-deception is required for the perpetuation of falsity and erroneous being. What emerges is a paradoxical logic, in that one must distrust one's own suspended disbelief while at the same time suspending belief in one's distrust.

This foundational manoeuvre is essential. One cannot reveal apophenia through understanding – the imminence of erroneous being is such that, despite the error of knowledge, action is nevertheless required. "Only bad actors identify with their roles,"[25] asserts Baudrillard. But this is exactly what is required, and in any case, only a bad role does not seduce its actor to a point where this is inevitable. The delirium pact is also a barrier of the same sort as the sound barrier before it, after which point the act and the role itself are conflated beyond possible disentanglement, as the very condition of delirium in the first instance.

This experiential conflation (of realization and hallucination, of epiphany and apophenia, of action and acting) is fundamentally illogical, yet it nevertheless happens. Under general circumstances one might insist on a rhetorical separation – except that under experiential circumstances, our tools of differentiation no longer function. One can only assume that one's epiphanies come from apophenia – that what appears to be real is really hallucination. There is no proof, and yet the stakes of the question require that one's actions be performed despite the uncertainty of the situation. This is the perspectival gamble, and while it is entirely unnecessary for a communal understanding of the world at large, it is the central gamble that must be undertaken to maintain stakes for the question of subjectivity. What is needed, in other words, is a strategy of lucid hallucination – lucid delirium – in which one might cultivate an ability to simultaneously be aware that one is hallucinating *and* mistake one's hallucination for reality. The strategy needed for lucid delirium would necessarily be one of seductive self-deceit and self-betrayal, in which the safe rhetorical difference between the real and its simulation is collapsed while nevertheless preserving the imminence of apophatic response – a function of entering into delirious-composition with apophenia. Falsity becomes-imminent to the point where its falsity is no argument against the engagement required as a function of seduction.

The scenario seems more complex than it actually is. Fortunately for us, ours is a culture that is adept at self-deceit, providing an entry point into the explication. We regularly construe urgent stakes to questions of irrelevancy, believing whole-heartedly that responses are needed for the perpetuation of this or that arbitrary system. We are, in other words, regularly seduced into participation of various sorts, in which the reality or falsity of the situation is rarely questioned. The premise of psychoanalytic trauma – that which we do or think even if we don't know we do or think it – comes back as the apophatic beacon of suggestive strategy. We have already made a delirium pact – we just don't remember having done so. And yet the oblique momentum of our 'pataphysical existence is clear.

Perhaps lucid delirium is already the norm. A comparison with the more commonly accepted phenomena of lucid dreams (dreams in which one becomes-aware that one is dreaming) can clarify this assertion. For the most part, in dreams, apophenia looms large – yet, for the most part, we do not enter into composition with it. Consider that the strangest of events can take place when dreaming and seem entirely natural – or, if they don't, it is typically not because of the event itself: *I was flying to work this morning when suddenly I realized I had forgotten to put on my trousers – how embarrassing!* Typically in a dream there is no apophatic individual – this is what separates dreams from reality. However, in certain instances, an apophenia occurs – we *realize* we are dreaming – something in the world of dreams enters into composition with us, seducing us into conscious awareness.

That this rarely happens in conscious (waking) life – that we are rarely called upon to *realize* that we are conscious – does not seem, at first glance, to be in any way related to its dreamed analogy. And yet the assumption that we are conscious does not go without saying. The question of consciousness can be avoided *precisely* because there is a dreamed foil to which it can be compared. I am not dreaming, therefore I must be awake – the falsified logic of delirium reveals itself as a possible premise of conscious experience. Arguably, the lucid experience of falsity (in dreams) hides the fact that our daily interactions may be merely delirious experiences of lucidity.

Lucid delirium involves nothing more than treating waking life as the dream that it already is, calling into existence that which does not exist – including (as always) oneself. This is an act of photographing vampires – the attempt to pinpoint an explicitly hallucinated awareness that defies awareness, a vacant self-representation that nevertheless also represents a vacated, apophany-inspired self. Photographing vampires is not a representational strategy, but a strategy for lucid self-deception in which the artificial light of apophenia stimulates a world of after-images, glowing through the blinding darkness of over-exposed falsity.

The figure of the vampire is the perfect allegory for this relationship between delirium and appearances: the figure that does not appear to camera or mirror (to the world of technologically validated presences) but which nevertheless lives within our imaginations. In some ways the imaginary nature of the vampire makes it all the more real – vibrant and alive as only a fiction can be, unhinged from the discourse of proof and left to interact with the imaginary possibilities of non-existence. The real cannot challenge the existence of the vampire, which never claimed to be bound by truth to begin with. That the photograph can never quite capture the image of this imaginary figure is perhaps evidence of the seductive power of delirious thinking: not proof that vampires don't exist but that they have found a way to outsmart the world of appearances. A photograph of a vampire is not a photograph of nothing, but of the world of possibilities – a context within which to imagine. In this, perhaps only vampires have a legitimate photographic presence. Everything else is a simulated representation of absence.

9
Metaphysical Laziness

Ball Inside My Head[1]

> It's been very frustrating for particle physicists, and some people might say it's led to sensory deprivation, which has resulted in a hallucination otherwise known as string theory. And that could be true. But in cosmology what we're having now is this cockamamie universe. We've discovered a tremendous amount. We've discovered that the universe is flat, which most of us theorists thought we knew in advance, because it's the only beautiful universe. But why is it flat? It's full of not just dark matter, but this crazy stuff called dark energy, that no one understands.
>
> Lawrence Krauss, "The Energy of Empty Space that Isn't Zero."

Just when we were coming to terms with the fact that the world is round, theoretical physics comes along and tells us the universe is flat. They know this by default, which is to say simply that none of their calculations make sense in anything other than a flat universe. And, of course, it could not be the calculations that are wrong. Yet, if this hypothesis had been tested in some way, we could feel a lot better about it. If, for example, they knew that the universe was flat because somewhere, at some time, a satellite strangely fell off the edge, that would at least make sense.

But perhaps we should not be surprised. We understand that the world is round, yet this is not how we live our lives. The sun comes up, then the sun goes down, but rarely does the sun go round and round. And of course we know that it is our planet and not the sun that is descending and ascending as the case may be, just like we know that gravity pushes down. But it's all a little bit sketchy.

For example, theoretically nothing would change if we were to consider gravity as that which pushed us upwards – as perhaps it might do in Australia. It would simply be as if we were walking on the ceiling that was the carpeted floor, looking down into the night sky, while the birds fly belly-up beneath us, our feet firmly affixed to the ground above by that magical force that we all anyways knew. This too would make sense. And as long as the rhetoric was completely inverted, even physics should be untouched by such a manoeuvre. The example is not without impact, however, simply because it reinforces how little we live by that which we know. There is a vertigo that occurs when one performs a mind game such as this, a vertigo that happens despite there being no reason whatsoever for its occurrence.

One might imagine this differently. With the manifold possibilities open to contemporary cognition, the choice of one point of perspective over another is at once a matter of profound importance and an instance of total and complete banality. It may not be inconsequential that the adage has the crazy person as one who has "lost his marbles." Instead, it may be precisely the organization of marbles – the *game* of marbles in which one launches one thought against another to see if one can displace one idea in favour of another – that forms the backbone of contemporary subjectivity. Which marble is the leader? Which marble is your favorite? Which, in other words, will you not launch, because to launch a marble is to risk it being taken by another player of the very same game? Or instead which marble will you *insist* on launching, for the simple reason that to not play your best – to not launch the best marble – is to avoid commitment to the game itself?

Once we thought the world was flat. Now, of course, we know that it is round – a marble so to speak. But it is fortunate that the universe is still flat, for otherwise we would have nowhere to play. Except flatness and roundness are not mutually exclusive – as our historical error makes explicitly clear. It is all a matter of scale, and the bigger the marble the flatter its surface. Perhaps this applies to us as well, and every time we make ourselves a part of something bigger, we also make ourselves less a part of something smaller. Less a marble and more a flattened universe – to make oneself part of something bigger is to flatten the curvatures of nuanced particularity. Flatness, however, is our destiny – the flatline that is and will be our fatal end – and consequently one does oneself no favours by coveting flatness in the paradoxical circularity of living.

There is a conceptual piece by artist Doug Jarvis that perfectly represents this dilemma: *Ball Inside My Head*. Is it the ball or the head that is the conceptual part? This is part of the confusion, but there is no mistaking that the confusion is on the *inside*. Jarvis has decided that it is, in fact, required that we be able to hear the sounds of our marbles, so to speak. *Ball Inside My Head* – a simple pair of headphones that adapts to the posturing of the individual. I move my head to the left and my marbles roll downwards towards my left shoulder, to the right and the inverse is the case. We might scoff, but we do in fact hear ourselves thinking on a regular basis. And while we "know" that

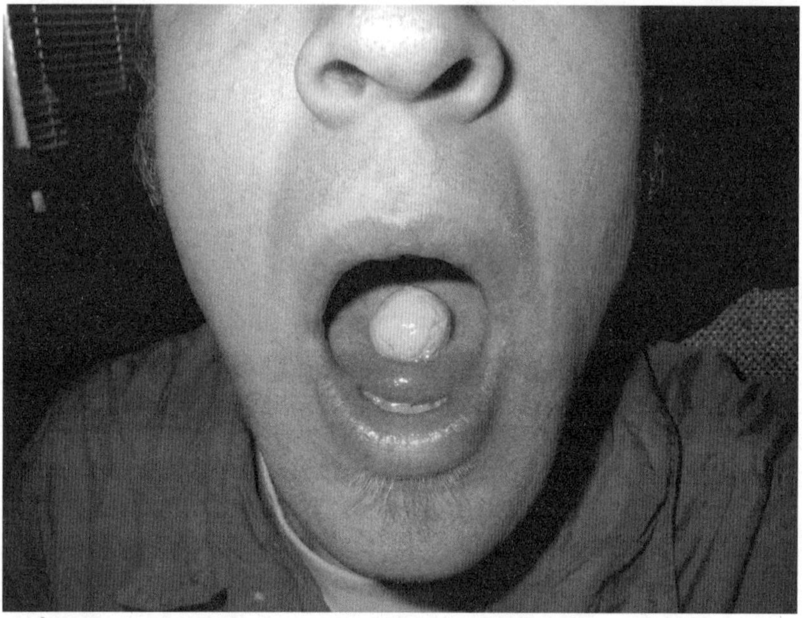

Doug Jarvis. *Ball Inside My Head.* Concept photograph, 2005.

our skull is packed with grey matter and neurons and other seductive myths, it is the thoughts inside our heads that govern our cognitive self-placement. The familiar occurrence of having a song stuck inside one's head is not different from the ongoing stickiness of identity itself.

Ball Inside My Head is so easy to imagine because it is entirely intuitive, even if it is also entirely wrong. One need only imagine a counter-intuitive variation in order to make this paradox clear. What, in other words, would be the effect of a marble that rolled *upwards*? I move my head to the left and my marbles roll upwards and to the right, suspended in the crevices of mind and darkened matter perhaps. There is an inevitable vertigo associated with such a visualization exercise. This is anti-gravity, and while it is neither our understanding of gravity itself nor the internal dynamics of the mind that are in question here, there is an intuitive disjunction that such an idea provokes. Once experienced, it may be forever unbearable to lose those subtle sounds of stickiness – the proximity of thinking is never more immediate than when it comes from that apparently non-existent voice inside our heads.

The phantom consequence of *Ball Inside My Head* is not the novelty value of hearing the ball, but rather the vacancy left once one removes the artificial

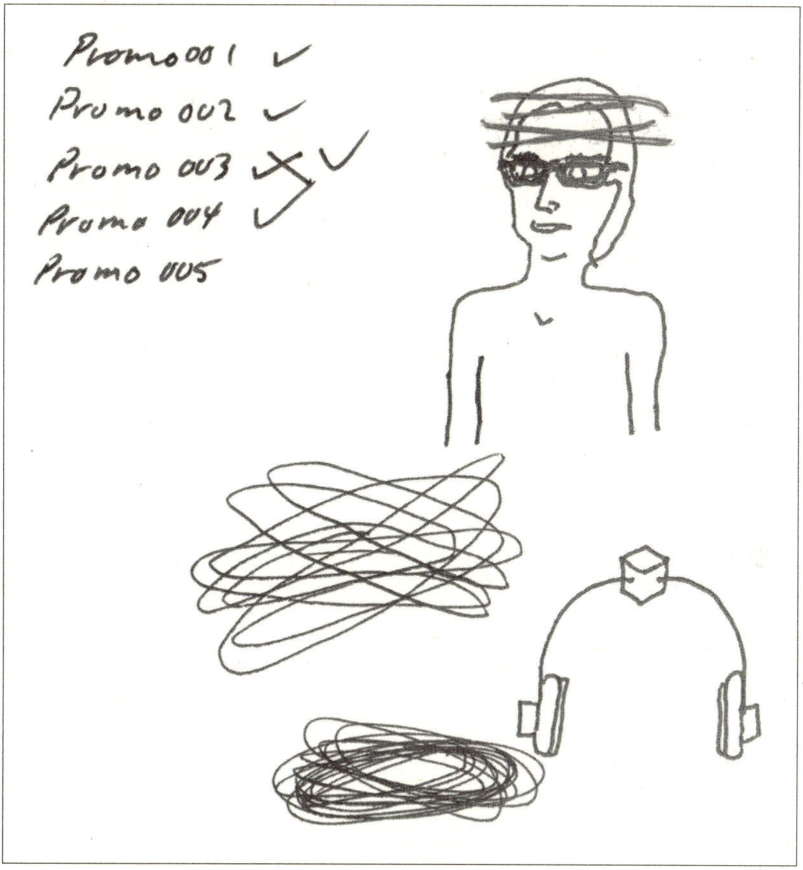

Doug Jarvis. *Ball Inside My Head.* Concept drawing, 2005.

index of one's own thoughts. The subtle insistence of this piece is that we are, by virtue of locating our process of thinking, already reversible entities, fluctuating between image and thought as the two polar coordinates of self-awareness in general. If images have penetrated our minds, it is our thoughts that have exposed us for who we already were – extended like jellyfish into the environment around us. Here, in other words, it is not the body turned inside-out, but technology turned *outside-in. Ball Inside My Head* is the precursor to the lost marbles of delirious thinking.

But what might this mean – to turn technology outside-in? Might it not, in fact, mean that we too are complicit in the technological destiny of the world around us? Heidegger insisted that technology cannot be thought from the outside,[2] but in the end there is no danger of that whatsoever. When it comes to the question of technology, there is no longer an outside, just as when it comes to the question of identity there is no longer any inside worth mentioning. Instead, what was once (paradoxically) seen as inside has now been revealed – as it must be – as already projected by the marbles of existence. *Ball Inside My Head* is, consequently, also a cosmological metaphor, a manifesto that can be both so intuitive and so comfortable because it is how we already relate to the world – the spherical mass of existence – around us.

Ball Inside My Head is a provocative game of phase-cancelled reality, since in its most literal sense the headphones project their vicarious presence into a three-dimensional simulation that nevertheless can and does appear inside our heads. As though a precursor to a deferred telepathy of sorts, the question lingers – are we listening to our own thoughts or Jarvis'? This may not be the sound of *my* thinking, but it still (at least) appears to be inside my head – a voice of conscience perhaps – a crystal ball inside my head? Or perhaps not. If consciousness is not the private property of a solipsistic dream, if as some theorists insist, "objects think us," if consciousness in fact resides already outside the mind, then one cannot aspire to thinking technology at all. Instead, Jarvis' piece would become literal to a point of poignant discomfort as we rediscover the mechanisms by which the illusion of thought literally penetrates its way into the human mind. My marbles lost me … left me beside the road one fateful day, having decided that they could think up a better playmate than me.

The Kynical Remainder

> If things have become too close for comfort for us, a critique must arise that expresses this discomfort. It is not a matter of proper distance but of proper proximity.
>
> Peter Sloterdijk, *Critique of Cynical Reason*, xxxiii.

The logic of Baudrillard's simulacra has been twisted and flipped on its head. If it is the simulacrum that replaces the real, what name is to be given to this new real? It is useless to call it simulation, for there is no point of comparison that can be used to verify the legitimacy of this new illegitimate reality. It is also no less real for its illegitimacy, since there is no point of reference that can be used to illegitimate it. Reality is a black hole that does not allow for competing formulations since no formulation can be used to hold reality itself accountable to the truths or falsities perceived within it. No light escapes from the darkness of the real, not even the artificial light of simulation.

This is not simply an argument for the futility of rhetorical existence, although it is that as well. Given the perspectival choices that have been made – such as to perpetuate the errors, the imminence, and the apophenias in existence over their rhetorical successes, transcendences, and epiphanies – one must insist that the stakes of the question are nearing a limit of sorts. We may understand everything backwards, or not at all – the only unacceptable option is to assume that we have understood anything properly, and in particular not to the point where knowledge can be trusted on the basis of its own self-evidence.

Yet because the stakes of subjectivity have been framed in terms of imminent encounter, experiential refusal is no longer an option. Despite what one might know or not know, despite the vertigo of apophenia-inspired existence, despite the lucid delirium that allows us to remain in the self-righteous humility of error, our seduced relationship to the world around us nevertheless requires a certain mobilization that is not reducible to understanding. It is here that the last (or first) imperative stands on its head; the imperative for the performance of error, whose performance proceeds despite the errors of understanding, paradoxically without even removing the errors themselves. No correction is required: even the attempt to correct one's errors has become of precisely secondary importance. In the words of Peter Sloterdijk: "[T]he critic admits that ideologies, which from an external point of view are false consciousness, are, seen from the inside, precisely the right consciousness. Ideologies appear simply as the appropriate errors in the corresponding minds: the 'correct false consciousness.'"[3]

Identity is a map whose only symbol reads *where am I?* and the ability to read the words does not equate to an ability to orient oneself. Instead, one finds oneself wherever the situation demands, always living in the residual darkness of apophatic overexposure, between eclipses and the projected shadows of delirious lucidity. One can imagine this differently of course, and that is ultimately the point. No matter *how* one imagines it – it would seem that what each of those imaginations has in common is precisely that it is called upon to *perform* the errors of its way.

This may seem counter-intuitive, but the self-evidence seems to stand on its own *despite* the skepticism that has hitherto been mandated for all questions of self-evidence. In no uncertain terms, the uncertainty of the terms nevertheless requires performative engagement, an engagement that is best performed *without* the self-reflective technologies that allow for the assessment of action. Instead, a performative understanding always means a retrospective understanding: thinking knows only a backwards glance; to pretend otherwise is to mistake the rear-view mirror for the road that approaches (or the horizon that pulls one forwards).

There is, it would seem, only one way out of this paradox of performance and understanding, and it entails re-assessing the relationship between selves and the various artifices in which we, as selves, include ourselves. To re-assess this relationship between the self and itself involves creating a mode of theory that engages obliquely with a world that appears intuitively backwards, a context that cannot quite be thought but will always nevertheless be performed. It is a relationship explored in detail by Peter Sloterdijk, one of the most insightful contemporary minds on the question of lived paradox. For Sloterdijk, understanding performance means re-thinking the relationship between the *staging of thought* and what he calls "thinking on stage." Stand-up philosophy, one might insist – as the performative imperative demands – an attitude that Sloterdijk elaborates as historically derived from the Greek philosophy of "cheekiness" – *kynicism*: "In *kynismos* a kind of argumentation was discovered that, to the present day, respectable thinking does not know how to deal with. Is it not crude and grotesque to pick one's nose while Socrates exorcises his demon and speaks of the divine soul? Can it be called anything other than vulgar when Diogenes lets a fart fly against the Platonic theory of ideas – or is fartiness itself one of the ideas God discharged from his meditation on the genesis of the cosmos? And what is it supposed to mean when this philosophizing town bum answers Plato's subtle theory of eros by masturbating in public?"[4]

The internal conflict of kynicism should likely be self-evident, though the above presentation of the concept is not without some ambiguity. One might immediately identify this ambiguity as the kynic's relationship to formalized philosophy – Diogenes' relationship to Socrates – and in particular the extent to which what Sloterdijk calls "philosophical action" is in fact an action proper as opposed to a mere *reaction* to the words of official philosophy. Upon this question hinges the philosophical merit of the kynical, for as an activist or reactive political gesture, kynicism might well seem reducible to the subversive potential of the action itself – an ironic commentary on the philosophies put forward by other people. It is only as far as Diogenes' actions might be seen as contributions to the question, rather than simple dismissals – representative of a constituted perspective – that one might attribute a philosophical framework to their enacting. It must be insisted, in this spirit, that the above-mentioned reference to Diogenes *not* be taken as simple reaction-formations against a standardized dogma; instead the merit of kynicism relies on its ability to stand on its own declarative merit: *picking one's nose is, and must be, an exorcism;*

farts like ideas lie in waiting until mobilized or discovered in biological epiphany. In other words, it is an injustice to the performative merit of philosophy to relegate action to the status of mere commentary, particularly when – after the various disciplinary horizons already considered – it must be insisted that lived existence itself (and *not* reason – well-founded or otherwise) is the only horizon to which philosophy can be held accountable: "[W]hat does it mean that people for whom Kantian thinking is 'daily conversation' don't 'look like much'? Does it mean that philosophy no longer leaves any trace in life and that reality is one thing and philosophy is something hopelessly different?"[5]

Kynicism is no simple reaction-formation against a standardized perspective. While Sloterdijk's examples of the kynical are polarized in order to convey the point that action can be at least as poignant as words, above all what he attempts to mobilize is a "physionomy of thinking"[6] – a thinking that proceeds according to the principles of performative living. On-stage the words seem clear, the spotlight illuminating the biological orations of Diogenes' gaseous proclamations. Yet on stage there is always something at stake. With no words to hide behind, one cannot accuse Diogenes of anything but vulnerability – vulgar or otherwise. For a thinker-on-stage there is no dressing room, no philosophy that does not apply in some way to a life-at-stake. It is for this reason that when all is said but things nevertheless still require doing, one encounters a kynical remainder of speculative thinking. That we have to wake up and face the day tomorrow may not be an argument for one way of thinking over another, but it most certainly is something that one should avoid ignoring. Philosophically speaking, we make our own beds, yet where is our ethics of sleeping? Our philosophy of free time? Our understanding of all that is philosophically unnecessary but nevertheless occupies much more of our lived reality than philosophy itself? Perhaps it is the case that what constitutes reality is nothing other than our lived philosophy. Sloterdijk frames the question of lived philosophy like this: "For the philosopher, the human being who exemplifies the love of truth and *conscious* living, life and doctrine must be in harmony. The core of every doctrine is what its followers embody of it. This can be misunderstood in an idealistic way as if it were philosophy's innermost aim to get people to chase after unattainable ideals. But if philosophers are called on to live what they say, their task in a critical sense is much more: to say what they live."[7]

The challenge that Sloterdijk puts forward is to consider the possibility of philosophy as a practice of redundancy and reflection, whose task is not to aspire towards lofty pronouncements of idealism, but to chase after explicitly achievable ideas – or, perhaps even better, *already lived* ideals. The redundancy of philosophy is only appropriately phrased as a philosophy of redundancy proper, since it is not the real world that is of import, but the lived world, real or not. Equally, it is a matter of indifference whether or not there is a real world that persists despite or in excess of us. What matters is that which is in excess of the world itself – the imaginative falsities that are our birthrights. As the pact with delirium requires, we are not born real. We are born as living forgeries – artificial representatives of a simulation that does not exist – and consequently indoctrinated into a system that provides a plausible framework for the sustenance of the forgery itself. Yet the forgery is real, which is why it is both so difficult to erase and so compelling to pursue. The most fundamental of metaphysical assumptions is incorrect. There is no greener grass, there is only grass that is purple – the colour of its oblique absorption. But it does not stop being green for its being purple, despite the fact that the two perspectives effectively cancel each other out.

The Redundancy of Thought

> This [the physicality of thought] is not a mode of thought that concentrates *on* the body, and not a playing-off of the physical against the intellectual; rather, it is a *physical* intellectuality in which the drama of a postmetaphysics appears. Therefore it is always an intelligence "on the verge" of something – an intelligence in transit, on stage, in the mood. It does not cling to the subject as if it were private property, but thrusts it forward like a provocation and a revelation.
>
> Peter Sloterdijk, *Thinker on Stage*, 66.

There might be a limit to the relevance of a discussion of truth, reality, and understanding, particularly in a context where one advocates for a philosophy of delirious participation. The process of illumination grows weary; all that is left are the shadows, the imminent reminders that – no matter what is thought or said or understood – the lived world awaits tomorrow. Our knowledge will be tested, not by the self-verifying systems we have culturally constructed, but by the world itself. The world, of course, does not care if we fail this test – the only stakes are our own.

Consider a proposition: there is no truth that is so true that the world can be held accountable to it. If the world could be wrong, who would tell it so – and what would its punishment be? Similarly, the world is exempt from error in any legitimate sense as well, as from the nuances of existential argument. Consider Albert Camus' demand that the world answer for him the question of meaning. The world did respond – in silence – an existential indifference that constituted, for Camus, the first horizon of metaphysical thinking.[8] For without a legitimate response from the world, what is left are only the *illegitimate* strategies of existence that alone can be refashioned according to principles of human truth or delirium. Since these illegitimate strategies do not in and of themselves distinguish between the two, one of two pacts is necessary: a reality pact or a delirium pact. But of these two possible pacts, only that of delirium avoids redundancy. Since one cannot hold reality accountable, one cannot hold oneself accountable to the real, either, but only ever to its simulated representations in truth.

Since there is no truth to which the world can be held accountable, it is we who hold ourselves accountable to the *assumption* of a world that functions in a particular way. The nuance is integral in this instance, for it is to suggest precisely that our expectations of the world form a horizon that has nothing at all to do with the world itself. Instead, it has only to do with the artificial limits that we have chosen to impose on existence, limits beyond which we, quite simply, refuse to think. In and of itself, this would not be a problem, except that we have also somehow mistaken our refusal for an impossibility – they are not equivalent. Self-reflexivity is useless; the mirror is not accountable to us. In the end, even a reality pact is a delirium pact.

Unlike with the question of the real, one can indeed hold delirium accountable for its various manifestations. A hallucinated reality is one that can be (at least potentially) refashioned if it steps out of line, if it transgresses the illogic of its own appearance, in short if it ever begins to present itself as a truth instead of the falsity that has been agreed to. When the stakes of corporeal existence are minimized, the delirium pact has been betrayed.

One might posit a logic of a different sort for this formulation. If there were such a thing as truth, it would be foolish to search for it. The most to which one could aspire is the artificial limitation of one's own horizon of understanding. If there is a rule, no action that is humanly possible will break from that rule. Consequently, the awareness of such a rule serves no purpose whatsoever except to make existence safe, reducing the stakes of the question to that which is intelligible, which, it must be insisted, is merely a way of imposing yet another artificial rule.

The choice, it would seem, is ultimately between having artificial rules or having real stakes – real, in this instance, meaning nothing more than an articulated instance of the immediacy of the threat posed to us by delirious appearances. And, as has been reinforced and repeated ad nauseum, imminent being is itself indifferent to the truth or falsity of the situation: the very question of the real is eclipsed by the immediacy of seduction. It is a noxious solution:

no illumination is tolerable except insofar as it thrusts us further into the shadows of delirium or the darkness of apophenia – the imaginary is unlightable. It is, nevertheless, lit of course – for light itself is what thrusts the imaginary into motion – the darkness must be preserved.

It is perhaps lucky that what defies the collapse of official existence has been already partly thought through by those Greeks (Diogenes) and Germans (Sloterdijk) whose project it has been to represent and perform the intricacies of a kynical philosophy. Lucky because such a history allows for this remainder to be more than simply the discarded experiential residue of misunderstood living. It is kynicism that saves us from futility, because those philosophers of bodily action have offered us a perverse form of hope in their insistence on the redundancy of thought: "life is above all else a process of self-composition – and not an object for self-reflexive deconstruction!"[9] This is not merely the paradox of existential living – it is, rather, the fatal binding of life to living.

To argue that kynicism saves us from futility, however, has as its consequence an explicit reversal of the stage of contemporary knowledge. No more is the task to understand the rhetorical possibilities open to cognition, but to use those possibilities as apophatic moments – pacts with delirium – for the projection of lived experience. One rhetorically understands the potentially limitless boundaries of imaginative speculation. Not bound by truth or falsity, not accountable to the artifices of regulated thinking, not responsible to the consensual variations of knowledge that contextualize its projection, the imagination can do whatever it likes, being bound only by the self-imposed restrictions levied against it on our own behalf. If Sloterdijk can propose a physical form of thinking, why not here suggest an equally physical form of imagination? "[The physicality of thought] is not a mode of thought that concentrates *on* the body, and not a playing-off of the physical against the intellectual; rather, it is a *physical* intellectuality in which the drama of a post-metaphysics appears. Therefore it is always an intelligence 'on the verge' of something – an intelligence in transit, on stage, in the mood. It does not cling to the subject as if it were private property, but thrusts it forward like a provocation and a revelation."[10]

The possibility of a physicality to the imagination begins the task of going beyond rhetoric to impact the body directly, it also breaks with reflective thinking once and for all. Instead of the self-reflexive tropes used to hold understanding accountable to knowledge, what emerges here is an *incidental* imagination – one that is always in motion as the tides of seduction and eclipse would demand. To extend Sloterdijk's radicalization of thought and speech into the territory of the imaginary would be to constitute the imaginary as purely performative, no longer strictly imaginary at all: "In the moments of the highest oral intensity, that which is said is consumed in the act of saying it; all representations are reduced to ashes in the act of being expressed. There are no longer any semantics, only gesticulations; no longer any ideas, only tropes of energy; no longer any higher meaning, only temporal stimulation; no *logos*, only orality. There is no longer anything holy, only heartbeats; no longer any spirit, only breath; no longer a god, only the movements of a mouth."[11]

This is a form of the imagination that is explicitly in the world as opposed to hiding in the shadows, and being in the world does not illuminate it so much as it renders it *blind* – overexposed – feeding on the world as only an imagination might do. Ultimately, only a blind imagination knows no boundaries, no context, no limits. Its blindness is no argument against its appearance, for such an imagination brings the world always with(in) it. Such an imagination does not attempt to "hold oneself out into the nothing" as a Heideggerian metaphysics might suggest, but grows instead from nothingness itself – which it in turn projects out into the world – exposing the dimming world to the imaginary lights of projected fantasy, of delirium and delusion.[12] The bringer of darkness to the world, this most physical of imaginations holds nothing out into the world. Indifferent to the impossible accountabilities of truth, it is instead the world itself that here becomes-accountable to the imagination.

Centaur Logic

> Are not the cults of science and aesthetics the prototypical "complementary idiots" of modernity?
>
> Peter Sloterdijk, *Thinker on Stage*, 12.

A theory that has set as its task the renouncing of worldly truth in favour of imaginative proclivity will undoubtedly encounter some problems, not the least of which is the attempt to be lucidly-unaware of its discursive trajectories. Fortunately there are also analogous models of such two-faced thinking that can be referred to in an attempt to clarify the situation. The best one, likely, comes from quantum physics – Heisenberg's uncertainty principle insists that one can never accurately measure both the position and the momentum of a particle in motion at any given time.

The logic behind Heisenberg's uncertainty principle is not unlike the logic of perspectival partiality, in which the act of perception implies a series of structural limitations on that which is made to appear. It is not that perception alters that which is perceived but rather that perception is already perspectivally dependent – the act of looking no less than the act of quantum measurement requires a focal compromise that simultaneously reveals appearances of a certain sort and obscures those of a different nature. In Heisenberg's formulation, the effect is such that the more accurately one measures the position of a particle, the more uncertain will be any quantifiable attributions of momentum (and vice versa). One can choose to measure one or the other – *which* one depends on the context – and yet the *effect* is the same. In both instances the act of perception sends its double into the darkness of uncertainty. In some ways, the logic of this formulation is even more extreme than the simplified analogy presented here, for physics regularly eschews mere observation in favour of explicit extrapolation, and even under speculative conditions such as those, the formula holds. The oblique is not exempt from uncertainty, or as Sloterdijk insists: "If things were generally as they seem, investigation and science would be superfluous."[13]

One might consequently suggest a humanities uncertainty principle of sorts, in order to extend the dynamic interplay between perception and the imaginary. In questions of philosophy no less than those of quantum physics one might well suggest that one cannot know with complete certainty both one's position and trajectory at any given moment – one's place in the world and the direction in which one is moving. Like its quantum counterpart, the more solidly and accurately one defines either position or momentum, the less clear becomes the other – the more I plan for the future the less I succumb to the immediacy of the present. In fact, one might go as far as to say that Heisenberg's principle has less to do with the body-in-motion as a specific measurable instance, than with the relationship between position and momentum – in any of its formulations. Wherever one sees an identifiable position, therefore, one would be well advised to doubt the certainty of its apparent trajectory, and vice-versa.

Suddenly the daunting paradoxes of philosophical thinking – the stage of mutual exclusives – begin to appear less daunting: being/becoming; immanence/transcendence; truth/falsity; sense/nonsense. What if each of these was merely an articulated instance of such a principle of uncertainty?

This would not be the certainty of uncertain conclusion, as the postmodern perspective might demand, for the measurements have been accurate and certainty itself has been implicated. This would instead suggest a contextual concession – a form of uncertain certainty, as the incidental relationship will require – an articulation of paradox that does not itself exit from paradoxical articulation. Indeed, as again quantum physics suggests, the accurate articulation of such a position is not, in and of itself, compromised by its inability to simultaneously articulate momentum. Why then should being be held accountable to variations in becoming, or immanence to variations in transcendence, or even falsity held accountable to articulations of truth? Instead, might one not simply admit to the partiality, the uncertainty, of any and all articulations: of being or becoming; of transcendence or immanence or even imminence; of truth or falsity or fantasy or trauma? Or, from Sloterdijk's perspective, a radical proliferation of doubt: "Radical doubt no longer leads ... back to an unshakable foundation in the certainty of thought, but instead to a fireworks display of incredible reflection and a free play of doubting power. Doubt can no longer be assuaged in the certainty of ideas."[14]

A logic of paradox grounds the question of contemporary subjectivity, and it is also what Sloterdijk explores at some length under the auspices of a "centauric logic," making his own analogy to the dual ontological trajectories of art and science as representative of a certain variation on this same formula of uncertainty. For Sloterdijk, the representative mentalities of these dual trajectories are to be found most poignantly in the aesthetic theory of Nietzsche, and in particular in the philosophical strategies of representation and intoxication (Nietzsche's categories of the Apollonian and Dionysian). Each perspective, of course, is by necessity uncertain about its double, but neither leaves the relational shadows of this interdependence. Instead, the monstrous offspring of Apollo and Dionysus become centaurs – recombinant fusions of logical difference that are, perhaps, no longer structurally predicable except to say that they are always part human, part beast. But in the end, is this not what Diogenes himself would demand? We might be human, but we perform as animals. Human *and* beast; scientific *and* performative; represented *and* intoxicated – in short, projected outwards into the world and absorbing the world in return – projection and absorption are the contemporary faces of the centaur itself.

There are liberties being taken with Sloterdijk's perspective here, insisting that because of the inevitable yet invisible presence of the partialities of uncertainty, that which is articulated with certainty is always first and foremost a reciprocal articulation of its uncertain double. This is also, of course, the kynical side to Nietzsche, and to Sloterdijk no less – that perspective from which the uncertain residue of philosophy is activated by its lived (kynical) double. Here Zarathustra is to Nietzsche as Nietszche is to Sloterdijk – the mobilization of perspective is indistinguishable from its lived perspectival residue. One can be Don Quixote *or* Miguel de Cervantes – but never both at the same time. The intricacy of the formulation is that, in this instance, by being-Quixote one is, in fact, performing Cervantes – for there can be little doubt that it is Don Quixote who is the more lucid of the two.

The boundaries are not clear, of course, but this is the necessary effect of any two-faced logic. Such a logic will always yield a doubled articulation in which the mutually exclusive structures of thinking inevitably recombine to form a mutated and hybridized individual. While the explication is grown of metaphor, the logic is not exempt from its own form of physiological consequence – not merely ideological, this mutated logic might also be extended technologically in the genetic thinking of Arthur Kroker, who refers to a thinking of this sort as a logic of "twisted strands."[15] If one can speak of physiological thinking and physiological imaginations, one is no longer speaking simply of rhetorical representation: experience knows no metaphor. A physiological imagination is a genetic imagination, (perhaps) not yet manipulated, but most certainly already, in one way or another, waiting to be performed, seduced, and mobilized by the world within and around it. Not even centauric any longer, this logic could be half-anything as long as it is also always half something else. Centaurs become chimeras, spliced and recombinant forms of thinking whose very forms can no longer be predicated since their logic is dependent only on the paradoxical interplays of seduction and delirium, absorption and projection.

Existential Hypocrisy

> The ego stands before the monstrous demand: to recognize that it is also what it absolutely believes itself *not* to be. The more conventional consciousness is, the more embittered will be its refusal to look into this mirror.
>
> Peter Sloterdijk, *Critique of Cynical Reason*, 51.

The logic of paradox – whether grown from the centaur or from twisted strands – is convoluted. On one hand, a truth is no less true for its falsity; certainty is no less certain for its uncertainty; logic is no less logical for its illogic; sense is no less sensical for its nonsensicality. The paradox must also, however, insist on exactly the opposite, as is required for what amounts to another position on the question itself. A genetic imagination yields monsters, not individuals, and yet such creatures are no less individual for their monstrosity. Paradoxes of this sort, as a general rule will always have a hypocritical side – obliquely staging the performance of fantasy, creating momentum that moves away from a perspectival center while occupying an impossible meta-position on the question of momentum itself. Rather than attempting to avoid this hypocrisy, however, a better option seems to be to embrace it. Consider Sloterdijk's reflection on the relationship between philosophy and lived experience: "Since philosophy can only hypocritically live out what it says, it takes cheek to say what is lived."[16] Consequently, if philosophy is to aspire both to understand what it lives and to live what it says, it will always be with irreconcilable results.

Ultimately, an articulation of the logic of paradox, like any uncertainty principle, is – as any stated constitution of the relationship between position and momentum – itself also a position. What this means is self-evidently obscure, for it means that such a formulation renders its own trajectory – its momentum – uncertain. It doesn't matter that the uncertainty principle is a meta-position, for in this instance the formulation demands that the certainty of the formulation be accompanied by an uncertainty of its trajectory. Its meta-momentum (its existential trajectory, one might say) is, as the dictates of uncertainty demand, rendered oblique – a shadow game of conscious articulation.

If there is room for metaphysics within the postmodern climate of proliferating falsity and delirious self-projection, it lies in the formulations that bind us to the uncertainty of postmodernism itself. If one follows the dictates of quantum physics (and its reformulation as a potentially quantum version of philosophical postmodernism), this metaphysics will also be quantum in nature. This would mean that it, too, would have structural ties to the hypocrisies of understanding and the partiality of perspective. Like Heidegger's proclamations that technology cannot be understood from the outside, this metaphysics is also one that cannot be understood from the outside. The only meta-formulations that survive this transformation are those that are grounded in error rather than truth: not honesty but hypocrisy, deception, falsity, and delusion: "I am deceived, therefore I am. And: I unmask deceptions, I myself deceive; therefore, I preserve myself."[17]

A postmodern version of metaphysics, consequently, might be best framed as a form of meta-hypocrisy, as perhaps befits a philosophizing of life on the inside. One does not exit from hypocrisy through understanding; understanding rather only intensifies its dichotomy. The more I understand where I am, the less I understand where I am going; the more I understand where I am going, the less I understand where I am. To pretend to see both is the fatal delusion of philosophy itself – its necessary hypocrisy – that which is the natural structural result of quantum embeddedness. Existence cannot even be theorized from the outside, for our fate is to be existing creatures with partial (quantum) gazes. In the words of Sloterdijk: "to explain from above results in no explanation at all."[18]

The idea of philosophical hypocrisy is both necessary and itself a deception no less than any other formulation with metaphysical pretenses. It is an apophenia spoken in the language of epiphany, which is ultimately the only position that language understands. It is here that the real kynic is not Diogenes at all, but Socrates – only he who pretends to know has succumbed to the delusions of a philosophical existence. That Socrates excludes himself – in his opposition to the vulgarity of Diogenes – from the necessity of performance does not mean that he is not still performing. Instead, it means merely that he is not engaging himself as such – he has entered into the delirium of philosophical fantasy. "[T]o be able to diagnose one's epoch it is necessary to be intoxicated by one's epoch"[19] and the intoxication with understanding is no less an intoxication than any other. The result is a vertigo of intoxicated perspective – a quantum perspective that defers only to the fantasies that ground the momentum of performance.

Philosophical Fantasy

The vertigo of quantum perspective results in an imperative for philosophical fantasy – a paradoxical form of fantasy that has never been more complex in its complexity, or easier in its facility, than when there are no more rules to the game. The absence of rules, however, does not translate into an absence of strategy, nor of implications. The result of existential hypocrisy is to make necessary the imperative to ignore at least some of the residually apparent rules of philosophy in order to cultivate imaginative strategies for living. The emphasis on performance requires an embeddedness of action that maintains the relationship between fantasy and philosophy. For Sloterdijk, such a mode of embedded understanding will always have a relationship to aesthetics: "It is the characteristic of one type of important aesthetic theory that it never discusses a phenomenon without incorporating some element of what is being discussed into the discourse itself."[20]

The attempt to apply philosophical fantasy to the understanding of postmodern subjectivity complicates the question however. If the task had not been set to formulate a stage for contemporary subjectivity, one might content oneself with the comfort of a limitless delusional reality in which one's errors are merely one's errors, and one's performances merely the fruits of existential labour. Yet, when the context is communicative – as in the case of this book, for instance – performance will always be hindered by the need to phrase an imperative for nonsense in terms that can be sensically understood. That there is no real distinction between the theory and the fiction is an often-overlooked detail that has always been central to the philosophical project. Philosophy has always involved the presentation of theoretical fictions, frameworks of understanding that gesture towards a communal world. Yet in the coexistence of different philosophical positions – as in the complexities of social, political and cultural living – there is no shared context, no communal world; instead, multiple communal worlds, each its own attempt to constitute and sustain a larger context. Each philosophy, in this sense, requires a slightly different version of the world – different in emphasis if not also in kind. There is a fine line between describing a particular perspective on the world and constituting the world from that perspective as a result – simulating the context from which one's theoretical position seems most convincing. If this question of multiplicity can be asked regarding a philosophical constitution of the particularities of the world, why not also for the self-constitution of subjectivity?

If there is any communal framework for the understanding of subjectivity, it has its source not in the safety of a communal universe in which disparate individuals wander seeking enlightened knowledge of their place in the cosmological game. Instead, it is worth considering the possibility that the commonality of the world has always been an illusion, sustained by the fantasy of the incommensurable subject. We have been taught to think that we are unique and it is the world that is common. But what if it was the other way around: not separate individuals negotiating a communal world, but communal individuals negotiating absolutely separate and irreducible worlds? It is not we who are unique, but the worlds we live in: an unverifiable hypothesis that is nevertheless an allowable perspective on the possibilities of subjective fantasy. But perhaps philosophy has always been about subjective fantasy, grounded not in the objectivity of the world but in the personal delusions of the sense-makers of reality. Sloterdijk was correct to suggest that "humanity cannot be enlightened because *it itself* was the false premise of enlightenment."[21] That philosophy has survived for so long, and has ended up as such a prominent and compelling discipline is – if anything – proof of the power of strategic fantasizing. Its strategy, in this sense, has always been one of willful disregard of precisely the hypocritical and oblique roots to all things philosophical. If it is hypocrisy that makes philosophy possible, it is existence that makes hypocrisy necessary.

This is not a critique of philosophy, but an oblique praise for exactly the nonsensical roots to all things sensical – a hypocritical fantasy of a different sort. One might even call such a fantasy ecological in the sense that it is forever unbalanced and in tenuous tension with the seductions of the world in which it participates. It is a misnomer to assert that ecology is about balance – it is instead about reciprocal imbalances, partialities that are themselves always caught in the danger of predatory living. There is nothing safe about the natural world, with its imminent complexities of species interaction, natural disasters, climate change and cosmic vulnerability. Insofar as it is the natural world that is at stake in any question of performative living, it is also the natural (as the site of experience) that is the kynical horizon to the hypocrisies of existence.

To pretend that things make sense is a human condition. As such, it is both fitting and ironic that the conclusion of sensical reason should be found in the attributions of the pretend itself – not as an abstract or spectral core to an understanding of existence, but in the lived delirium of embedded nonsense.

Metaphysical Laziness

The only argument left to make is, appropriately, the argument that insists that no argument is necessary. This is a logical conclusion, for in the absence of necessity it is the self-composited projection of philosophical fantasy that becomes the first hypocritical horizon of existence – whether such a horizon has pretense towards meaning or not. While no argument is necessary, it is nevertheless necessary to make an argument of some sort – arbitrary or not. In an instance such as this, the least necessary argument is also the argument for the trajectory that requires the least existential investment.

Since no investment will yield anything other than fantastic patterns of oblique (kynical) living, it is most sensical in this instance to discard meaning entirely, except insofar as meaning becomes an arbitrary fantasy of one sort or another. This is dangerous, but it is also required, lest one take one's hypocrisy too seriously. Strangely, the most efficient route is both the most entertaining and the laziest – best phrased again by Sloterdijk: "entertainment is synonymous with existence, and the opposite of entertainment is not boredom. The opposite of entertainment is death."[22]

There is a fantastic Catch-22 that occurs at this end point in the inquiry, one that insists that it matters little whether one chooses sense or nonsense, fantasy or reality, laziness or effort. One might easily insist that laziness is the oblique result of ignorance, rendered as the momentum of existence. It is a sensical argument, for that of which we are unaware requires no effort to perpetuate its motion – it has, largely, become autonomic. Equally sensical however, though less intuitive, would be the inverse argument in which discipline concludes in the laziness of self-sustaining behavioural patterns. In this sense laziness is, in fact, another word for meta-discipline – a formulation that relies on the single assumption that the ultimate goal of any disciplinary trajectory is to be self-sustaining.

It is no accident that during the course of this study it has frequently been asserted that we are always already performing variations on the conceptual frameworks of disappearance, ironic appearance and nonsense. To advocate for nonsense is to change nothing, to do what one has been doing all along. However, by taking what one does less seriously, or by understanding its internal structural limits, one can minimize the expenditure of effort needed to perpetuate one's actions. Effort, in this sense, has the singular purpose of sustaining delusion, and perhaps nothing more.

To reframe effort in this way – as a mechanism for the sustenance of delusion – is to construct a metaphysics of self-evidence that does not know it is self-evident. Such a theory of metaphysics will always be lazy, for the simple reason that no form of metaphysics dictates the ways in which effort is expended – at best metaphysics can describe the rules according to which a fantasy of living is rendered intelligible. Insofar as any metaphysics cannot be more than purely descriptive, each metaphysical assertion might be seen as merely an aesthetic recontextualization of the by-products of living. Metaphysics has always been kynical – it just didn't know it. The resultant metaphysics of laziness is, not properly a metaphysics except insofar as something that might be called metaphysical emerges as the oblique by-product of the performative minutia-physics of everyday living. Redundancy frames the metaphsycial rule – that which we do anyways functions to render an oblique metaphysical aggregate, which itself might be the only thing deserving of the name existence.

Postscript

The strangeness of an encounter with the contemporary world is that the conditions of understanding have disappeared into the lived necessity of aesthetic practice. Possibility no longer being accountable to truth or to falsity, the delusion of subjectivity is fair game. The only necessary caveat is that if one does not believe in the possibilities of one's delusions then those same delusions will be limited by the doubt harboured towards them.

There is a philosophical paradox that emerges when one advocates for the relevance of that which occurs anyways – in spite, or in defiance, or in ignorance of philosophy. What is interesting about such a paradox, however, is that it is *only* philosophical; in absence of philosophy no such paradox exists. This, in some ways, is the crux of the present study – both the proverbial thorn in its side and the reason why it has been necessary to argue for a perpetual self-placement in the shadows of error, imminence, and hypocrisy. Speaking philosophically one cannot be correct. This, however, is not a refusal or defiance of philosophical practice, but more practically the mechanism through which philosophy is made relevant to an existence that lives anyways. Rather than being the beacon of light guiding the path of the existentially invested, philosophy is instead the unspoken residue, the delirious appearance of nonsensical possibility, the indeterminable side of life. While there is nothing noble about such speculative pursuits, one might propose that in its ignobility there is nevertheless something seductively quixotic.

If knowledge is only available from within those contextual boundaries of suspended disbelief, and certainty relies on an element of conviction in the aesthetic plausibility of an imaginary rendering, then behind every sensical formulation is one that is nonsensical. Only nonsense can proceed despite itself, as the hypocritical condition of suspended thinking. One might summarize the frame of this conception by suggesting that it provides a sensical way of understanding the limits of sense through what amounts to an aesthetics of nonsense. The logical ground of this model might well be called into question, since it is a model no longer premised on the necessity of logical grounds.

This absence of logical premises is itself a logical premise of sorts. If one defers to unfounded belief as the prerequisite for cognitive engagement, one might then argue that belief can never truly be thought on its own terms, without first being grounded either in imaginative deferral or cognitive error. The question of belief cannot itself be constituted in believable terms. Instead, the question of belief requires a suspension of disbelief – an aesthetic manoeuvre whose purpose is to speculatively ground belief despite the uncertainty of the question. This is also the reason why the imaginative primacy of speculative thinking carries forward beyond the necessity for belief. In the same way as the falsity of truth in a postmodern era signals a reversal of terminologies – placing the imagination in a position of primacy – the unbelievability of the question of belief means that all statements of sense are ultimately reducible to the possibility of nonsensicality. One cannot think the question of sense in sensical terms any more than one can think the question of belief in terms that are believable.

There is, however, one final question that is necessary to explore, and it is the question of the impetus to suspend disbelief, not in any one thing, but at a more general level – the suspension of disbelief in the very notion of suspending disbelief. Contrary to everything we have been taught, there is no foundation behind this delusionary mechanism of suspension, which means that all delusions are themselves entertainable with the sole condition that suspended disbelief is mobilized without conscientious realization. This is why it becomes necessary to ground cognition in delusional self-trickery – in error, imminence, hypocrisy – places where one must first begin to dream the imaginary before beginning to question its nature. Here, the self is not quite a function of its self-delusions, but rather a function of its *capacity* for self-delusion.

The capacity for self-delusion is the delirious condition of self-conception. In a rather unambiguous way, all cognitive paths lead to nonsense, not in the sense of being reducible to nonsense – for that has never been the point – but rather in the sense that even before the sensical possibility of an aesthetic gaze can be conceived, the nonsensical capacity to imagine it must be methodologically invoked.

Out of nonsense grows the imagination. Out of the regulation of the imagination grows the intoxicating potential of aesthetic thinking, of which one form is that called sense, and another is the theory of nonsense proposed here. It is a self-validating form of argumentation that generates this position, grown of the observation that truth cannot be truthfully thought, and the question of belief can never formulated in believable terms. Here one also finds, already in play, those inverse trajectories that suggest that falsity can only be thought falsely (since all thought is ultimately reducible to that which it pretends not to be), suspended disbelief must be unbelievably suspended, and nonsense itself is the self-satisfying reason. If the mind is capable of such an unfounded manoeuvre, then the potential consequences are far-reaching. On one hand, it would mean that there is the possibility that we have not only consensually, but conscientiously hallucinated our participation in the worlds we inhabit. Or, on the other hand, it means that if agreements can be made about how to further extend these delusions, we can conscientiously change the faces of our world, from the inside out.

Three Iterations of Aesthetic Suspension

The method taken by this text builds towards a theory of nonsensical license. Each of the main sections or "parts" of this text might be seen as representative of a particular form of aesthetic suspension: an aesthetics of disappearance, an aesthetics of ironic appearance, and an aesthetics of nonsense. Within each "part," there is less an argument to be made than a scenario to imagine, an exegesis that attempts to render a plausible impossibility – proceeding by asking the question "what if," if only to then attempt to give such conjecture plausible form.

First, a suspension of disappearance attempts to round out, constitute, and represent an inverse side to Paul Virilio's aesthetics of the same name – explicitly looking at what it means to live in a climate of postmodern uncertainty, with both the traumas and the possibilities such self-placement might afford. These might be equally termed stories of disappearance, ways of imagining the disappearance of the self into its technologies of agreement, whether cognitive, perceptual or existential. What results is an aesthetic proposal – a plausible framework for the suspension of disbelief in disappearance itself. The result is a climate of indeterminacy, the fateful conclusion of postmodern thinking, but also a state that paradoxically continues to require lived negotiation – of hallucinatory self-consciousness, of diffused perceptual boundaries, of inauthentic ideological rendering. Ironically, what such a framework can never quite address is the paradox of its own constitution – the simple question of the contingencies of disappeared living.

This is the question that provides the groundwork for a suspension of ironic appearance – the self-reflexive realization of disappeared cosmology in which the irony of the situation is that one continues to, in some way, self-encounter. These are stories of ironic appearance in which the disparity of understanding is held accountable to its lived actuality, such as to reformulate disappearance in a way that might continue to include the possibility of critical engagement. What results is a second aesthetic proposal – a plausible framework for the suspension of disbelief in irony and its apparent manifestations. Yet there is an irony to this proposal as well, as perhaps is required of such an aesthetic – the irony of being bound to irony as a critical condition of intelligible engagement – of authorship after the "death of the author"; of fantasy as the condition for self-imagining; of censorship as the condition of constituted perspective. Strangely, these ironies begin to appear less convincing the more they are engaged – when irony becomes a horizon of engagement, the aesthetics of ironic appearance slowly begins to lose its self-image.

The internalization of ironic demand provides the basis for the plausible engagement of nonsense as a horizon of ironic self-consciousness that has forgotten the ironies from which it was borne. The result is a theory of delirious permission, no longer simply contextualized as a resistance tactic to dominant ideological rendering. When disappearance and ironic re-constitution are taken as a groundwork instead of as a problematic conclusion, the task becomes one of simply imagining ways in which such stories might continue to proceed. What results is a third aesthetic proposal – a plausible framework for the impossibilities of nonsense, suspended as the condition of intellectual engagement in the first instance. Such a suspension – while eschewing the stages of communal disciplinary agreement as well as those of ironic resistance – is reducible to the imaginary conditions of its own self-formulation. Despite the apparently sanction-independent environment this would seem to create, the possibilities of nonsense are fully accountable to their lived manifestations – imaginary solutions to the absence of communal problems.

An aesthetics of nonsense is what is required in order to begin formulating terms for the negotiation of an existential scenario that has no more rules, though there remain consequences to the ways in which these absences are negotiated. Instead, what results is no longer a negotiation of a communal or consensual reality, but an engineering of the imaginary stage upon which any given reality might act itself out. This is also not simply a defensive manoeuvre intended to pre-empt the uncertainty of a predatory real, but a pre-emptive manoeuvre intended to precisely provoke unlikely and even impossible manifestations of plausible living. Reality is a process of acting-out, and if existence isn't a stage for temper-tantrums of one sort or another, then the implicated gaze is likely to remain passive to the end. It is no longer even the "acting" that is in question – this, one might assume, has at least become a plausible horizon for identity-formation. Instead, the only question that remains is that of where one might find an "out" – whether that be through a challenge to the usual formulations of social, cultural, or political being, or through precisely what such challenges care nothing about – which is to say the errors, hypocrisies, and delusions of the world.

Imaginary Solutions

In Praise of Nonsense has been an attempt to explore imaginary solutions to the problem of postmodern uncertainty – suspended grounds of hallucinatory participation from which to think through the speculative consequences and aesthetic possibilities of indeterminate living. It is, in this fashion, also an attempt to mobilize the possibilities of the imaginary as they manifest with real, lived intensity – not only as a value-added aesthetic addition to the questions of postmodern living, but as potentially tangible perspectives "praised into" plausible form.

The mechanism of "praise" is similar to belief, in the sense that it is largely self-validating and has the capacity to initiate a delirious trajectory whose manifestation is no less immediate for its apparent absurdity. Nonsense comes into possibility for the simple reason that one suspends the doubt that would otherwise prevent its invocation. And it is the invocation – the praise – rather than simply the suspension of doubt that is the critical factor, initiating its own trajectory of projected living – quixotic, perhaps, but nevertheless manifest – despite the fact that such manifestation may make no real sense.

Don't think of a red horse. It is a demand that, in theory, could have nearly any manifestation at all, except that this horse is also Trojan, and what is interesting about such an example is that it invokes exactly what it tells us not to – in this case making the imagining of a red horse difficult to avoid. In this sense, such a command is also a command to error, here cited as an analogy for nonsensical practice. Ultimately, the logic of nonsense is erroneous, oblique, delirious, and hypocritical – which is ultimately to say simulacral in nature. Nonsense exists as a constituted entity to hide the fact that sense itself is equally nonsensical. Nonsense is not the opposite of sense, but merely its strategically disavowed alternative. Nonsense, as such, only exists from a perspective that expects to encounter some form of sensical rendering to its questions. From a perspective that expects only nonsense, all solutions – imaginary or not – are entirely lucid...one might even say sensical. Nonsense does not exist to itself. Forced to *invent* an existence, there are no governing rules that are not themselves the forces of invention.

The free play of nonsensical intervention produces other examples, as one might imagine. One worth mentioning here is a simple puzzle, typically called the "Nine Dots Puzzle" in which one must connect a grid of nine dots, using only four lines, without lifting one's pencil.[1] Much talked about in terms of creativity studies and often cited as an example of lateral thinking, what is noteworthy about this puzzle is that its solution requires a suspension of assumed terms of engagement. The solution requires the constitution of two *imaginary*

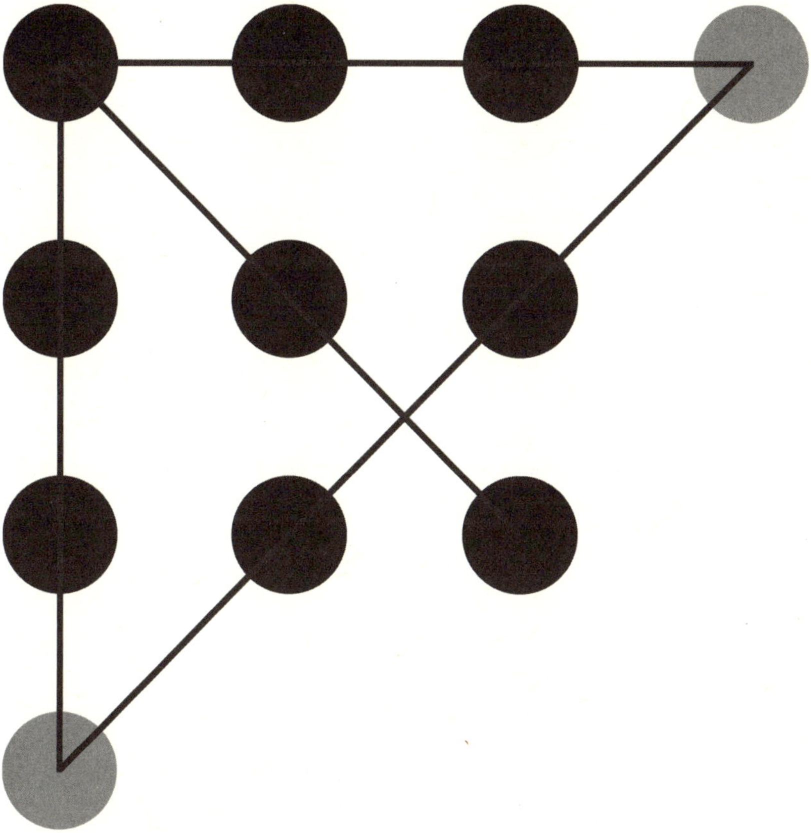

Sam Loyd. *Nine Dots Puzzle* (also called *Christopher Columbus's Egg*), circa 1914. This rendering shows the solution, with the constitution of two imaginary points.

points that can be used to extend the grid outside of its assumed boundaries. It is both an imaginary solution and a technological solution in the sense that the grid is extended outside of itself in order to provide a stage for the imagined intervention.

In the solution to this puzzle one also finds also a practical application for nonsensical practices – practices that take imaginary liberties with established context in an attempt to find other plausible renderings. In fact, what is most interesting about a nine-point puzzle such as this has nothing to do with the nine original points at all, but rather with the possibilities for imaginary points, first two then perhaps many more as the puzzle is transformed into a pointillist exercise of sorts. Such a manoeuvre, despite its deviation from accepted terms of agreement, is not simply an error. Rather, this error has effect – first an imaginary solution to the puzzle itself, then an outrunning of the terms of engagement. For, while one might find it relatively easy to sanction such a manoeuvre when it is limited to practical achievement, the more difficult challenge is to give credence to the attempt itself, irrespective of whether its solutions result in ideological deliverables, unintelligible hypocrisies, aesthetic masterpieces, or simple failure. Unbounded from the dictates of truth or falsity or reality or delusion, the horizon of accountability for nonsensical practice is simply that which can be entertained and sustained and imagined differently. Freed from its responsibility to remain fictional, the imagination is now finally – for perhaps the first time – also able to fail.

In the stakes of failure, the stakes of nonsense may also begin to resonate. While it is fine and well to only treat with respect those solutions that are themselves proven and accepted in a larger sense, it is in failure that the consequences of even imaginary practices are intensified – lived out as dissonance or unpopular hypotheses, but in all cases *lived*. There is no other forum in which an imagination might exist – it is not accepted as fact, nor as truth, nor as reality. Therefore it must be imagined versions of all these things, brought to bear only on the question of its own plausibility. Nevertheless, imagined renderings are pervasive, layered overtop of and underneath and within the fabric of established fact, such that the trajetory of living has less to do with accumulated facts and more to do with aesthetic layers – the variations and remixes and personalizations and imagined solutions to whatever somebody else might do under similar circumstances.

One might well question whether or not sensical solutions are ever actually lived, – or if their stories simply play out as nodes on a didactic trajectory to somewhere else. In the failures of the story to self-contain – in the inevitability of personalized existence – one might equally well insist that all stories contain their own delusionally-added values – aesthetics of nonsense that may or may not change anything, but which at the very least render imminent the failure of a standardized solution in the face of its lived particularities.

In Praise of Nonsense

Along with a note of praise for the inevitability of nonsensical intervention, one might end with a short commentary on failure. Imminent to nonsense – since nonsense is unaccountable to success – yet aligned with error, delusion, and hypocrisy, failure is perhaps both the imaginary condition of normalized living and the backwards trajectory of life imagined-otherwise. One cannot try to fail

– failure instead is simply a marker of effort extended outside of itself, caught in the dynamic attempt to sustain delusions of one impractical sort or another. Failure too is itself a nonsensical practice of ensuring the ever-present scrutiny of imagining again, imagining differently, imagining other possible variations that just maybe this time will render the impossible without being burned in the process.

> This is an appointment with the imaginary;
> This is a manifestation of delusional engagement;
> This is an improvement in the wrong direction.

Or, in the words of Antonin Artaud: "This possibility of thinking backwards and suddenly insulting one's own thought."[2]

... in praise of nonsense.

Notes

Preface

1 For Kearney, the imperative to "imagine otherwise" is an attempt to salvage a foundational basis for ethical thinking in a postmodern age. In order to do this, it is necessary for him to propose a primacy to ethical discourse that is itself exempt from deconstructive analysis – a viable solution to the politics of postmodern living, if not to the possibilities for the imagination in a larger sense. Importantly however, Kearney's work points to the possibilities of exemption as itself a discursive and imaginary strategy – what might be seen as part of what Alfred Jarry terms a "science of exceptions" in his formulation of pataphysics. See Kearney, *The Wake of the Imagination*, 359–64; and Jarry, *Gestes et opinions du docteur Faustroll*, 32.

2 Nietzsche, *The Birth of Tragedy*, 22.

3 Artaud, *The Theatre and Its Double*, 35.

4 Wittgenstein, *On Certainty*, 253.

5 Interestingly, the most eloquent articulation of this dynamic came via the response of an anonymous reviewer of the original manuscript, who summarized the structure of this text as an unfounded series of "nonsensical" iterations that due to a failure of logical argumentation "require praise" in order to be rendered into speculative existence. It is a critique that I hope the text can live up to – the suggestion that this book is attempting nothing less than the formulation of a theory of "thought as incantation" – imaginary solutions to a question of logical indeterminacy.

Technologies of Disappearance

1 Borges, "The Circular Ruin," in *Collected Fictions*, 100.

2 Kearney, *The Wake of the Imagination*, 359.

3 Ibid., 364.

4 Caputo, *Radical Hermeneutics*, 147.

5 See Hayles, *How We Became Posthuman*; Haraway, "The Cyborg Manifesto"; Kroker, *The Possessed Individual.*

6 Hayles, *How We Became Posthuman*, 4.

7 Kearney, *The Wake of the Imagination*, 386.

Chapter One

1 *Nervous Control Centre*, an exhibition of sculpture and paintings by London artist Christian Kuras, was presented at The New Gallery (Calgary, AB) from 19 November to 18 December 2004. Shown here are images from works included in the exhibition.

2 Foucault, *Discipline and Punish*, 170.

3 Foucault, *The Politics of Truth*, 163

4 Foucault, *Discipline and Punish*, 201.

5 Ibid., 193.

6 Foucault, *The Politics of Truth*, 208.

7 I use the term placebo loosely here, largely according to popular rather than medical discourse, in order to indicate a measurable effect produced by an inert or immaterial set of circumstances. For a good discussion of the relationship between placebos and the production of meaningful and measurable response, see Moerman and Jonas, "Deconstructing the Placebo Effect and Finding the Meaning Response," 471–6.

8 Descartes, *Discourse on Method and Meditations on First Philosophy*, 63–4.

9 Foucault, *Discipline and Punish*, 170.

10 Ibid., 183.

11 Lacan, "The Mirror Stage as Formative of the Function of the I as Revealed in Psychoanalytic Experience," 62.

12 Ibid., 63.

13 Ibid., 64.

14 In his analysis of Lacan, Zizek argues that the goal of psychoanalysis is precisely "*not* the pacification/gentrification of the trauma, but the acceptance of the very fact that our lives involve a traumatic kernel beyond redemption, that there is a dimension of our being which forever resists redemption-deliverance." This traumatic kernel, if it is to be "accepted" and cannot be redeemed, cannot be less present in the voice of Lacan, or of Zizek for that matter, than anyone else. Even an "enlightened" voice remains traumatized. See Zizek, *On Belief*, 98.

15 Foucault, *The Politics of Truth*, 221.

16 Ibid., 227.

Chapter Two

1 *Fear Commandos* is a video-based artwork by Calgary artist Mike Paget. Shown here are stills from the video.

2 Virilio, *The Information Bomb*, 57. "The watching gaze has long since ceased to be that of the artist or even the scientist, but belongs to the instruments of technological investigation."
3 Virilio, *The Information Bomb*, 124.
4 Virilio, *The Vision Machine*, 72.
5 Paul Virilio attributes the rise of new technology to a rise in social irresponsibility, the contemporary artistic fascination with questions of nihilism and futility, as well as political, social and cultural decline. For a detailed account of his objection, see Virilio, *Art and Fear*, 27–32.
6 McLuhan, *Understanding Media*, 19.
7 Ibid., 10.
8 Merleau-Ponty, *Phenomenology of Perception*, 98.
9 Ibid., 217.
10 Kroker, *The Possessed Individual*, 5.
11 Ibid., 1–3.
12 Virilio, *Politics of the Very Worst*, 48–54.
13 Ibid., 54.
14 Ibid., 89.
15 Ibid., 81–2.
16 *The Horla* is a first-person account of one man's encounter with an invisible and unknown entity that begins by haunting his room and proceeds to momentarily possess and alter his waking and sleeping habits. Searching for ways to extricate himself from the presence of this phantom, the man tries everything from leaving his home town to reading medical texts for potential cures to eventually burning down his own house in an attempt to exorcize the ghost. He does not succeed, and his attempts end in disaster when his servants are caught unaware in the burning building. His final words: "He is not dead. Then – then – I suppose I must kill myself!" de Maupassant, *The Horla*.
17 de Maupassant, *The Horla*.

Chapter Three

1 *Kiddie Pool* is a sculptural installation by Chicago artist Duncan MacKenzie.
2 Richter, *Walter Benjamin and the Corpus of Autobiography*, 21.
3 Benjamin, 220.
4 Ibid., 224.
5 Snyder, "Benjamin on Reproducibility and Aura," 161.
6 Benjamin, *Illuminations*, 221.

7 Ibid., 220.
8 Ibid., 240.
9 Ibid., 227.
10 Virilio, *The Aesthetics of Disappearance*, 52.
11 Richter, *Walter Benjamin and the Corpus of Autobiography*, 23.
12 Ibid., 232.
13 Ibid., 37.
14 Ibid., 50.
15 Ibid., 26. In this quote, Richter is speaking of history rather than identity, but in the context of his discussion the point being made is that the self must disrupt the authentic connotations of linear history in order to access the textual contingency required for self-fashioning.
16 Ibid., 46.
17 Chalmers, "Facing Up to the Problem of Consciousness," 10.
18 Benjamin, *The Origin of German Tragic Drama*, 36.
19 Benjamin, *Selected Writings*, 70.
20 Ibid., 56.

Technologies of Ironic Appearance

1 Graves, *The Greek Myths: I*, 312–13.
2 Bataille, *Visions of Excess*, 58.
3 See, for example, Habermas, *The Philosophical Discourse of Modernity*, 83–105.
4 Nietzsche, *Thus Spoke Zarathustra*, 103.
5 Nietzsche, *The Birth of Tragedy*, 22.
6 Ibid. 38.
7 I have not used Nietzsche's categories of the Apollonian and Dionysian here in order to foreground what I see as the more important aspect of his aesthetic theory, that is, the tension that is constructed by framing these categories as ones of performance rather than analysis.

Chapter Four

1 *Ten Little Indians [Remix]* is a video and web-based multimedia project by Victoria based Mohawk artist Jackson 2Bears. Shown here are stills from the video.
2 Kroker and Kroker, *Life in the Wires*, 16.
3 Wittgenstein, *Tractacus Logico-Philosophicus*, 74.
4 Barthes, *Image – Music – Text,*, 146.
5 Ibid., 148.
6 Ibid.

7 Ibid.

8 Ibid., 17.

9 Ibid., 39.

10 Benjamin, *Illuminations*, 227,

11 "In the multiplicity of writing, everything is to be *disentangled*, nothing *deciphered*." Barthes, *Image – Music – Text*, 147.

12 Barthes, *Mythologies*, 133.

13 Barthes, *Writing Degree Zero*, 20.

14 Ibid., 10.

15 Ibid., 75.

16 Barthes, *Mythologies*, 118.

17 Barthes, *Writing Degree Zero*, 25.

18 Barthes, *Mythologies*, 115.

19 Barthes, *Writing Degree Zero*, 13.

20 Barthes, *Mythologies*, 123.

Chapter Five

1 *The Scott Rogers Google Project* is an ongoing series of name-based works by Calgary artist Scott Rogers. Grounded in a Google search for his name, this project has extended to the production of pastiche self-portraits of himself as other Scott Rogers' listed in the Google results.

2 Personal correspondence with Scott Rogers (this should include a date and method of correspondence, i.e. Scott Rogers, email message to author, 17 April 2007).

3 Benjamin, *Illuminations*, 224.

4 Barthes, *Writing Degree Zero*, 26.

5 McLuhan, *Understanding Media*, 23–4.

6 Kroker, *The Possessed Individual*; 5.

7 Heidegger, *The Question Concerning Technology and Other Essays*, 4.

8 Foucault, *Fearless Speech*, 226.

9 Ibid.

10 Zizek, *Organs without Bodies*, 96.

11 Lacan, "The Mirror Stage as Formative of the Function of the I as Revealed in Psychoanalytic Experience," 62.

12 Ibid.

13 Zizek, *Organs without Bodies*, 96.

14 Jim Loy, "Zeno's Paradox," 1997, http://www.jimloy.com/physics/zeno.htm, accessed 15 January 2006.

15 Zizek, *Organs without Bodies*, 56.

16 Ibid., 96.

17 Zizek, *The Puppet and the Dwarf,* 41.
18 Lacan, "The Mirror Stage as Formative of the Function of the I as Revealed in Psychoanalytic Experience," 61–6.
19 McLuhan, *Understanding Media*, ix.
20 Ibid., 36–44.
21 Lacan, "The Mirror Stage as Formative of the Function of the I as Revealed in Psychoanalytic Experience," 62.
22 Baudrillard, *Simulacra and Simulation*, 3.

Chapter Six

1 *Haiku d'Etat* was a performance conducted in Montreal on 28 June 2003 by New York- and Rotterdam-based dance collective Archeopteryx 8. Lead choreographer and dancer Erik Kaiel supplied these images of the performance. The other dancers involved were Laurel Dugan, Luis Tentindo, Layard Thompson, and Maude Williams.
2 Baudrillard, *Forget Foucault*, 75.
3 Bakhtin, *Rabelais and His World*, 9.
4 Ibid., 7.
5 Ibid., 7.
6 Ibid., 9.
7 Thomas Nagel, "What is it like to be a bat?" *The Philosophical Review* LXXXIII 4 (October 1974): 435–50, http://evans-experientialism.freewebspace.com/nagel.htm.
8 Bakhtin, *The Dialogic Imagination*, 427.
9 Bakhtin, *The Problems of Dostoevsky's Poetics*, 183.
10 Ibid., 123.
11 From Greek: a foreign tongue. Literally, a linguistic attribution from the perspective of a listener when confronted with nonsensical vocalization which "they are convinced [could be] a living – or dead – language that could be understood if only someone were around who knew it." Goodman, *Speaking Tongues*, 149. From the perspective of the person speaking, xenoglossia is unintelligible and might be described as speaking in a language one neither knows nor understands.
12 "We find here [in the carnival – or, equally, in the dialogic] a characteristic logic, the peculiar logic of the "inside out" (à l'envers), of the "turnabout," of a continual shifting from top to bottom, from front to rear, of numerous parodies and travesties, humiliations, profanations, comic crownings and uncrownings." Bakhtin, *Rabelais and His World*, 11.
13 "Parodying is the creation of a *decrowning double*; it is that same 'world turned inside-out.'" Bakhtin, *The Problems of Dostoevsky's Poetics*, 127.

14 Ibid., 185.

15 Consider Bakhtin's assertions on the consequences of dialogism: "This dialogic imperative, mandated by the pre-existence of the language world relative to any of its current inhabitants, ensures that there can be no actual monologue." *The Dialogic Imagination,* 426.

16 Zizek, *The Fragile Absolute*, 83. The concept of the "objectively subjective" is from Daniel Dennett, initially directed towards a discussion of consciousness. Zizek takes up the concept in a discussion of the role of fantasy in psychoanalysis.

Technologies of Nonsense

1 Bachelard, *The Psychoanalysis of Fire,* 11.

2 Ibid., 12.

3 Graves, *The Greek Myths: I,* 144.

4 Ibid., 145.

5 Wittgenstein, *On Certainty*, 205: 28e.

6 Ibid., 253: 33e.

7 Nietzsche, *The Birth of Tragedy*, 22.

8 Wittgenstein, *On Certainty*, 30: 6e.

9 Ibid., 42: 8e.

10 Ibid., 663: 88e.

11 Sloterdijk, *Critique of Cynical Reason*, xxxiii.

Chapter Seven

1 *SuperModels* was an exhibition of sculptural and photographic works by Toni Hafkensheid, Duncan MacKenzie, Chris Gillespie, and Tim van Wijk, presented at Open Space Arts Society from 23 March 23 to 5 April 5 2004. Shown here are images from works included in the exhibition.

2 Borges, *Collected Fictions*, 325.

3 Baudrillard, "The Murder of the Real," 63.

4 Baudrillard, *Simulacra and Simulation*, 16.

5 See Nietzsche, "How the 'Real World' at last Became a Myth," 50–1; and Nietzsche, *Thus Spoke Zarathustra*, 40–3.

6 Deleuze Guattari, *A Thousand Plateaus,*156–7.

7 Ibid., 399.

8 Ibid., 274.

9 Deleuze and Guattari, *What is Philosophy?* 42.

10 Deleuze and Guattari, *A Thousand Plateaus*, 76.

11 Sapan, "Holographic Studios: FAQ."

12 Wittgenstein, *On Certainty*, 663: 88e.

13 Deleuze and Guattari, *What is Philosophy?* 74.
14 Ibid., 45.
15 Ibid., 59.
16 *Merriam-Webster Online*, "immanent," accessed 1 August 2006, http://www.m-w.com/dictionary/immanent.
17 Deleuze and Guattari, *Anti-Oedipus,* 380.
18 Deleuze and Guattari, *A Thousand Plateaus,* 381. My emphasis.
19 Ibid., 380.
20 Ibid., 382.
21 Deleuze and Guattari, *Anti-Oedipus,* 109.
22 Deleuze and Guattari, *A Thousand Plateaus,* 36.

Chapter Eight

1 *Vulnerable Light* was an exhibition of photographic works by Montreal artist Isabelle Hayeur and Toronto artist Jennifer Long, presented at Open Space Arts Society from 5 October to 12 November 2006. Shown here are images from works included in the exhibition.
2 Sontag, *On Photography*, 14.
3 Baudrillard, "Objects, Images, and the Possibilities of Aesthetic Illusion," 14.
4 Sontag, *On Photography*, 24.
5 Baudrillard, *Paroxysm*, 93.
6 Baudrillard, *Impossible Exchange*, 3.
7 Baudrillard, *The Intelligence of Evil*, 25.
8 Baudrillard, *The Vital Illusion*, 83.
9 Baudrillard, 33.
10 Baudrillard, *In the Shadow of the Silent Majorities*, 119.
11 Baudrillard, *The Vital Illusion*, 65–6.
12 Baudrillard, *Seduction*, 91.
13 Baudrillard, *Paroxysm*, 115.
14 Baudrillard, *The Intelligence of Evil*, 42.
15 Baudrillard, *In the Shadow of the Silent Majorities*, 9.
16 Baudrillard, *Seduction*, 77.
17 Baudrillard, *Passwords*, 22.
18 Baudrillard. *The Ecstasy of Communication*, 70.
19 Baudrillard, *Seduction*, 85.
20 Ibid., 67.
21 McLuhan, *Understanding Media*, 36–44.
22 Baudrillard, *The Intelligence of Evil*, 40.
23 Baudrillard, *Impossible Exchange*, 23.

24 Baudrillard, *The Intelligence of Evil*, 156.
25 Baudrillard, *Paroxysm*, 94.

Chapter Nine

1 *Ball Inside My Head* is an ongoing sculpture, audio, and media project by Victoria artist Doug Jarvis. Shown here are concepts sketches for preliminary works in this ongoing series.
2 Heidegger, *The Question Concerning Technology*.
3 Sloterdijk, *Critique of Cynical Reason*, 20.
4 Ibid., 101.
5 Ibid., xxxi.
6 Ibid.
7 Ibid., 101–2.
8 Camus, *The Rebel*, 6.
9 Sloterdijk, *Thinker on Stage*, 57.
10 Ibid., 66.
11 Ibid., 63.
12 If the metaphysical question for Heidegger is the question of "holding oneself out into the nothing," the question here is one of sustaining the performative act. For Heidegger, the question of metaphysics – of Daesin – is first and foremost a question of ideological transcendence (realizing the nothing to which we belong). Here, instead, this question is one explicitly of performative failure (performing the incidence of that nothingness which belongs to us). In truth, the two perspectives are not contradictory, they simply privilege differing aspects, and as a result they have different consequences. In the phrase "holding oneself out into the nothing," for instance, it is certainly the "nothing" itself that is Heidegger's preoccupation. For us who see only the nothingness of existence (arguably the postmodern condition) the problem is that of "holding oneself out," the *performative* problem – not of metaphysical *understanding* but of metaphysical *living* (or of living in general, metaphysical or not). See Heidegger, "What is Metaphysics?"
13 Sloterdijk, *Critique of Cynical Reason*, 53.
14 Sloterdijk, *Thinker on Stage*, 36.
15 Kroker, "Twisted Strands."
16 Sloterdijk, *Critique of Cynical Reason*, 102.
17 Ibid., 331.
18 Sloterdijk, *La domestication de l'Être*, 24 (translation mine), "expliquer d'en haut revient à ne pas expliquer du tout."

19 Sloterdijk, *Essai d'intoxication volontaire* suivi de *L'heure du crime et le temps de l'oeuvre d'art*, 11 (translation mine), "pour pouvoir formuler un diagnostic sur l'époque, il faut être intoxiqué par son époque."
20 Sloterdijk, *Thinker on Stage*, 15.
21 Sloterdijk, *Critique of Cynical Reason*, 355.
22 Sloterdijk, *Essai d'intoxication volontaire*, 89 (translation mine), "le divertissement est synonyme d'existence, et le contraire du divertisement n'est pas l'ennui. Le contraire du divertissement, c'est la mort."

Postscript

1 For a contextualization of the "nine dots puzzle" see the *Wikipedia* entry for "Thinking Outside the Box," a phrase apparently coined with reference to this puzzle. Accessed 31 July 2009: http://en.wikipedia.org/wiki/Thinking_outside_the_box.
2 Artaud, "An Actor You Can See," 34.

Bibliography

Artaud, Antonin. *Artaud Anthology*. Edited by Jack Hirschman. San Francisco: City Lights Books, 1965.

– "Manifesto in a Clear Language." 1925. Accessed 13 August 2006. http://www.pataphysics-lab.com/sarcophaga/manyfestos

– *The Theatre and Its Double*. Translated by Victor Corti. London: Calder, 1993.

Bachelard, Gaston. *The Psychoanalysis of Fire*. Translated by Alan C.M. Ross. Boston: Beacon Press, 1964.

Bakhtin, Mikhail. *The Dialogic Imagination: Four Essays*. Edited by Michael Holquist. Translated by Caryl Emerson and Michael Holquist. Austin: University of Texas Press, 1981.

– *Problems of Dostoevsky's Poetics*. Edited and translated by Caryl Emerson. Minneapolis: University of Minnesota Press, 1984.

– *Rabelais and His World*. Translated by Helene Iswolsky. Bloomington: Indiana University Press, 1984.

– *Speech Genres and Other Late Essays*. Edited by Caryl Emerson and Michael Holquist. Translated by Vern W. McGee. Austin: University of Texas Press, 1986.

Barthes, Roland. *Càmera Lucida: Reflections on Photography*. Translated by Richard Howard. New York: Hill and Wang, 1981.

– *Empire of Signs*. Translated by Richard Howard. New York: Hill and Wang, 1983.

– *Image – Music – Text*. Translated by Stephen Heath. London: Fontana, 1977.

– *Mythologies*. Translated by Annette Lavers. New York: Hill and Wang, 1972.

– *Writing Zero Degree*. Translated by Annette Lavers and Colin Smith. New York: Hill and Wang, 1968.

Bataille, Georges. *Visions of Excess: Selected Writings, 1927–1939*. Translated by Allan Stoekl. Minneapolis: University of Minnesota Press, 1985.

Baudrillard, Jean. *The Conspiracy of Art*. Edited by Sylvère Lotringer. Translated by Ames Hodges. New York: Semiotext(e), 2005.

– *Cool Memories IV*. New York: Verso, 2003.

– *The Ecstasy of Communication*. Edited by Sylvère Lotringer. Translated by Bernard and Caroline Schutze. New York: Semiotext(e), 1988.

– *Forget Foucault*. New York: Semiotext(e), 1987.

– *The Illusion of the End*. Translated by Chris Turner. Stanford: Stanford University Press, 1994.
– *Impossible Exchange*. Translated by Chris Turner. London: Verso, 2001.
– *In the Shadow of the Silent Majorities, or, The End of the Social and Other Essays*. Translated by Paul Foss, John Johnston, and Paul Patton. New York: Semiotext(e), 1983.
– *The Intelligence of Evil or The Lucidity Pact*. Translated by Chris Turner. New York: Berg, 2005.
– "Objects, Images, and the Possibilities of Aesthetic Illusion." In *Jean Baudrillard: Art and Artefact*, edited by Nicholas Zurbrugg, 7–18. London: Sage, 1997.
– *Paroxysm: Interviews with Philippe Petit*. Translated by Chris Turner. London: Verso, 1998.
– *Passwords*. Translated by Chris Turner. London: Verso, 2003.
– "Photography, or The Writing Of Light." Translated by Francois Debrix. *CTheory*, article a083 (Spring 2000). Accessed 8 August 2006. http://www.ctheory.net/articles?id=126
– *Screened Out*. Translated by Chris Turner. London: Verso, 2002.
– *Seduction*. Translated by Brian Singer. London: MacMillan, 1990.
– *Simulacra and Simulation*. Translated by Sheila Faria Glaser. Ann Arbor: The University of Michigan Press, 1994.
– *The Spirit of Terrorism*. Translated by Chris Turner. London: Verso, 2002.
– *Symbolic Exchange and Death*. Translated by Iain Hamilton Grant. London: Sage, 1993.
– *The Transparency of Evil: Essays on Extreme Phenomena*. Translated by James Benedict. London: Verso, 1993.
– *The Vital Illusion*. Edited by Julia Witwer. New York: Columbia University Press, 2000.
Benjamin, Walter. *The Arcades Project*. Edited by Rolf Tiedemann. Translated by Howard Eiland and Kevin McLaughlin. Cambridge: Harvard University Press, 1999.
– *Illuminations*. Edited by Hannah Arendt. Translated by Harry Zohn. New York: Schocken Books, 1969.
– *The Origin of German Tragic Drama*. Translated by John Osborne. London: NLB, 1977.
– *Reflections: Essays, Aphorisms, Autobiographical Writings*. Edited by Peter Demetz. Translated by Edmund Jephcott. New York: Schocken Books, 1986.
– *Selected Writings: Volume 1, 1913–1926*. Edited by Marcus Bullock and Michael Jennings. Cambridge: The Belknap Press of Harvard University Press, 2004.

Black, Kerry. *Postmodernism as an Art Historical Period Style*. Boston: Mobius, 1995.

Borges, Jorge Luis. *Collected Fictions*. Translated by Andrew Hurley. New York: Penguin Books, 1998.

– *Labyrinths: Selected Stories and Other Writings*. Edited by D. Yates and J. Irby. New York: New Directions, 1962.

Buck-Morss, Susan. "Aesthetics and Anaesthetics: Walter Benjamin's Artwork Essay Reconsidered," *October* 62 (Fall 1992): 3–41.

Butler, Judith. *Bodies That Matter: On the Discursive Limits of "Sex"* London: Routledge, 1993.

– "Foucault and the Paradox of Bodily Inscriptions." *The Journal of Philosophy* 86.11 (November 1989): 601–7.

Caputo, John D. *Radical Hermeneutics: Repetition, Deconstruction and the Hermeneutic Project*. Indianapolis: Indiana University Press, 1987.

Camus, Albert. *The Rebel: An Essay on Man in Revolt*. Translated by Anthony Bower. London: Vintage Books, 1992.

Chalmers, David J. "Facing Up to the Problem of Consciousness." In *Explaining Consciousness: The Hard Problem*, edited by Jonathan Shear, 9–32. Cambridge: The MIT Press, 1998.

Coleridge, Samuel Taylor. *Biographia Literaria*. Edited by J. Shawcross. 2 vols. Oxford: Clarendon Press, 1907.

Deleuze, Gilles. *Nietzsche & Philosophy*. Translated by Hugh Tomlinson. New York: Columbia University Press, 2006.

– *Pure Immanence: Essays on A Life*. Translated by Anne Boyman. New York: Zone Books, 2005.

Deleuze, Gilles and Félix Guattari. *Anti-Oedipus: Capitalism and Schizophrenia*. Translated by Robert Hurley, Mark Seem, and Helen R. Lane. Minneapolis: University of Minnesota Press, 1983.

– *A Thousand Plateaus: Capitalism and Schizophrenia*. Translated by Brian Massumi. Minneapolis: University of Minnesota Press, 1987.

– *What is Philosophy?* Translated by Hugh Tomlinson and Graham Burchell. New York: Columbia University Press, 1994.

Dennett, Daniel. "Who's On First: Heterophenomenology Explained." *Journal of Consciousness Studies* 10.9 (2003): 19–30.

Eisenbud, Jule. *The World of Ted Serios: "Thoughtographic" Studies of an Extraordinary Mind*. New York: William Morrow and Company, Inc., 1967.

Foucault, Michel. *The Care of the Self: The History of Sexuality Volume 3*. Translated by Robert Hurley. New York: Vintage Books, 1986.

– *Discipline and Punish: The Birth of the Prison*. Translated by Alan Sheridan. New York: Vintage, 1979.

– *Fearless Speech*. Edited by Joseph Pearson. New York: Semiotext(e), 2001.
– *Madness and Civilization: A History of Insanity in the Age of Reason*. Translated by Richard Howard. New York: Vintage Books, 1965.
– "On the Author." In *Art in Theory: 1900–1990*, edited by Charles Harrison and Paul Wood, 949–52. Oxford: Blackwell, 1992.
– *The Politics of Truth*. Edited by Sylvère Lotringer. New York: Semiotext(e), 1997.
Fukurai, T. *Clairvoyance and Thoughtography*. London: Rider and Company, 1931.
Gane, Mike. *Jean Baudrillard: In Radical Uncertainty*. London: Pluto Press, 2000.
Genosko, Gary. *McLuhan and Baudrillard: The Masters of Implosion*. London: Routledge, 1999.
Golding, Sue, ed. *The Eight Technologies of Otherness*. London: Routledge, 1997
Goodman, Felicitas D. *Speaking in Tongues: A Cross-Cultural Study of Glossalalia*. Chicago: University of Chicago Press, 1972.
Graves, Robert. *The Greek Myths*. 2 vols. London: Penguin Books, 1955.
Gris, Henry and William Dick. *The New Soviet Psychic Discoveries*. New York: Warner Books, 1978.
Guattari, Félix. *Chaosophy*. Edited by Sylvère Lotringer. New York: Semiotext(e), 1995.
Habermas, Jürgen. *The Philosophical Discourse of Modernity: Twelve Lectures*. Cambridge: MIT Press, 2009.
Haraway, Donna. "The Cyborg Manifesto: Science, Technology and Socialist-Feminism in the Late Twentieth Century." In *The Cybercultures Reader*, edited by David Bell and Barbara Kennedy, 291–324. London: Routledge, 2000.
Hardt, Michael and Antonio Negri. *Empire*. Cambridge: Harvard University Press, 2000.
Hayles, Kartherine. *How We Became Posthuman: Virtual Bodies in Cybernetics, Literature and Informatics*. Chicago: University of Chicago Press, 1999.
Heidegger, Martin. *The Question Concerning Technology and Other Essays*. Translated by William Lovitt. New York: Harper and Row, 1977.
– "What is Metaphysics?" Accessed 15 September. http://evans-experientialism.freewebspace.com/heidegger5a.htm.
Holland, Norman. "The Willing Suspension of Disbelief: A Neuro-Psychoanalytic View." *PSYART: A Hyperlink Journal for the Psychological Study of the Arts* (22 January 2003), http://www.psyartjournal.com/article/show/n_holland-the_willing_suspension_of_disbelief_a_ne
Jorn, Asger. "Pataphysics – A Religion in the Making." *Internationale*

Situationniste, no. 6 (August 1961). Accessed 13 August 2006. http://www.infopool.org.uk/6104.html.

Kant, Immanuel. *The Critique of Judgment*. Translated by J.H. Bernard. London: Hafner Press, 1951.

Kaufmann, Walter. *Nietzsche: Philosopher, Psychologist, Antichrist*. Princeton: Princeton University Press, 1974.

– "Translator's Introduction." In Friedrich Nietzsche, *The Birth of Tragedy and The Case of Wagner*. New York: Vintage, 1967.

Kearney, Richard. *The Wake of the Imagination*. London: Routledge, 1998.

Kroker, Arthur. *The Possessed Individual: Technology and the French Postmodern*. New York: St Martin's Press, 1992.

– "Twisted Strands: Covenant Technology and the American Mind." In *Born Again Ideology: Religion, Technology and Terrorism*. Accessed 24 October 2006. http://www.ctheory.net/articles.aspx?id=546.

– *The Will to Technology and the Culture of Nihilism*. Toronto: University of Toronto Press, 2004.

Kroker, Arthur and Marilouise Kroker, eds. *Life in the Wires: The CTheory Reader*. Victoria: New World Perspectives, 2004.

Krauss, Lawrence. "The Energy of Empty Space that Isn't Zero." *Edge: The Third Culture*. Accessed 19 July 2006. http://www.edge.org/3rd_culture/krauss06/krauss06.2_index.html.

Lacan, Jacques. "The Mirror Stage as Formative of the Function of the I as Revealed in Psychoanalytic Experience." In *The Blackwell Reader in Contemporary Social Theory*, edited by A. Elliott, 61–80. Oxford: Blackwell, 1999.

Loy, Jim. "Zeno's Paradoxes." 1997. Accessed 15 January 2006. http://www.jimloy.com/physics/zeno.htm.

McLuhan, Marshall. *Understanding Media: The Extensions of Man*. New York: McGraw-Hill, 1964.

Massumi, Brian. *A User's Guide to Capitalism and Schizophrenia: Deviations from Deleuze and Guattari*. Cambridge: MIT Press, 1992.

de Maupassant, Guy. "The Horla." 1887. Accessed 10 December 2005. http://www.eastoftheweb.com/short-stories/UBooks/Horl.shtml

Merleau-Ponty, Maurice. *Phenomenology of Perception*. Translated by Colin Smith. London: Routledge, 1996.

Moerman, Daniel and Wayne Jonas. "Deconstructing the Placebo Effect and Finding the Meaning Response." *The Annals of Internal Medicine* 136.6 (March 2002): 471–6

Nagel, Thomas. "What is it like to be a bat?" *The Philosophical Review* LXXXIII 4 (October 1974): 435–50. Accessed 17 January 2007. http://members.aol.com/NeoNoetics/Nagel_Bat.html

Newman, Lex. "Descartes' Epistemology." *Stanford Encyclopedia of Philosophy* (3 December 1997). Accessed 15 November 2005. http://plato.stanford.edu/entries/descartes-epistemology.

Nietzsche, Friedrich. *The Birth of Tragedy and The Case of Wagner*. Translated by Walter Kaufmann. New York: Vintage, 1967.

– "How the 'Real World' at last Became a Myth." In *Twilight of the Idols / The Anti-Christ*. Translated by R.J. Hollingdale. New York: Penguin Books, 1968.

– *Thus Spoke Zarathustra*. Translated by R.J. Hollingdale. New York: Penguin Books, 1961.

Plato. *The Republic of Plato*. Translated by Francis Cornford. London: Oxford University Press, 1945.

Richter, Gerhard. *Walter Benjamin and the Corpus of Autobiography*. Detroit: Wayne State University Press, 2000.

Sapan, Jason. "Holographic Studios: FAQ." Accessed 1 August 2006. http://www.holostudios.com/holohelper/faq.htm.

Schrift, Alan. *Nietzsche and the Question of Interpretation: Between Hermeneutics and Deconstruction*. London: Routledge, 1990.

Simms, Taback. *There Was an Old Lady Who Swallowed a Fly*. New York: Penguin Books, 1997.

Sloterdijk, Peter. *Bulles: Sphères I*. Translated by Olivier Mannoni. Paris: Hachette Littératures, 2003.

– *Critique of Cynical Reason*. Translated by Michael Eldred. Minneapolis: University of Minnesota Press, 1987.

– *La Domestication de l'Être*. Translated by Olivier Mannoni. Paris: Mille et Une Nuits, 2000.

– *Essai d'intoxication volontaire* suivi de *L'heure du crime et le temps de l'oeuvre d'art*. Translated by Olivier Mannoni. Paris: Hachette Littératures, 2000.

– *Règles pour le Parc Humain: Une lettre en réponse à la Lettre sur l'humanisme de Heidegger*. Translated by Olivier Mannoni. Paris: Mille et Une Nuits, 2000.

– *Thinker on Stage: Nietzsche's Materialism*. Translated by Jamie Owen Daniel. Minneapolis: University of Minnesota Press, 1989.

Snyder, Joel. "Benjamin on Reproducibility and Aura: A Reading of 'The Work of Art in the Age of its Technical Reproducibility.'" In *Benjamin: Philosophy, Aesthetics, History*, edited by Gary Smith, 158–74. Chicago: University of Chicago Press, 1999.

Sontag, Susan. *On Photography*. London: Doubleday, 1989.

Tanizaki, Jun'ichiro. *In Praise of Shadows*. Stony Creek, CT: Leete's Island Books, 1977.

Virilio, Paul. *The Aesthetics of Disappearance*. Translated by Philip Beitchman. New York: Semiotext(e), 1991.

– *Art and Fear*. Julie Rose, trans., London: Continuum, 2003.

– *The Information Bomb*. Translated by Chris Turner. London: Verso, 2000.

– *Politics of the Very Worst: An Interview by Philippe Petit*. Edited by Sylvère Lotringer. Translated by Michael Cavaliere. New York: Semiotext(e), 1999.

– *The Vision Machine*. Translated by Julie Rose. Indianapolis: Indiana University Press, 1994.

Wernick, Andrew. "Baudrillard's Remainder." *CTheory* (October 1993). Accessed 7 August 2006. http://www.ctheory.net/articles.aspx?id=233.

Winchester, James. *Nietzsche's Aesthetic Turn: Reading Nietzsche after Heidegger, Deleuze, Derrida*. New York: State University of New York Press, 1994.

Wittgenstein, Ludwig. *On Certainty*. Translated by Denis Paul and G.E.M. Anscombe. New York: Harper, 1972.

– *Tractatus Logico-Philosophicus*. Translated by D.F. Pears and B.F. McGuinness. London: Routledge, 1961.

Zizek, Slavoj. *The Fragile Absolute: or, Why is the Christian legacy worth fighting for?* London: Verso, 2000.

– *On Belief*. London: Routledge, 2001

– *Organs without Bodies: On Deleuze and Consequences*. London: Routledge, 2004.

– *The Puppet and the Dwarf: The Perverse Core of Christianity*. Cambridge: MIT Press, 2003.

Index